P9-CEU-139

Swing Kings

THE INSIDE STORY OF BASEBALL'S HOME RUN REVOLUTION

JARED DIAMOND

WILLIAM MORROW
An Imprint of HarperCollins*Publishers*

HarperCollins books may be purchased for educational, business, or
sales promotional use. For information, please email the Special Markets
Department at SPsales@harpercollins.com.

Page 311 serves as an extension of the copyright page.

FIRST EDITION

Designed by Bonni Leon-Berman

Library of Congress Cataloging-in-Publication Data has been applied for.
ISBN 978-0-06-287210-4

20 21 22 23 24   LSC   10 9 8 7 6 5 4 3 2 1

To all the people ever told they
weren't good enough

CONTENTS

SWING KINGS FAMILY TREES

The Williams School

Ted Williams

Mike Bryant

Bobby Tewksbary

Chris Colabello   Josh Donaldson

Kris Bryant   Joey Gallo

Craig Wallenbrock

Doug Latta   Joe Borchard --- **Greg Walker**   **Robert Van Scoyoc**

Marlon   Justin   Cord Phelps   Paul Konerko   Chris Taylor
Byrd   Turner

Jason Castro

J. D. Martinez

The Lau School

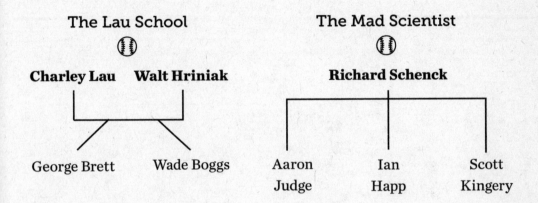

Charley Lau   **Walt Hriniak**

George Brett   Wade Boggs

The Mad Scientist

Richard Schenck

Aaron   Ian   Scott
Judge   Happ   Kingery

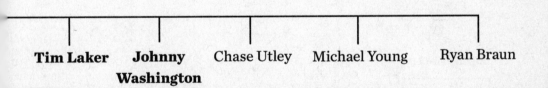

Tim Laker   **Johnny   Chase Utley   Michael Young   Ryan Braun
              Washington**

KEY
Coach
Player

Swing Kings

PROLOGUE:
THE DAY I CONQUERED THE SWING

The sun shone bright over Dean Field one warm weekend morning, bathing Scarsdale High School's baseball park in a beautiful summertime glow. I was 15, representing my town in a travel league against teams from around the area. There was no fence in right field at this point in my life. One would be constructed later. For now, there was just a large, steep hill, the base of which sat more than 300 feet from home plate and extended straight up until it reached Post Road high above the outfield. It took quite a drive to reach that hill, and as a left-handed batter, I had always dreamed of hitting a ball up onto it. That hill seemed so far away yet so close, as if it were mocking me every time a fly ball fell short. Reaching that hill represented strength. It represented power. It represented the culmination of all the hours I had spent in my life thus far playing a game that would never love me anywhere near as much as I loved it. If I could just drive a ball onto that hill, all the work I had put in would mean something.

Our opponent that day was Dobbs Ferry, a little village located on the Hudson River. As I warmed up, nothing felt any different than it ever had before. It was just another game in a summer full of them. Except this game was different from any other I had ever played in. In my first at-bat, I crushed a majestic fly ball well beyond the reach of any defender's glove. When I stepped up to the plate the next time, the opposing right fielder took a couple of steps back out of respect for my newfound power stroke, and again I rocketed a pitch well over his head, the ball bouncing up the hill. By my third at-bat the right fielder had decided that my first two bombs were no fluke, and he played so deep that it would be almost impossible for any ball to land behind him. Yet some-how, for the third time that day, I once again sent a thunderous fly ball to the hill, another mammoth hit that nobody could cor-ral. Three at-bats, three titanic blasts, each one farther than the last, and farther than any other balls I had ever hit before.

I grew up in Scarsdale, New York, a small town located in Westchester County, about a half-hour ride from Midtown Man-hattan on the express train. More than anything, I wanted to play baseball, long before I set my sights on a career covering the game for the *Wall Street Journal,* which I've had the pleasure of doing since 2013.

I was practically born with a bat in my hands. A near-congenital love of baseball had been passed down to me by my father and my grandfather before him. My birth announcement was a photograph of me as an infant, swaddled in blankets, on a pretend baseball card, with a full collection of statistics on the back. I never stood a chance.

The problem was that while I knew how to hold the bat just fine, I wasn't all that good at swinging it. When I was a child, my dad would bring me out to a field somewhere for solo batting practice practically every night from the time the winter's last snow melted until the next year's frost arrived. He is blessed with the sort of magical right arm that never seems to tire, so I would swing and swing and swing until my hands were bleeding and covered with blisters. I still have the calluses to show for it.

In spite of my limited athletic ability—my awkward, lumber-ing "running" style remains a source of great mockery among my friends—I worked myself into a decent enough hitter. I smacked a few home runs in Little League, batted in the middle of the lineup for teams through my early years of high school, and spent a year on the varsity roster. I was good. Or at least, I wasn't abjectly terrible by the standards of my little corner of suburbia. But true hitting, that indescribable feeling of the bat connecting with the ball and then watching it soar over everybody's heads, the kind of hitting that forces people to look at each other and say, "How far did that *go*?" remained elusive and tantalizing. I wanted to experience it more and more with each boring ground-ball single up the middle. I just didn't know how to do it.

Except for that one magical day.

My teammates, who thought that they knew my skill set after nearly a decade of watching me hit, were thrilled. The umpire was shocked. It was like a fantasy. Anybody who had seen me at the plate that day would've walked away from the field convinced that I had a future as a ballplayer, that I was something special. But here's the thing: I had no idea how I managed to pull that off. As far as I knew, I wasn't doing anything differently from what I had always done. I was swinging the same way I always had— only the ball was exploding off my bat and flying to places I never previously imagined I could reach. It was like a scene out of *The Natural,* with me filling in for Robert Redford.

I returned for my next game a few days later emboldened, ready to continue my new life as a superstar slugger destined for greatness. But when I stepped up to the plate, it was like the previous game had never happened. The thunder in my bat had reverted once again to a gentle breeze. I was a mere mortal, tapping grounders to second base like I always had.

I spent the rest of my baseball-playing days trying to recapture the magic of "The Game" that afternoon at Dean Field. I replayed the at-bats over and over in my head, desperate to unlock the secret to what I had done. The Game continued to haunt me long after I put away my spikes for the final time. My father and I had countless conversations about it through the years, until our words were largely replaced by longing sighs for what could have been. I've relayed the story to my wife, to my friends, to my colleagues enough times that they have it memorized. I'm not entirely sure if they all believe it happened in quite the way I tell the tale, but they're usually polite enough to humor me. Sometimes I wonder if I imagined the whole thing, if it's some false memory created in the deepest recesses of my sub-conscious. Even now, playing in beer-league softball games on unkempt fields scattered around New York City, I cling in vain to the belief that the power I kindled on that day more than 15 years ago will somehow return. It never has. It probably never will. But for one day, for reasons I may never fully understand, I conquered the skill that is widely considered to be the toughest in all of sports.

I had found the perfect swing—completely by accident. The only question was: How?

INTRODUCTION:
THE REVOLUTION

The Los Angeles Dodgers entered the 2019 baseball season saddled with pressure, facing the wrath of an enormous and passionate fan base across Southern California unwilling to accept any more heartbreak. For the past six years, the Dodgers had served as the ultimate tease, raising expectations only to tear them down, leaving behind the sort of profound discontentment that comes only with unconsummated success.

From 2013 through 2018, the Dodgers won more games than any other team in the sport. They won six consecutive National League West titles, a reign of supremacy unmatched in any division in the decade. In their last two playoff runs they had reached the World Series.

But despite all of that, the Dodgers couldn't escape one simple fact: both times they went to the Fall Classic, they lost. In 2017, the Houston Astros outlasted them in a seven-game thriller. A year later, the Boston Red Sox steamrolled them in five. All told, the Dodgers—one of baseball's most storied franchises—hadn't won a championship since 1988. Over time, frustrations about the Dodgers gave way to anger that appeared to be on the verge of boiling over as 2019 was set to begin. It reached a fever pitch when the Dodgers sat out the sweepstakes to acquire two of the most heralded free agents in recent memory, Bryce Harper and Manny Machado, showing surprising austerity for a team with a budget as gigantic as the Dodgers'. Sure, the Dodgers were good. There was no doubt about that. But were they as good as they could be?

That was the major question that hovered over Dodger Stadium on the afternoon of March 28, 2019. The Dodgers' opponent on opening day was the Arizona Diamondbacks, who sent ace right-hander Zack Greinke to the mound. The Dodgers countered with a lineup that looked eerily familiar: Eight of their nine starters had played for them the year before, with outfielder A. J. Pollock the lone exception. Seven of the nine had been on the Dodgers for at least the past two seasons. It felt like a rerun.

Then the game started. With two outs in the second inning, mercurial outfielder Joc Pederson stepped up to the plate. On the first pitch, Greinke flipped up a curveball at about 72 miles per hour—and Pederson slammed it far over the 395-foot sign in straightaway center field. Two innings later, Greinke tried another curveball, this time to Kiké Hernández. He sent it soaring into the left-field bleachers. And that was only the beginning. The very next batter, catcher Austin Barnes, turned on a fastball and put it in almost the exact same spot. Three batters after that, shortstop Corey Seager, appearing in his first regular-season game since April 29, 2018, following elbow surgery, blasted the Dodgers' third home run of the frame, a 407-foot drive to right-center.

Once Greinke came out, the onslaught continued. In the sixth inning, Pederson homered again. One inning after that, Diamondbacks reliever Matt Koch surrendered three more home runs in the span of four batters, hit by Max Muncy, Cody Bellinger, and Hernández for the second time. By the time the game ended two hours and forty-nine minutes after it began, the Dodgers had set an opening day record with eight home runs on their way to a 12–5 win.

The Dodgers' home run barrage on opening day in 2019 was only the beginning of what would be a historic season, one that wouldn't just rewrite record books but would throw the record book into a blazing inferno and start it again from scratch. Players across the sport combined to bash an utterly ridiculous 6,776 home runs, or one every 24.6 at-bats. It was a record-setting power surge that bordered on the unfathomable. Even in 2000, the heart of the steroid era, a time when baseball players resembled Incredible Hulk monsters, "only" 5,693 homers were hit.

And that's not even the craziest part. The craziest part is that by the time the year finished, with the Washington Nationals winning the World Series, the idea of many baseballs soaring over fences in stadiums across the league somehow didn't seem all that crazy. Because just the season before, players had hit 5,585 home runs. The season before that, they hit 6,105, an all-time high that stood for exactly two years. In fact, of the five seasons that have seen the most total home runs in major league history, four were the 2016 to 2019 seasons. There has been no indication that 2020 will be any different.

The 2019 season was just further proof that baseball has fundamentally changed in ways that have led to an entirely new version of the game. Sure, the trappings have remained the same: players throw the ball, they hit the ball, and they catch the ball, just as they've done for 150 years. But the product on the field is unlike anything the sport has ever seen, forcing a $10 billion industry to consider how much further the state of play can continue this way before the sport that has for so long been known as "America's pastime" becomes completely unrecognizable. As home runs have soared, so have strikeouts, with Major League Baseball setting a new record in that department every year since 2008. The humble single has fallen to record lows. Baseball today is about one thing: power—and how to cultivate it.

The rise of data analytics in the early portion of this century ushered in a paradigm shift nearly as radical as this one, though in a different way. The prior shift was about making the game better by making the game smarter. The tidal wave of outsiders with advanced degrees who poured into front offices used numbers to reshape how teams approached scouting, the draft, and in-game strategy. Player evaluation has never been more accurate than it is right now. In fact, many executives around the league believe that there is hardly any advantage to be won anymore in that realm. Every team is so good at data analytics that player evaluation is no longer a market inefficiency.

Today's changes are about making the game better by making it, well, better. Literally. It is about taking baseball players who were already evaluated and actually making them more talented baseball players than they were before. In other words, *Moneyball* was all about finding players with a higher ceiling than anybody realized. What's happening now is about raising the ceiling altogether.

When the Dodgers blasted eight homers on opening day of 2019, it wasn't totally a surprise. The players who hit them and their capabilities were already well known to baseball fans. The surprise was who was there waiting for them in the dugout after they trotted around the bases.

Around Thanksgiving, the Dodgers had made what might have been the most important acquisition any team in baseball would make all off-season—and almost nobody had noticed or cared. Robert Van Scoyoc wasn't part of the Dodgers' active roster. In fact, he had *never* been on the Dodgers' active roster. Or the active roster of any other major league team. Or minor league team. Or even a four-year college team. His entire baseball-playing career consisted of a so-so stint in high school, followed by an undistinguished couple of years at a community college in California. Yet there he was, sitting in the Los Angeles dugout as the Dodgers' freshly minted hitting coach, wearing uniform number 6, watching with joy as his players turned Dodger Stadium into their personal launching pad. It was the first game he had ever coached in professional baseball at any level, and it could not possibly have gone any better.

Robert Van Scoyoc might have been the least accomplished baseball player ever to land a job on a modern major league coaching staff. He also might have been the most important coaching hire in baseball history.

Robert Van Scoyoc sitting on the Dodgers' bench was the ultimate proof that what was happening in baseball was real, wasn't going anywhere, and was growing. All across the major leagues, players were proving that they could elevate their performance—that they could be better than they had been before. They had done it not with chemical assistance, as players had done when steroids were at their most rampant, but by changing their technique in ways that went against baseball's stubborn conventional wisdom, with the help of people that the industry had long shunned.

For evidence of that, look no further than the Dodgers. The man who batted in the coveted third spot of the lineup for them on opening day 2019 was third baseman Justin Turner. In December 2013, Turner had been on the outskirts of the baseball landscape. A fringe utility player heading into his age-29 season with no clear future, he had been cut by the Mets. Now he was one of the best hitters in baseball.

The revolution is what landed Van Scoyoc his job, as bizarre as it seemed. Though he was just 32 at the time and had accomplished virtually nothing on a baseball field as a player, Van Scoyoc had proven himself in nerdy baseball circles as one of the most sophisticated hitting minds on the planet. As an independent instructor, he had earned the opportunity to work directly with J. D. Martinez, another player who nearly found himself out of baseball at the exact same time as Turner. A few months after the Mets let Turner go, the Astros released Martinez, casting him aside as yet another player not cut out to survive in Major League Baseball. Only after Martinez found Van Scoyoc did he transform himself into a hitting monster. Martinez didn't just belong to the revolution—he was an evangelical, espousing the gospel to anybody who would listen.

The way Robert Van Scoyoc, Justin Turner, J. D. Martinez, and so many others reached their remarkable heights is the story of an industry in transition. For most of history, it was generally accepted that the players who ascended to the highest rung of baseball had maxed out their talent and reached the full scope of what they were capable of. The caliber of player they were in the major leagues was who they were destined to be.

But today is the dawn of a new model. The last few years have proven that the perception that professional athletes can't still dramatically improve is a fallacy. They can get better. They just need the right training, as baseball has only now started to real-ize. This incredible shift has forced a multibillion-dollar indus-try to completely rethink how it develops talent and redefine the concept of who is qualified to nurture that talent—a realization with applications that extend far beyond sports, and it comes down to one easy sentence: Just because something has always been done a certain way doesn't mean it's the best way to do it. It was a lesson already learned in the executive suite. Now it was happening in the dugout.

For people like Robert Van Scoyoc, the journey from obscurity to superstardom started with a question that is notable for both its simplicity and its profundity: What if everything you thought you knew about how to swing a baseball bat was fundamentally wrong?

BROKEN SWINGS

Hitting always came naturally to J. D. Martinez, and he has no problem saying that. He's never been afraid to speak his mind. Born in Miami of Cuban heritage, Martinez is the rare professional baseball player who doesn't shy away from saying what he believes, whether on the baseball field or off it. That is J. D. Martinez: one of the most passionate people in baseball and in everything he does. But nothing in his life compares to hitting.

Martinez can't explain why. He just knows that when he first picked up a bat, his body innately understood how to wield it in such a way that the barrel struck the center of the ball and sent it flying. Ty Van Burkleo, one of Martinez's old hitting coaches, would often tell him that he was "born with the hitting sperm."

"Some guys just have that gift, that hand-eye coordination," Martinez said. "It's that hitter gene."

Whatever nature failed to give Martinez in regard to hitting he learned from Paul Casanova. Casanova, a catcher from Cuba, spent 10 seasons with the Washington Senators and Atlanta Braves in the 1960s and '70s. Casanova was never much of a hitter at the major league level, posting a meager .225 batting average in 2,786 at-bats, but he was a veteran contributor who even made the All-Star team in 1967.

For years after his playing career, Casanova gave lessons in South Florida alongside former major league infielder Jackie Hernández. Together, they mentored countless young people in the area, on baseball and life. Martinez first connected with "Cassie" when he was in grade school, and Casanova became a second father to him. Casanova helped Martinez fall in love with baseball, regaling him with stories about playing with Hank Aaron and facing Mickey Mantle. Casanova's stories excited Martinez in the most profound ways, leaving him dreaming about one day having baseball stories of his own.

Casanova also taught Martinez how to hit, imparting the wisdom that enabled him to connect on home runs against the likes of Steve Carlton, Bert Blyleven, and Catfish Hunter. To his students, Casanova's home doubled as a Cuban museum, because it also served as a shrine to Cuban baseball history. The walls were lined with photos of all the great old-time Cuban major leaguers throughout history, from Minnie Miñoso to Tony Oliva to Tony Pérez. Since he came from a Cuban family himself, this baseball history resonated with Martinez, and he spent almost as much time at Casanova's house as he did at his own.

Martinez was at Casanova's hitting academy—also known as Casanova's backyard—almost every afternoon, honing his swing. Nothing else mattered. Nothing else brought him so much joy.

Casanova's lessons clearly paid off. Martinez hit well enough at Charles W. Flanagan High School for the Minnesota Twins to select him in the 36th round of the 2006 draft. Instead of signing, Martinez brought his bat to Nova Southeastern, a Division II college in nearby Fort Lauderdale, where he rewrote the record books, hitting .394 with 32 home runs and 142 RBIs in three seasons with the Sharks.

That performance caught the attention of the Astros, who grabbed Martinez in the 20th round of the 2009 draft. When he arrived in professional baseball, he did what he always did: he flat-out raked. In 2009, he hit .348 with a .997 on-base-plus-slugging percentage (OPS) in 72 games split between rookie ball and Single A. In 2010, he hit .341 with a .937 OPS at Single A and Double A. In 2011, he hit .338 at Double A and earned a promotion to the majors, a well-deserved honor for a player with numbers like those.

On July 30, 2011, at Milwaukee's Miller Park, Martinez reached the pinnacle. He entered his first major league game in the top of the eighth inning as a pinch hitter for pitcher

J. D. Martinez during his college days at Nova Southeastern.

Aneury Rodríguez. On the second pitch he saw from Marco Estrada of the Brewers, Martinez launched a majestic fly ball that short-hopped the wall in straightaway center field for a double, scoring Humberto Quintero from first base. He was just 23 years old.

As he stood on second base, Martinez could see his future in front of him. He had hit everywhere he had ever been, and now he had hit at the highest level of the game. And it wouldn't be long until he'd be back on second base again—and jogging right past it. A couple of days after his debut double, on August 3, Martinez walked into the home clubhouse at Houston's Minute Maid Park and saw something amazing: not only was he starting in left field, but manager Brad Mills had decided to bat him in the prestigious third spot in the lineup, an incredible honor for any player, let alone a rookie appearing in just his fifth major league game.

In his first at-bat in the bottom of the first inning, Martinez dug in against Cincinnati's Dontrelle Willis. After working the count to 2–2, Willis hung an off-speed pitch. Martinez pounced, driving the ball over the left field fence for a home run, the first of his career. Later he would say to the *Houston Chronicle* that before the game, he told Astros pitcher Jordan Lyles he would homer that day. Then, facing Willis again in the third, he laced a line drive to left for a single. After a fly-out to deep center, he ended his workday with a ground-ball double that plated two more runs, giving him a three-hit night with four RBIs.

In fact, RBIs would be a theme for Martinez for the rest of 2011. He had three more on August 6 when he hit a three-run home run off Milwaukee's Chris Narveson. He had a two-run double off Arizona's Joe Saunders on August 11. On August 20, he beat up on San Francisco's Madison Bumgarner for a two-run double in the third, followed by a two-run homer in the seventh.

Martinez drove in 28 runs that August in what was essentially his first month in the major leagues. Only three players in all of baseball had more: Carlos González of the Colorado Rockies and Curtis Granderson and Robinson Canó of the New York Yankees. It still stands as a franchise rookie record. By the time the 2011 season ended, Martinez had appeared in 53 games for the hapless Astros. Though the team finished with a dismal 56–106 record, Martinez hit .274 with an above-average OPS of .742, to go along with six homers and 35 RBIs.

As Martinez went into the off-season, the possibility of failure was the furthest thing from his mind. He had just shown that he could hit in the major leagues, and as far as he was concerned, he was embarking on the career he had always dreamed about and would continue hitting. The fact that he had hit just .250 with a .622 OPS in September was of no concern. It was just a bad month, a run-of-the-mill slump. In spring training of 2012, Astros hitting coach Mike Barnett told the *Chronicle* that the team attributed Martinez's struggles to the fatigue of playing into September for the first time in his pro career, causing him to lose about 25 pounds. Martinez had gained the weight back, Barnett insisted, and the problems had nothing to do with pitchers figuring out how to attack him. The Astros viewed Martinez as a fixture in the middle of their lineup for years to come.

But the cold, hard reality that Martinez wasn't considering was this: in baseball, everybody eventually reaches a wall. There's a moment in every player's life when suddenly the best of his ability no longer suffices. For most of us, that moment arrives sometime between Little League and high school. A small portion of superhuman athletes advance to college and an even smaller portion continue to have success all the way to the professional ranks, but eventually everybody collides with that wall that tells them they're not good enough.

In the major leagues, Martinez smashed into that wall at full speed and splattered all over the pavement. In spite of his strong start, this was the big leagues, the league with the best pitchers in the world and an army of really smart people whose sole job was to watch players and discover their weaknesses. It turns out that Martinez's weaknesses weren't hard to spot. He could still pummel mistakes, but his struggles with his timing and consistency left him susceptible to the changing speeds and movement of big league pitching. Before long, Martinez's production plummeted. He hit .241 in 395 at-bats in 2012, and his OPS dropped to .685. In 2013, his numbers (and his playing time) fell even further, with his OPS sinking to .650—more than 20 percent below the league average.

Martinez couldn't understand why he suddenly was struggling. His new hitting coach with the Astros, John Mallee, had an idea. Right after the Fourth of July in 2013, before a game against the Rangers in Arlington, Texas, Mallee first put the thought in Martinez's head that maybe—just maybe—his swing was the problem. He approached Martinez and tried to level with him: Martinez's swing had betrayed him. It was long. It was choppy. It had too many moving parts that were difficult to replicate. It simply wasn't working. The proof was in the declining numbers. Mallee told Martinez that all of the evidence—both empirical and subjective—suggested that he probably would not have success in the major leagues with it. Something needed to change.

Martinez, understandably, was defensive. His swing had gotten him all the way to the major leagues. Who was John Mallee to tell him differently? Mallee had never played baseball at anywhere near the level Martinez had reached as a rookie; he had never even made the big leagues, fizzling out after hitting .188 in Single A. Paul Casanova, the man who had taught Martinez almost everything he knew and believed about hitting, had spent a decade in The Show.

Moreover, would Mallee even be there for Martinez if he tried to make changes and failed? Would anybody with the Astros be there for him or care? No, Martinez figured. They'd just replace him with the next young outfielder they could find. Martinez was content to figure out his problems his way. He'd get his career back on track by himself, doing what he had always done. After all, doing things his way had always worked before.

Except Mallee's message stuck with Martinez. He was struggling. The Astros were disappointed in his progress and were clearly at least laying the groundwork to find somebody new to man a corner outfield spot. A year earlier, they had traded for outfield prospect Robbie Grossman, and he was showing early signs of success in the majors in 2013. At the 2013 trade deadline, they acquired L. J. Hoes, a former third-round draft pick. Most terrifying for Martinez, first-round draft pick George Springer was zooming through the system and putting up big numbers in Triple A. Springer

Martinez's Astros swing, which he defended to John Mallee.

was the future. If Martinez didn't start hitting soon, he'd be part of the Astros' past. Actually, not even that. He'd be a blip in the history of baseball, ignored and forgotten, not even relevant enough to be considered worth remembering. And it was all happening in public, for the world to see. Martinez had to improve—or fade away.

That's when he thought about Jason Castro, one of his teammates. Castro was enjoying a breakout season with a swing that, to Martinez's eyes, looked . . . strange. At the very least, it didn't look anything like his. He had asked Castro about his swing earlier in the year and heard a little bit about a coach in California who had taught him the mechanics and a whole bunch of wacky drills to hone them. This coach had never worked as a hitting coach for a professional team. In fact, he had never played professional baseball at all. He was just that: a random dude in California. Naturally, Martinez dismissed it at the time. How Castro learned his funky new swing simply sounded too bizarre.

But something happened that month, just weeks after Mallee's ultimatum, that not only changed Martinez's mind but changed Martinez's life. And when it happened, Martinez ran straight back to Castro to ask him again about that guy in California.

On July 26, 2013, in the sixth inning of a meaningless game in Toronto, Martinez lined a single to center field against Blue Jays knuckleballer R. A. Dickey. The next Astros batter, Marc Krauss, banged a ground ball to second base—a routine double play. Martinez, running from first to second, slid to avoid being smacked by the throw back to first. But the slide was awkward. He came up in pain. He had sprained his left wrist and ultimately had to leave the game. He wouldn't play again until the middle of September. Martinez couldn't believe his bad luck. "Right when I start to get going, every time I start to feel like I'm getting hot, something happens," he told the *Chronicle* afterward. "It just drives me crazy. It's very frustrating."

It turns out the freak injury was the best thing that ever happened to him.

The extended stint on the disabled list gave Martinez ample time to partake in his favorite hobby: thinking about hitting. By that point, the mystery of Castro's swing had imprinted in his brain. He had to understand it. One day as he watched Castro smoke yet another ball off the fence, he thought to himself, *Dude, what the heck? How is this guy banging right now?*

So as he languished on the DL, he pored over video of Castro. He still wasn't convinced. Though he was willing to admit at that point that maybe—maybe!—that strange-looking swing somehow worked for Castro, he couldn't fathom how it could possibly work for anybody else.

"I said to myself, 'This doesn't make any sense, because when we were in Double A, Jason's numbers could never keep up with mine,'" Martinez said.

The Astros returned to Houston early in August, and the mystery of Castro's swing continued to confound Martinez. He couldn't figure it out, and it was burning him up inside. He found himself spending more time holed up in the video room rewinding clips of Castro's swings, playing them at different speeds and at different angles. Nothing worked.

One night, a few minutes before a game, Martinez finished yet another futile session of studying Castro in the video room and started heading out to the field to join his teammates. The fastest way to get from the video room to the dugout at Houston's Minute Maid Park was a shortcut through the weight room. As he was weaving through the exercise machines, Martinez glanced up at the TV and froze. At that time, the biggest story in the baseball world involved Brewers slugger Ryan Braun, who had recently been suspended for 65 games for violating the sport's drug agreement. This startling turn of events ultimately prompted Braun to admit publicly that he had used performance-enhancing drugs.

Given the magnitude of a former MVP getting popped for PEDs, the sports channels devoted tons of airtime to Braun, running clips of him hitting seemingly on an endless loop. When Martinez looked up at the screen, he was stunned. He couldn't believe what he was seeing. It wasn't the discussion of Braun's suspension that had fazed him. It was Braun's swing. Braun's swing looked exactly like Castro's—and nothing like his own. The same bat path. The same hand movements. The same, well, everything.

The Astros' trainer, manning the weight room, started to turn off all the televisions in the area. As he was about to turn off the final TV in the room, Martinez barked at him to keep it on. The trainer said he couldn't—the National Anthem was about to start on the field outside. He warned Martinez that he could get in trouble for missing it. Martinez didn't care and told him so. He had to watch Braun. Nothing was going to stop him.

For J. D. Martinez, this was the lightning bolt moment. He hustled back to the video room, armed with a piece of information that had rocked his entire worldview to its core. He pulled up video of the best hitters from around the league, with a special emphasis on Miguel Cabrera and Albert Pujols, perhaps the two finest right-handed sluggers on the planet and the players Martinez aspired to become. The results were uncanny: their swings all looked like Castro's. And Braun's.

J. D. Martinez spent the entire game in the video room. All of it. He didn't see a single pitch. As the innings passed by, some other Astros players walked through, wondering what Martinez was doing. Martinez tried to show them what he was seeing, but he couldn't explain it, and nobody really seemed all that interested in his rantings and ravings. But Martinez's entire life had just changed. He needed to learn that swing.

When the game ended, Martinez made a beeline to Castro's locker. He had been in the video room for three hours, lost in his epiphany as he realized that he had cracked the code: Castro's swing, the one he had dismissed earlier in the year, wasn't weird—it suddenly made perfect sense. "I know exactly what it is," Martinez said to Castro. "You changed your bat path." Castro leaned over and took off his shoes. Then he looked back up at Martinez, standing over him. There was a smirk on his face. "That's exactly what I did," Castro responded.

Martinez had a follow-up question: Who taught him that bat

path, the bat path he had seen deployed by Ryan Braun and Miguel Cabrera and Albert Pujols? The answer, of course, was that guy in California Castro had tried to tell him about months before. Only this time Martinez was ready to listen. "Text him right now," Martinez implored Castro. It was late at night in Houston, but not in California, and Martinez didn't want to wait until morning. Castro said he would do it the next day, not wanting to bother anybody after hours. Martinez grabbed Castro's phone and ordered him to unlock it.

Calm down, Castro told him, but that only riled up J. D. Martinez more. Again he demanded, more forcefully this time, that Castro unlock his phone. Castro relented, and Martinez fired off a text from Castro's phone informing the California guru that now that he had his number, he would reach out to him from his own phone.

J. D. Martinez had just connected with Craig Wallenbrock for the first time. When the 2013 season ended, Martinez didn't go home. He flew to Los Angeles straight from Houston. It was time to go to work.

The same summer J. D. Martinez was beginning to realize he might have a problem, Justin Turner was on the verge of a crisis of his own. He just didn't know it yet.

Turner looks more like a surfer than a baseball player. He has flaming red hair, a long, bushy beard, and a cool-kid demeanor cultivated in the beach culture of Southern California. In conversation he gives off a fun, laid-back vibe. He seems like he'd be a good person to have along for a weekend in Las Vegas. He doesn't seem like the type who would emerge as a hitting pioneer.

That was especially true in 2013, because that year Turner didn't look like much of a hitter by major league standards. He was a spare part who had already bounced from the Cincinnati Reds to the Baltimore Orioles to the New York Mets without making much of an impact at any stop. He could reliably play any infield position, which made him a valuable backup, but nobody expected much more than that out of him. From 2009 through 2013, he had hit a respectable, but unspectacular, .260 in 318 big league games. He had virtually no power, managing just eight home runs in 841 at-bats.

When the 2013 season ended, Turner was less than two months away from celebrating his 29th birthday. By normal human standards, that's still pretty young. Plenty of 29-year-olds are still acquiring the skills required to build a successful career. Not expected to be finished products, they have plenty of time to improve and grow. But baseball players operate in a very different universe. In their world, 29 is teetering on the edge of old. It's around the age when teams expect players to start slipping from the height of their prime. It's around the age when players begin to have trouble landing long-term contracts in free agency. It's not "old" exactly—but it's certainly not young either. In baseball, by the age of 29, conventional wisdom says you are who you are. The time for meaningful improvement on the field has passed.

For Justin Turner, that was a big problem. Yes, he was a professional athlete. He had been since the Reds drafted him in the seventh round in 2006. He had made his major league debut with the Orioles in 2009 and established himself to an extent with the Mets, appearing in 297 games from 2011 through 2013. But while Turner was a major leaguer, he certainly hadn't accomplished enough to stabilize his life. He had earned, before taxes, less than $2 million as a big leaguer. That's not nothing, but it certainly wasn't enough to sustain him. The reality was that he didn't know what his life looked like without baseball. He knew he didn't want to find out, though he didn't know if he had a choice. Turner was, at best, a so-so major leaguer—an interchangeable part in the giant machine of professional baseball. He was about to turn 29, and he had a lifetime OPS of .684. If he didn't change that soon, it would be too late. In fact, in the eyes of much of the baseball world, it already was.

At that time, Turner's future seemed preordained: He would bop around the majors for as long as his defensive versatility allowed him to. With hard work, the right circumstances, and a bit of good fortune, he might forge a respectable baseball career, a remarkable accomplishment in its own right. But he wouldn't be a star. He wouldn't become rich. He wouldn't be remembered. Not with what he was working with at that time.

Every major leaguer, from the top of the roster to the bottom, has something in common: they are all phenomenal, world-class athletes. They have to be. No normal human being could even dream about making contact with a baseball traveling at close to 100 miles per hour, zooming toward the plate with spin and movement. The hand-eye coordination, reflexes, and body control that requires is almost impossible to fathom for all but the elite of the elite.

Even though Turner was far from a consistent hitter at the major league level, he had one skill that's virtually impossible to teach: he could put his bat on the ball. Turner rarely struck out. He had earned a reputation for putting together professional at-bats, making pitchers work, and generally being a nuisance at the plate. This skill suggested that there was an even better hitter somewhere inside him who just needed to be brought to the surface.

The issue was that Turner had no way of recognizing this possibility in himself. He had been conditioned his entire life to think he was a certain kind of player, a hitter with limitations that he couldn't surpass, for one superficial reason: the way he looked.

Turner is five-foot-11 and doesn't have the traditional muscle-laden body of a monster slugger. Players like that are told from a young age to avoid trying to hit for power, to not concern themselves with home runs and extra-base hits. They are meant to hit singles. Growing up, Turner said, he was often told, "Don't hit the ball in the air. You're not going to hit a home run if you hit it in the air. Those are outs. Someone is going to catch it."

Turner had generally followed this advice. In four years of college baseball at Cal State Fullerton, he hit a total of eight home runs. But somewhere within him, that better hitter *did* exist—and Turner himself had even caught a glimpse. As a senior at Mayfair High School in Lakewood, California, his team one day held a home run derby against a pitching machine. Turner didn't expect much out of himself. Neither did his teammates. Even in high school, power wasn't something Turner was known for. At that point in his life, Turner was about five-foot-nine and 130 pounds. He didn't even think he had the physical ability to hit home runs.

"I was a serviceable player," he said. "But I didn't do a lot of damage."

In that home run derby, however, something strange happened. Turner surprised himself, sending quite a few balls soaring over the fence. He didn't know he could do that.

Looking back now, Turner focuses on something he once heard from former major league outfielder Shawn Green, who hit 328 home runs in his 15-year career. Green never started hitting homers . . . until he started practicing hitting homers, consciously and intentionally.

"And I wasn't smart enough to realize, 'Hey, maybe I should continue to practice hitting homers,'" Turner said.

But in 2013, the same year Jason Castro opened J. D. Martinez's eyes to another way, another player on the Mets was having the same effect on Turner. Marlon Byrd had a swing that was unlike anything Turner had seen before—and it was working. Byrd was new to the Mets in 2013, a 35-year-old veteran who had been suspended for failing a performance-enhancing drug test the year before. He had accomplished far more than Turner had in his career, but at that point Byrd, at best, was a reclamation project. At least that's what Turner figured when Byrd showed up. But then Byrd started hitting home runs, more than he had ever hit before. And Turner couldn't help but notice that swing.

Justin Turner at Cal State Fullerton.

For most of his life, Turner had simply lacked the information necessary to build an ideal swing. He had grown up in Southern California hearing all of the traditional phrases and buzzwords: "let the ball get deep" and "stay back" and "squish the bug" and "swing down through the ball." It was what he knew, and it generally worked for him, all the way into the majors. What he didn't do, however, was produce any power. He didn't "do damage," as he often says. He'd hit singles, often up the middle or to the opposite field. Plus, he rarely walked.

Pitchers weren't concerned about him driving the ball, so they would routinely challenge him with fastballs and dare him to hit them.

"Knowing how to maximize my swing, I didn't really have a clue," Turner said.

When Byrd showed up on the Mets in 2013, Turner was intrigued. At first, Turner just watched, in part because Byrd was all but banned from discussing hitting with his teammates, so he wouldn't corrupt them with his radical new swing. The Mets were happy it was working for Byrd and didn't want him to change a thing, but that didn't mean they were convinced it would work for everybody else.

But as the season went on, Turner started asking Byrd questions. One day in the cage, following a question from Turner, Byrd pointed out that the barrel should drop underneath the hands on every swing, because that's the only way to hit the ball in the air. Turner didn't agree. He didn't disagree. He just said, "Huh," and walked off. A lightbulb had started flickering in his head. Maybe, even though his coaches didn't approve, there was something there.

It took Turner a while to truly put his faith in what Byrd was saying and implement some of his ideas. He knew where he stood: Turner was one of the last players on the Mets' roster. If he started telling a coach, as he puts it, "'Hey, I don't like your way, I'm going to do it a different way,' that's playing with fire." That leads to a coach telling his bosses that a player is uncoachable, and that leads to being cut.

Just as important, he still wasn't convinced he was capable of doing what Byrd did. Byrd might not have been a Hall of Famer, but he had been an All-Star in the major leagues before any of his swing changes, even hitting 20 homers in a season. So when Byrd would tell Turner, "You've got to slug," Turner could think of nothing else to say besides, "Man, I don't slug."

And yet as the summer wore on and Byrd kept hitting, it was impossible for Turner not to look up at the scoreboard and see the truth. As the calendar turned to September, he hadn't hit a home run in 172 plate appearances. His OPS was .645. It wasn't good enough. Something had to change.

"The more conversations I had with him, the more and more what he was talking about made perfect sense to me," Turner said, and what he had been doing his whole life seemed to make less and less sense. "I wanted to punch myself in the face and say, 'Why have I been doing this? This makes no sense.' And I knew it didn't make sense. But it took four or five months of being with him to even give it a go."

The catalyst for Turner to finally try something different came on August 27. That's the day when the Mets traded Byrd to the Pittsburgh Pirates. Suddenly, Turner's guru was gone. He hadn't spent any time actually changing his swing at that point. He hadn't taken the thousands of swings Byrd had taken to refine what was an entirely new way of doing something he had been doing his entire life. All he had was a few months of watching Byrd and a whole bunch of conversations with Byrd as he tried to understand how he went about his business. Although he had sometimes tried out Byrd's swing in batting practice or in the cage, it wasn't the same as bringing it out in the game.

So understandably, Turner was nervous about what would happen when he tried to swing Byrd's way. But he wasn't too worried about repercussions or consequences. Nobody thought much of him anyway. He was far from an expert, but he didn't care. There was a month left in the season. There was nothing left for him to lose. It was time.

"He was ready to hit," Byrd said. "He was ready to get it right."

What Turner had learned was that, just like Jason Castro, Byrd had a guy in California too, another obscure coach who had taught him to swing in a way that defied all conventional wisdom. Turner knew he had to see this miracle worker for himself. So that winter he did just that. He was barely 20 miles away from the batting cage where J. D. Martinez was meeting his guru, in the cradle of the most explosive innovation in the realm of hitting in decades. The 2014 season would begin in a few months.

THE ORACLE OF SANTA CLARITA

In the summer of 1971, Craig Wallenbrock was a self-described "pot-smoking hippie" living by his personal creed: walk lightly and leave no footprints. He was residing in San Clemente, California, where he surfed all day and stocked shelves at a grocery store at night so he had more time to ride the waves when the sun rose again.

Wallenbrock had moved there a year before in a fit of frustration. He had spent the last four years living with the surfers on Mission Beach, staying enrolled at nearby San Diego State mostly so he could avoid the draft and stay out of Vietnam. Then, when he thought he was on the verge of graduating, he found out he still needed a foreign language credit to finish his degree in English. He decided he didn't care about school anymore, so he left, moved up the coast, and paddled out to sea.

Now he needed a change. He was 25 years old, and it was time for his life to begin. Wallenbrock had a brother, Judd, 11 years his junior. They didn't know each other all that well; Craig left the house when Judd was a small child. But Judd knew one thing about Craig: he loved baseball—or at least he used to.

Craig Wallenbrock was a baseball player once. He arrived at San Diego State in 1966 with a coveted spot on the team there following a successful two-season stint playing at Pasadena City College. Those were challenging times, however. War was raging. The culture was changing. So was Wallenbrock. Before he played in a single game for the Aztecs, he quit, leaving the game he had loved behind forever. Or so he thought.

Now Judd was entering high school. He was starting to get serious about baseball, and as far as he was concerned, Craig was the best player he had ever known. So he asked his older brother to coach him up. Wallenbrock wasn't sure. "I don't know what I can do for you, because I failed at this game," he told Judd.

But the more he thought about it, the more the idea appealed to him. At a time when Wallenbrock wasn't exactly on good terms with his family, given the pot-smoking and the surfing, this seemed like an opportunity to bond with his brother. He was starting to patch things up with his father. He was ready, as he put it, to "reenter society."

Craig Wallenbrock left the ocean behind and returned to Pasadena to throw batting practice to his brother. It was the most important decision he would ever make.

Craig Wallenbrock was born in St. Charles, Missouri, in 1946, but he grew up near Pasadena. He loved all sports, but particularly baseball, and he was good at it, mostly playing on the streets with his friends. He had no formal coaching. "I could just hit," he said. "Naturally. I was athletic and had hand-eye coordination, so that's what I did."

As Wallenbrock got older, his father, a scholarship quarterback at the University of Missouri before a broken hip derailed his football career, thought it was time for some professional assistance. "He said, 'Well, he's going to have to improve to get to the next level,'" Wallenbrock recalled. Suddenly, he was working with the best coaches in the area his dad could find.

They were mostly local guys with some playing experience themselves, maybe in the minor leagues. They taught what virtually every coach taught back then—and many still do to this day: stay back, swing down, bring your knob on a straight line to the ball, be short and quick, "squish the bug"—the oft-cited cue to a hitter to rotate his back foot upon swinging, as if he were smooshing an ant. Every drill Wallenbrock remembers was in service of those cues.

One that stands out was a coach placing a baseball behind his right heel. When Wallenbrock swung, he was supposed to try to kick it between the catcher's legs. This was supposed to teach "squishing the bug." There was a two-tee drill, where the coach would put one tee up tall and another tee, with a second ball, below it. The object was to hit the top ball into the bottom ball by—quite literally—swinging down on the ball.

"I just continued thinking I was going to be better by working with these people," Wallenbrock said. "They're pro players. I'm 13 years old."

The coaching didn't work. Wallenbrock regressed. By the time he got to high school, the natural swing that had served him well on the streets of Southern California was gone.

"It seemed like the higher I went, the more I struggled," Wallenbrock said. "I put that to the fact that the competition was getting better, but really, looking back, the coaching was getting worse."

Still, Wallenbrock's athleticism carried him through high school, to Pasadena City College, and ultimately to San Diego State on a partial baseball scholarship. He wasn't a bad hitter, he said, but he was declining, and it was his defensive versatility, rather than his bat, that helped him reach the college level.

This was the late 1960s, during the heart of the Vietnam War. Wallenbrock was studying and practicing baseball in San Diego, a military town, but living in Mission Beach, bunking with "a bunch of hippie surfers." Wallenbrock came from a conservative background, a worldview only reinforced by the rigid construct of collegiate sports. But during those years, he became disillusioned, first with baseball, then with the world. He had a falling-out with his father. He severed ties with the baseball team. He left everything behind and rode the waves.

"I quit, spent as much time as I could at the beach, surfing down in Mexico as a pot-smoking hippie," Wallenbrock said. "I was frustrated. I thought I was better, but I wasn't producing. And I felt, 'There's something wrong. Maybe I'm not cut out to be a baseball player.' I looked at myself as a failure, that I couldn't learn to hit. And I thought I was doing everything right, and so I blamed myself."

After Craig Wallenbrock quit the baseball team at San Diego State, the game that once consumed his life became an afterthought. For the next five years, he went to class when he wasn't surfing. A year later, he stopped with the classes altogether. Baseball was a thing of the past.

His brother Judd brought him back, even though Wallenbrock had no idea how to help him. The good news was that he had a secret weapon: even though Wallenbrock hadn't made it very far as a player, some of his teammates had. He'd played with guys like Darrell Evans, a two-time major league All-Star who went to Pasadena City College, and Tom Hutton, a 12-year veteran who also grew up in the Pasadena area.

"I started contacting those guys, and the next thing I knew it was, 'Yeah, I can give you some advice for your little brother,'" Wallenbrock said. "Then it was, 'Hey, you still got a good arm?'"

Just like that, Craig Wallenbrock was a batting practice pitcher for major leaguers. If not for his BP throwing skills, he probably never would have returned to baseball at all. Somehow, for Wallenbrock, that serendipity made perfect sense.

"My own belief is that the world is ruled by randomness, and we have to understand that," he told me. "What's that old song by Paul Simon? 'Believe we're gliding down the highway, when in fact we're slip-slidin' away.'"

A book he would read later in life, Leonard Mlodinow's *The Drunkard's Walk,* only reinforced that worldview. Wallenbrock described it as being about "how randomness rules the universe."

"Rather than try to make order out of things, instead embrace the randomness of it," he said. "And as I embraced the randomness of things, I became interested in Eastern philosophy, living in the moment. And then the surfing came in." Wallenbrock was clearly slip-slidin' away now, off on another tangent that he swore had something to do with baseball.

"The surfer realizes that every wave is different, and you can't have a set of rules," he continued. "You can have some general ideas, but you've got to be able to react in the moment, and you have to be totally in the moment. Well, that's Eastern philosophy. How do you live totally in the moment?"

These are the philosophies that guided him as he slowly gravitated back toward baseball. He believes randomness brought him to that point, not a grand unifying plan of the universe. His life was about baseball, then it wasn't. He surfed and went to school, then he just surfed. Now he was back into baseball. That's how life works. The important part is what a person does at each stop, and a person uses all of his or her previous experiences to influence the next one. Wallenbrock had plenty of experiences, brought about by a wide array of interests that extended far beyond sports.

At one point, Wallenbrock became fascinated by Wu Li, a

Chinese landscape painter and poet who was believed to have been born around 1632. Wu Li's ideas about learning became a source of guidance as Wallenbrock moved into the realm of coaching.

"Wu Li said, if we put a number on your abilities right now—let's put that number as four—and you want to move up to a five, what do you have to do?" Wallenbrock said. "Everybody answers, 'Well, you add one.' And Wu Li said, 'Yes, but one is made up of an infinite number of fractions, and each of those fractions has a universe of knowledge contained within it.'

"So we have to learn to look at fractions, and study those little fractions and the little particles. Sometimes we get so absorbed in the particles and the little things that we're learning and fascinated by, that we no longer care if we get to five, because the process has become so enchanting. And then one day we wake up, and we realize we were so involved with the process, we went by five and we never knew we reached it, and now we're at six."

This isn't the way people who dedicate their lives to baseball usually think. That's not a criticism. But the reality is that, for most people in sports, there was never any room in their lives for anything else other than the game and the singular pursuit of excelling in it. Athletes—and coaches—are obsessed with their craft, closed off to everything else in the world that isn't directly in service of it. To reach the highest level of athletic achievement, that's what is required.

But Craig Wallenbrock is different from just about everybody else. His path to baseball was roundabout, and it provided him with the opportunity to experience a world that didn't involve the game. When he first started coaching his brother, Wallenbrock had accumulated knowledge from so many other disciplines that made him more than a coach. It made him a teacher. And clearly, even then, Wallenbrock understood teaching.

The question was whether he understood hitting. But, hey, he understood Wu Li. So how hard could it be?

It was the early 1970s when Wallenbrock agreed to help his brother become a better hitter. Taking advantage of his BP side gig, Wallenbrock bought an early video camera, a big clunky thing that he said resembled an "old-time movie projector." He decided he would start filming the major leaguers he pitched to and review the footage with his brother, searching for clues. This was a seminal moment, for both its impact and its simplicity. The idea of filming hitters sounds obvious now, but back then it was unheard of. This is where Wallenbrock's unusual background gave him a remarkable advantage. It's also an example of why diversity of thought and experience is so crucial in any field. So often those ensconced in their bubble become blind to new thoughts and ideas. I can speak from experience: my wife, who isn't a baseball fan, often comes up with the most interesting story ideas for me to pursue for the *Wall Street Journal,* because she sees things I take for granted and asks, "What is that?"

Wallenbrock approached the teaching of hitting as an out-sider, free of biases and preconceived notions about the "right way" to do it. With fresh eyes sharpened by his other interests and hobbies, it was obvious to him that the ability to play back a swing on film, to watch it again and again, would be beneficial. And what he saw once he started watching made him rethink everything he thought he knew about how to hit.

For starters, none of the major leaguers he was looking at swung down, or "chopped wood," as Wallenbrock was taught to do. They were doing something different. Wallenbrock started seeking out video of any great hitter he could find, from Hank Aaron to Stan Musial to Ted Williams to Mickey Mantle. Their swings also looked different from what he had been taught. But when he told the guys he was pitching to about his discovery, they didn't believe him.

"All of the good ones were not doing what they said they were doing," Wallenbrock said. "And they would describe it, and they would show me what they were doing. And then I'd watch video and look at them, 'No, you're not doing that.' And they would get frustrated with me—'I know what I'm doing.'"

Wallenbrock started noticing other things too. His next big breakthrough came when he started throwing not just to pro hitters but to kids and teenagers as well. With the younger, more inexperienced hitters, he could see the barrel of the bat from the mound early in the process of their swing, so he felt comfortable pitching without a protective screen guarding him from comebackers. He didn't need one. He could see the ball clearly coming off the bat and could react accordingly.

With the more advanced hitters, however, it was the exact opposite: not only was the ball coming off the bat faster, but he couldn't see the barrel at all until the absolute last moment. Only then would it whip into view, having zoomed through the hitting zone too fast for Wallenbrock to react. Often, he said, he would flinch when they swung, even on balls that weren't hit anywhere near the mound. For those hitters, he would stack trash cans in front of himself, just in case. What had they figured out that the less impressive hitters had not?

At first, he thought maybe great hitters just had greater bat speed and therefore didn't need to start their swing as early as lesser hitters. But when he slowed down the video (he had brought his camera here too), he saw something else: the great hitters didn't propel their bats forward with their top hands, as he had been taught to do. The swing didn't start with a forward motion at all. Instead, they kept their barrel behind the ball for

THE ORACLE OF SANTA CLARITA   37

as long as possible. He called it the "lag position," and he soon came to realize that it was perhaps the single biggest thing that separated great hitters from everybody else.

With excitement, Wallenbrock brought this revelation to his BP crew. He wanted confirmation that he was on to something, some validation that maybe he had started to crack the code. He received a lot of blank stares.

"They didn't know what I was talking about," Wallenbrock said. "Yet I saw them do it. And so they were doing it without knowing what they were doing."

That was it. Wallenbrock went back to his brother and declared they were going to scrap everything and start over. No longer would they solicit advice, not even from major leaguers. They would watch video of great hitters, make observations, and teach themselves how to hit. The camera didn't lie. This was perhaps the most important realization of Craig Wallenbrock's life.

Judd Wallenbrock, Craig's younger brother, wound up landing a scholarship to play baseball at UCLA. He eventually left the team, Craig told me, "for the same reason the Beatles split up—a woman."

Craig Wallenbrock was on to something big. But still, he didn't envision a life in baseball. He worked in the mornings for his father, an industrial food broker, with whom he had forged a fragile reconciliation, and pitched to pro hitters in the afternoons when they were in town. He was still in his midtwenties.

For the next eight years, Wallenbrock had what could be best described as a normal job, selling sugar and corn syrup to bakery and dairy companies. He was good at it too. In the early 1980s, after Wallenbrock stopped working for his father, he fielded job offers from a vanilla company and a cocoa company.

Baseball was no longer necessarily an afterthought for him, but it was certainly on the periphery. After Judd went off to college, Craig continued to help out with coaching in some local youth leagues, not with any intention of turning baseball into a career, but for fun. He wasn't all that different from any Little League coach.

In 1979, nearly a decade after he moved back home to Pasadena, that started to change. His old baseball coach, Ron Robinson, was now working as an administrator at Pasadena City College. The baseball team needed an extra body, and with Wallenbrock's reputation as a batting practice pitcher, he seemed like an obvious choice. This wasn't a career change. Wallenbrock was still a salesman first, but one who helped out with a junior college baseball team in the afternoon. Nevertheless, it was a step up.

"I kind of got the baseball bug," he said.

Wallenbrock spent three years at Pasadena City College. As time passed, he found himself increasingly more interested in coaching than in sales—and other teams started noticing him. In 1982, he became an assistant coach at Cal State LA. That job eventually led to a conversation with Art Mazmanian, a legend on the junior college circuit. Mazmanian spent more than three decades as the head coach at Mount San Antonio College, a junior college near Los Angeles. He won more than 700 games there. Mazmanian also managed 18 seasons in the minor leagues. He had been Don Mattingly's first professional manager and one of his biggest champions as a young player. Now Mazmanian, who died in March 2019 at the age of 91, needed a hitting coach at Mount San Antonio and thought Wallenbrock might be a good fit. Wallenbrock wasn't so sure.

"I went, 'Oh, no. No, I failed at that, Art,'" Wallenbrock recalled. "And he said, 'Well, you don't have to be good at it.'"

So Wallenbrock took the job, and it opened up a treasure trove of willing and available test subjects for exploring his ideas and theories about the swing. Not only did he have a roster of players at his disposal, but lots of pros would come back to train at Mount San Antonio in the winter. That's how Wallenbrock met longtime Los Angeles Angels manager Mike Scioscia and Ron Roenicke, a former big league manager and, as of late 2019, the bench coach for the Red Sox. Wallenbrock was throwing more and more BP—and, of course, filming everything.

That last part was key for Wallenbrock. The idea of using film as a training tool, as ubiquitous as it is today, was then still a relatively novel concept even in the major leagues, let alone in junior college.

"The attitude was, 'I played this game for 20 years. I don't need video to tell me what I did. I know what I did,'" Wallenbrock said. "Then people would make fun of me: 'Well, he has to use video, because he never played pro ball.'"

Wallenbrock didn't mind. He had long rejected traditional ideas about the swing and how to teach it. He was more comfortable operating outside the system.

"I failed in the system," Wallenbrock said. "I failed trying to do it the system's way. I wasn't going to stay in it, I was going to do something else."

The more video he watched, the more he discovered. He broke the swing down into parts, one move at a time. He watched how great hitters gripped the bat, how they moved their legs and their hips and their shoulders.

To this point, coaching hitting, to whatever extent the concept even existed, was done mostly by feel. Coaches would simply tell their pupils what they did—or what they thought they did—and ask them to repeat it. Wallenbrock already knew the folly of that method. Because of his obsession with video, he understood that hitters routinely didn't actually do what they thought they did. He didn't want to teach by feel. He wanted to teach universal truths.

As a cross-disciplinarian with a vast collection of interests, Wallenbrock came to realize that generating power in hitting a baseball was no different from generating power in anything else. So he began studying predators from nature, the big cats and the wolves, to see how they generated so much power as they ran and jumped through the air. It was immediately clear to him that the force was generated in their heels. This ran counter to the common wisdom about hitting: "Be on the balls of your feet." When he started watching the great hitters through that lens, he saw that they in fact strode off their heel, not the balls of their feet. Suddenly, it all made sense: In surfing, he had always been taught to keep his whole foot on the board to maintain balance on the water. If he was on the balls of his feet, he would fall. Why would it be any different in baseball?

He then became interested in karate, not to earn belts, but to mine its precepts and apply them to the swing. A strong punch, he learned, comes from rotating the core, not the legs and the shoulders, as hitting coaches often taught. A powerful swing, he figured, should follow the same principles as a strong punch.

Although the baseball bat was a relatively modern invention, humans had been swinging weapons for millennia. Might Japanese samurais have something to teach Wallenbrock? He became fascinated by *The Book of Five Rings,* a text believed to have been written around 1645 by the swordsman Miyamoto Musashi, shortly before his death. The samurai, Wallenbrock learned, had to maintain control of his blade to fend off multiple assailants. He had to go through, not to, his opponents. If he went to the opponent, the opponent would slay him. So why did the conventional wisdom hold that hitters should swing *to* the ball? If they swung *through* it, Wallenbrock theorized, launching from the lag position, they were more likely to generate power, in much the same way a samurai could kill multiple attackers with one swing of the sword.

Wallenbrock didn't make all these observations at once. They came to him slowly, one piece at a time, until he had figured out the foundations of an elite swing. For Wallenbrock, who *Sports Illustrated* baseball writer Tom Verducci would one day call "The Oracle of Santa Clarita," these revelations were like looking at the paintings created by his cherished Wu Li. They were large and often had no central component, no portrait subject or vase of flowers, like a Rembrandt or Van Gogh. Instead, Wu Li painted small segments that came together to form a whole. That was how Wallenbrock studied the swing.

To demonstrate this idea, Wallenbrock gave me a challenge: he would recite a series of numbers, and I had to say them back.

"Seven, four, one, nine, one, one, two, five, seven," he said.

I paused for a moment.

"Um, seven, one, four, nine, two, five, one, one, seven? Was I close?"

Not close enough. I did have the right digits, but all out of order.

"Now I'm going to teach you how to do it," Wallenbrock said. "Instead of thinking in terms of individual numbers, I want you to think in terms of sets. And the first set I want you to think of is, *seven, four, nineteen.*"

I repeated it back.

"Okay, now, the second set I gave you was one, one, two, five, seven. Again, reduce that to three sets: *eleven, two, fifty-seven.*"

"So," I responded. "It's *seven, four, nineteen, eleven, two, fifty-seven,* or seven, four, one, nine, one, one, two, five, seven."

I realized I was beaming, way too proud of my ability to memorize a few numbers.

"You can do it because you've mastered the set," Wallenbrock said, validating my pride. "So each time we master a set, we can go on to a greater set. But what most people try to do is they try to master, back to Wu Li, the whole thing at once. And when you tried to do that, you couldn't do it. But when I gave you the little trick as to how to do it, it was pretty simple. Let's look at the parts, and let's figure out the parts and figure out how those parts now can be put together."

And there it was, a cogent theory of the swing, from surfing to Wu Li, that actually kind of, sort of made sense. But if you strip away all the stuff about samurais and karate and alpha predators from the African veldt, Craig Wallenbrock's breakthrough had basically entailed watching video of great hitters swinging. Couldn't anybody have done that?

Well, yes. And other people eventually did, but not as early as Wallenbrock. So why did it take everyone else so long?

For Wallenbrock, that answer all comes back to Cat Stevens. There is a line in "Father and Son" that resonated with Wallenbrock, a man who had a rocky relationship with his own father. The line is: "From the moment I could talk, I was ordered to listen."

"The Korean War, for the first time, the soldiers were coming back questioning the war, questioning why we were there: 'Why do we have to do this?'" Wallenbrock said. "Up until that time, patriotism had been invoked, and we just did it because we were patriotic. That's what we did.

"And then the Vietnam War comes along, and it looks like it's Korea all over again. But my generation, having now talked to the veterans of Korea, had a different view than my father's generation had of World War II. And I think that started that questioning, and we started asking why."

Craig Wallenbrock had always questioned authority. He was

fiercely committed to forging a path that differed from that of his father, and the generation his father represented. That burning desire to talk when he felt pressured to listen inspired him to always ask why. He vividly remembered asking his high school coach to explain why he told the pitchers to try to induce ground balls while also telling the batters to swing down in order to hit the ball on the ground. It made no sense to him. "He just looked at me like, 'God, have you started smoking pot already?'" Wallenbrock said.

Growing up, he'd modeled his swing off some of the great sluggers from his childhood, players like Hank Aaron and Roger Maris, who had classic power strokes. Coaches would tell him not to swing that way. Wallenbrock would ask why. The answer, invariably, would be, "Those guys are freaks. You need to copy a guy with a classic swing." That someone, one coach told Wallenbrock, was Ron Fairly, a solid if unspectacular player who spent 21 seasons in the major leagues with what would be described as a classic swing.

"I'm thinking, let's see—Ron Fairly, .260, not much power. Henry Aaron, 40 home runs . . . ," Wallenbrock said. "And I said, 'Yeah, but the freaks always seem to be the best players. So I want to study the freaks.'"

Little did Wallenbrock know back then that he would one day be responsible for creating freaks of his own.

When Craig Wallenbrock became the hitting coach at Mount San Antonio, he still didn't know all that much about hitting. But he was starting to generate some ideas. And most important, it turns out he had a pretty good eye for underappreciated talent.

Wallenbrock recruited a first baseman out of South Pasadena

High School named Rob Nelson, whose dyslexia had limited his collegiate options. Nelson wound up appearing in 76 games for the Oakland Athletics and San Diego Padres between 1986 and 1990.

Around the same time, Wallenbrock uncovered another hidden gem. He first met Keith Lockhart at Hollenbeck Park near Los Angeles at a high school state championship tournament. Lockhart was, as Wallenbrock remembered it, "just this little pipsqueak."

Lockhart was about to graduate from Northview High School in nearby Covina. He had nowhere to go from there. Nobody had recruited him, and he didn't know enough about the system to put himself in front of the right people to make sure he got noticed. But at least one recruiter noticed him: Wallenbrock. At Mount San Antonio, Lockhart received a most unusual hitting education.

"Craig was, even back then, an outside-the-box type of guy," Lockhart told me. "He had these little gadgets, little things we did with the tees. He'd have two or three balls on two or three tees to help us keep our bat path. He had another drill with a towel to get us to whip our bats."

Whatever Wallenbrock taught Lockhart, it clearly worked. Lockhart went from Mount San Antonio to Oral Roberts to pro ball. Lockhart, the player whose baseball career might have ended after high school if not for Wallenbrock spotting him, wound up playing 10 years in the majors and appeared in all four games of the 1999 World Series for the Braves.

After retirement, Lockhart didn't see Wallenbrock for a while. Lockhart moved into other aspects of the game, eventually taking a scouting job with the Chicago Cubs. But the specter of his old teacher remained. One day a few years ago, Lockhart's son Daniel, a minor-leaguer, asked him, "Dad, have you ever seen anything from this guy Craig Wallenbrock?" "I said, 'Danny, he was my junior college hitting coach,'" Lockhart recalled.

That's how, about 30 years after Craig Wallenbrock recruited that "little pipsqueak" to junior college, he taught hitting to that little pipsqueak's son.

"Craig is a guy where you have to trust his success. He can be quirky. He might not do it the way you would do it. But you can't argue with the success," Lockhart said. "Sometimes you scratch your head and say, 'Why is this guy not a big league hitting coach?' Maybe he was just ahead of his time."

Craig Wallenbrock was having success helping hitters with an approach that went against conventional wisdom. But outside of his little pocket in Southern California, almost nobody knew who he was. Wallenbrock was an unknown, operating in complete anonymity, espousing ideas that couldn't have been more different from trendy teachings of the day. At the time, that meant Charley Lau. The first celebrity hitting coach, Lau was the first swing "guru" to receive widespread mainstream recognition.

Charley Lau was a catcher who played 11 seasons in the major leagues between 1956 and 1967. He wasn't much of a hitter. He had a lifetime batting average of .255 and an OPS of .683, well below league average for the time. He hit 16 total home runs, topping out at six for the Orioles in 1962. He was, by any objective measure, not much more productive than any random call-up from Triple A would have been. This is the man who would become the most famous hitting coach in history.

After playing, Lau plied his trade for the Orioles, A's, Kansas City Royals, Yankees, and Chicago White Sox. Over that time, he became something of a coaching superstar in an era when the very idea of a hitting coach was still relatively novel. The Red Sox had Hall of Famer Hugh Duffy, an outfielder who hit .440 for the Boston Beaneaters in 1894, serve as a coach as early as 1932. That same season the Reds employed Harry Heilmann as a coach, and a year later the Pirates brought on Honus Wagner in that role, keeping him on their staff into the early 1950s. But it would be decades before a dedicated hitting coach became the widespread norm across the major leagues. And if there was any doubt about the value of the role, Charley Lau silenced it all.

Lau wrote books called *The Art of Hitting .300* and *The Winning Hitter*. He had instructional videotapes. He even appeared in the 1983 film *Max Dugan Returns,* written by Neil Simon, in which he was Matthew Broderick's on-screen tutor.

It should go without saying by now that you don't have to be a great hitter to be an expert hitting instructor. Wallenbrock and Robert Van Scoyoc never played above junior college. They accomplished far less as players than Charley Lau did. But Lau's ideas about hitting and the swing couldn't have been more different from what Wallenbrock was starting to discover inside his burgeoning Southern California laboratory.

Like Wallenbrock, Lau was an early advocate of film study. He'd been mining video for information since the early 1970s, if not before. But his review of the footage had led him to markedly different conclusions. Lau developed a list that he called the "absolutes of hitting," truths that all hitters must abide by to be successful. These included striding with the front toe closed, shifting weight from back to front, and having the bat in the launch position when the front foot touches down. He believed power derived from the stride, not from the rotation of the hips and torso. Lau taught a swing that had the barrel going in a straight line down to the ball. It can best be described as a classic swing, the one most people learn in Little League from cues like "be short to the ball" or "pull the knob through the ball." Today Lau's methods are known as "linear hitting."

And without a doubt, these ideas worked for hitters. Tony La Russa, the Hall of Fame manager, told me that he considered Lau to be "the greatest hitting coach of all time." When La Russa convinced White Sox ownership to hire Lau as the team's hitting coach for the 1982 season, he compared the acquisition to signing three players. Lou Piniella was a disciple of Lau's. So was Hal McRae. Reggie Jackson, while not necessarily a full-blown believer in the Tao of Lau, was known to seek Lau out for advice when he was slumping. Walt Hriniak, Lau's protégé, became a successful major league hitting coach in his own right, working with batters like Wade Boggs and Harold Baines, among many others.

But there was no greater advocate of Lau's teachings than George Brett. Yes, that George Brett, the one who played 21 years for the Royals, had 3,154 hits, and is widely considered to be one of the best hitters in the history of baseball. He believed in Charley Lau, once telling the *New York Times,* "Charley made me a hitter."

That endorsement alone made Lau a force of coaching impossible to ignore. His pioneering approach laid the foundation of hitting instruction for decades. It created generations of hitters who were convinced that they knew the correct way to swing a bat, because they had it straight from a coach renowned for his expertise. That is what Craig Wallenbrock was up against.

Wallenbrock didn't know it then, but some people were beginning to notice him. Important people. People who had the ability to elevate his profile to heights he never could have imagined years earlier, when all he cared about was finding good dope and riding the waves. One of those people was Duane Shaffer.

Shaffer is the very definition of a baseball lifer—a veteran scout who spent decades driving around dusty fields across the nation in search of the next big thing. In the mid-1980s, he was working for the White Sox, and Southern California was part of his territory.

Shaffer spent most of his time at the big-name colleges, places like UCLA and USC, scouting the most coveted players in one of the most fertile areas of the country for amateur baseball talent. But a couple days a week, when the major schools had no games, he often found himself at smaller programs like Mount San Antonio. That's where he first met Craig Wallenbrock.

As time went on, Wallenbrock started offering Shaffer his thoughts not just about players on his team, but about players on teams throughout the league. Few of them ever signed professional contracts; the talent discrepancy with the bigger colleges was just too much to overcome. Still, Shaffer quickly realized that when it came to hitters, Wallenbrock knew his stuff.

"When you're a scout, you need a big network," said Shaffer, who as of 2019 worked for the Padres as a scout. "Craig became a part of my network."

For Shaffer, that meant occasionally checking in with Wallenbrock for tips about little-known players who might be worth checking out. Sometimes Shaffer would even visit Wallenbrock's home in Pasadena, where there was a batting cage in the backyard for hitters seeking a little extra work.

Wallenbrock handed out all of this advice pro bono, never expecting anything to come of it. He loved watching hitters and talking about hitters, so he viewed recommending hitters to a professional scout as his pleasure, not extra work for which he deserved compensation. The arrangement certainly benefited Shaffer, who decided after a while it was time to make the relationship official.

"It got to the point where it was, 'Hell, I might as well just put him on,' so I hired him as a part-time scout," Shaffer said.

And just like that, barely a decade after quitting his college baseball team and putting the game behind him, Craig Wallenbrock had a job in professional baseball.

For a while, scouting became Wallenbrock's life. He stayed with the White Sox until 1988, when he took a job with the A's, and then he moved to the Cleveland Indians in 1994. Two years after that, he left scouting and took a job with player agent Jim McDowell, the brother of former big league pitcher Jack McDowell, helping him evaluate amateur players who would become potential clients. He had made his own strange way in an industry notoriously hostile to outsiders. But being a talent evaluator wasn't bringing him closer to solving the riddle that had originally drawn him back in, the one that still enchanted him: the swing.

Wallenbrock continued studying video and analyzing the swings of the greatest hitters in history. But he didn't have an outlet for all the thoughts careening around in his head, a laboratory where he could test his theories. Maybe, he thought, he could make one. He had a growing network in the baseball community and access to young players and their parents who increasingly thought of him as some sort of authority.

"People started saying, 'Why don't you charge for this?'" he said.

Wallenbrock had taught hitting before, of course, to Judd, and at junior college. This was something new, though. For the first time, Craig Wallenbrock was going to dedicate his time to teaching the swing, to one-on-one instruction with players serious about improving their performance at the plate. But first he needed a dedicated space, an indoor batting cage that was his.

As it turns out, an extra cage was available to rent at the Ball Yard, an establishment in Chatsworth, California. The proprietor of the facility was a man named Doug Latta.

THE BALL YARD

Marlon Byrd needed a place to hit. It was the 2012 season, and he and his family had just moved from the Chicago area to Calabasas, California. The first priority was finding a facility where he could keep his swing in shape. Byrd had lots of time on his hands in those days. On June 25 of that year, he had received a 50-game suspension from Major League Baseball after testing positive for a drug called tamoxifen.

Tamoxifen is not a steroid. It is a selective estrogen receptor modulator typically prescribed to treat breast cancer. A man—like Marlon Byrd, for instance—might take it to treat a condition called gynecomastia, an endocrine system disorder that leads to a noncancerous growth of breast tissue. Tamoxifen is on the banned substance list because gynecomastia is a common side effect of steroid use. In other words, tamoxifen isn't a performance-enhancing drug itself, but it treats the symptoms of performance-enhancing drugs, which explains why it is prohibited.

Byrd had gynecomastia. He said he only took tamoxifen for a legitimate medical reason and insisted that his only crime was negligence, not malice. Later on in his career, Byrd said, he had a therapeutic-use exemption for the drug, allowing him to take it.

"All I had to do was look at the banned list," Byrd told me. "I didn't."

If Byrd really was trying to cheat, he wasn't doing a very good job of it. At the time of the suspension, Byrd, then 34, had played in 47 games in 2012 for the Cubs and Red Sox, hitting .210 with just one home run and a .488 OPS. His bat speed had deteriorated to the point that he had to switch to a lighter model, one used by Boston's five-foot-nine second baseman Dustin Pedroia—and even that still felt heavy. A couple weeks before the suspension, without any knowledge of the positive test and impending suspension, the Red Sox released Byrd. No other team was jumping at the opportunity to sign him.

Byrd had been in the major leagues since 2002, when he was a speedy outfielder with the Philadelphia Phillies. He developed into a solid player, even making the All-Star team with the Cubs in 2010. When his production started slipping in his thirties, he thought he was just getting old. Then, when the suspension was handed down, he figured he'd never get another chance. The way he had been playing, he didn't deserve one, even without the stigma that comes from failing a drug test.

"I'm thinking, *I'm not good. I'm a pariah in baseball. I'm not going to get another job,*" Byrd said. "I stunk, plus I supposedly was trying to cheat. So that's how baseball looked at me."

That's why Byrd decided to uproot his family and move to Calabasas. He needed a change of scenery. Maybe it was the sunshine or the California breeze, but once he settled into his new home, Byrd decided he wasn't ready to quit baseball. He wanted another chance—if the game would give him one.

Those are the circumstances that led to Marlon Byrd showing up at the Ball Yard. He checked out a facility in Westlake Village called Boost Your Average and was impressed with how it looked. Everything was new and state-of-the-art, the equipment pristine. It was beautiful—but Byrd rejected it. "It didn't seem like a place of work," he said.

Then Google led him to the Ball Yard. Byrd drove over to Chatsworth, following his GPS to a parking lot, and saw . . . nothing. He was confused. Where was this place? Eventually he got out of his car and walked around a bit until he found a locked door with the address he found online. He swore there was no sign, or if there was he didn't see it. Byrd knocked on the door. Then he knocked again, louder. No answer.

Disappointed and a little annoyed, Byrd returned to his car to drive home. Then, just as he was about to back out and leave, a forest green Dodge Durango pulled up next to him, with a gray-haired, middle-aged man in the driver's seat.

"What are you looking for?" the man asked.

"I'm looking for the Ball Yard," Byrd responded.

"Oh! Come in!"

Doug Latta had arrived just in time. If he hadn't, and Byrd had left, he probably wouldn't have come back. He probably would have found another spot to hit. Maybe he would have made it back to the major leagues. Maybe not. But as Latta unlocked the door and welcomed Marlon Byrd to the Ball Yard, neither of them realized that Byrd had just met the man who would re-make his career.

Like Craig Wallenbrock, Doug Latta grew up in the baseball hot-bed of Southern California, attending Fairfax High School in Los Angeles, right on the border of West Hollywood. As a child, he loved baseball, but his family didn't have much by way of re-sources to support his burgeoning interest in the sport. Most of his baseball education came in the form of pickup games with his friends in an empty lot on the site of a burned-down house in his neighborhood, like a re-creation of *The Sandlot*. When he couldn't find enough kids to play a game, he went to the front lawn of his house with whomever he could round up to emulate the stances and swings of their favorite big leaguers. Latta idolized Steve Garvey, the great Dodgers first baseman in the 1970s. He still vividly recalls that in the first game he ever attended at Dodger Stadium, on June 5, 1971, Garvey bashed a home run off Mets lefty Ray Sadecki. He also remembers New York's starting pitcher that night: a young Nolan Ryan.

Though Latta played on his high school team, mostly as a reserve, by the time he graduated baseball was nowhere near his mind. That summer his mother, who raised him and his two older sisters alone, passed away, essentially leaving Latta on his own. He went to UCLA not to pursue baseball, but just to figure out a way to carve out a life for himself, balancing school and work.

"There was no safety net," Latta said. "I was now an adult taking care of myself."

Harsh reality didn't cure him of the baseball bug. If anything, it strengthened his desire to be on the field, playing the game he loved—to escape from the challenges he faced every day. He joined a weekend league in town, just for fun, until one day it became a little more serious. While warming up on the field at Los Angeles Valley College, the baseball coach from the school saw Latta throwing and approached him, asking him which college he played for. "One thing I had that would definitely stand out, I had a very strong arm," he said. The coach was impressed. He saw in Latta the tools of somebody good enough to play in community college. Latta informed him that, in fact, he wasn't playing anywhere.

Before too long, he had an offer to join the team. It was tempting, but ultimately, Latta declined. He lived 45 minutes to an hour away from the campus, and he didn't feel comfortable commuting that far, preferring instead to stay close to his sisters in the wake of their mother's death. Fortunately, the Valley coach had a friend at Los Angeles City College, a 15-minute drive from Latta's house. After a few phone calls, Doug Latta was officially a college baseball player, living out a dream that he thought he had already abandoned.

Latta's college baseball career was anything but a straight line. He spent a couple of months playing on the Pepperdine summer team. He was at San Jose State for six months, but an issue in the transfer of his previous credits from UCLA cut that short. Ultimately, he found a home at California Lutheran, a school in nearby Thousand Oaks, outside of Los Angeles. He would go on to graduate from Cal Lu.

As a hitter, Latta was inconsistent. His first year playing in junior college, he hit okay. In the second, he struggled, worrying too much about generating power and not enough about making contact. His swing was unrefined, to say the least. In his third year, his first at Cal Lu, he opened the season in the zone, hitting better than he ever had before. Then he suffered a grade 3 ankle sprain while trying to turn a double play in the field. Doctors initially told him the injury would end his playing career. He proved them wrong, making it back to the field, but he never fully regained his swing.

Believing baseball to be in his rearview mirror once and for all, Latta focused on business after finishing school. His business was swimming pools—constructing them, remodeling them, repairing them, and everything in between. By the mid-1990s, he had served stints as the president of the Swimming Pool Trades and Contractors Association and the National Association of Gas Chlorinators. Doug Latta had carved out a life for himself, and it didn't involve baseball.

Well, it *mostly* didn't involve baseball. Latta always missed playing. He missed the competition. He missed the sound of the crack of the bat and the smell of freshly laid dirt. Before long, he'd joined a semipro team called the Pasadena Redbirds. For Latta, playing for the Redbirds was just a way to stay connected to the game, but others in the league took it a lot more seriously. Ex-pros would play, looking for one more shot at major league glory, so the competition and stakes were high. Once in a while, pro scouts would come by, hoping to uncover a diamond in the rough. One day Latta met a scout who had just started working for the A's. His name was Craig Wallenbrock.

They quickly became friends and, before long, officemates, because at the end of 1998, Doug Latta decided he needed more in his life than the pool business. He wanted to see if he could make a job out of baseball. That dream turned into the Ball Yard, the facility for hitting training that he opened in a warehouse in Chatsworth, California. At the beginning, Latta had exactly one batting cage reserved for high-level training. A year later, he would have six. When Wallenbrock asked for a cage, Latta was happy to bring him in.

"It was like going into a graduate program," Latta said. "Having Craig in was perfect—someone I knew, someone I trusted, obviously, someone who wanted to be there."

The partnership wasn't quite Jobs and Wozniak—their bank accounts made that perfectly clear—but in many ways, the Ball Yard was the baseball equivalent of a garage tech startup, an underground club dedicated to progress and innovation in the realm of hitting. No matter who was in the cage, whether a Little Leaguer or a professional, the message was the same: this is a place for serious hitters who are willing not only to work but to explore new ideas often far different from what any other coach teaches. "First of its kind," Latta said proudly.

The Ball Yard.

At this point, Wallenbrock had already been honing some of his more unusual philosophies of the swing for decades and, at least within nerdy hitting circles, had made something of a name for himself. Latta was still new to Wallenbrock's ideas. But he was ready to learn.

With the addition of Wallenbrock, top players, even big leaguers, were now training at the Ball Yard. At this point in his life, Latta really didn't have an expert knowledge of swing mechanics. He knew that what he had been taught throughout high school and college was flawed. Small observations had convinced him that there was a ton he was still missing.

At the Ball Yard, working with clients and absorbing some of Wallenbrock's knowledge, that changed. Latta worked mostly with kids at the beginning. Then Wallenbrock brought in his ever-growing roster of clients, players like Michael Young and Brad Fullmer. When he had time, Latta would watch what Wallenbrock taught and how he taught it. Then he'd go back and watch video of the swings, breaking them down until he understood why hitters swung the way they did. As time passed, Wallenbrock began to turn to Latta and ask, "Hey, Doug, what do you see?" further bringing him into the discussion. Suddenly, Latta, a so-so college ballplayer who made his living building swimming pools, had a front-row seat to some of the most sophisticated hitting discussion in the world. Wallenbrock was his tenant. He also was his teacher. It went on this way for about a decade.

By around 2001, the Ball Yard had become the host of an annual hitting summit that featured current and former big leaguers gathering to discuss their ideas about the swing and where it was going.

As the years passed, the reputation of the Ball Yard grew. On most days, from 9:00 a.m. until 3:00 p.m., the facility hosted a steady stream of elite hitters—major leaguers, minor leaguers, top college prospects. It got big enough that by 2006 Latta was able to sell his pool business and focus all of his professional attention on baseball.

"The key to the Ball Yard was that it was always a place to work," Latta said. "It was like a sanctuary."

By that time, Latta had learned enough from Wallenbrock to start formulating some of his own ideas. He became obsessed not only with video but also with kinesiology and physiology as he tried to figure out how the body moved in a high-level swing and why it moved that way.

"For 12 years, I had been watching video out the wazoo," Latta said. "I had been watching major leaguers hit in our cages. I'd been watching their trials and tribulations."

And in the summer of 2012, something would happen that would bring Doug Latta out of obscurity and into the forefront. That's when Marlon Byrd walked into the Ball Yard for the first time.

Doug Latta might have owned the Ball Yard, but at that time it was his tenant who was in high demand. Craig Wallenbrock never advertised his services as a private hitting instructor. He believed his work spoke for itself. The baseball community is small and insular, especially in Southern California, and he was confident that if he helped players improve their swings, they would talk and others would seek him out.

That's exactly what happened when Wallenbrock started training hitters out of the Ball Yard early in 1999.

"I'd work with 13- or 14-year-olds in this real small local area," Wallenbrock said. "Then as I branched out, it just became a bigger area of Southern California. And then, as the reputation spread, guys would fly in. Every once in a while I'd have a guy come in from Arizona or come down from Northern California, and I thought that was coming a long way."

Even in those early days, the list of players who worked with Wallenbrock in their youth is astounding. Not long after signing his first professional contract in 1997, an infielder named Michael Young sought out Wallenbrock and worked with him every off-season through the minor leagues. He wound up making seven All-Star teams and winning a batting title with the Texas Rangers.

Not long after that, while playing college ball at UCLA, another infielder found Wallenbrock: Chase Utley. He went on to make six All-Star teams and win four Silver Slugger awards with the Phillies, a major league career that will almost certainly garner Hall of Fame consideration. A couple of years later, Wallenbrock began teaching a high school slugger in nearby Granada Hills named Ryan Braun. He too developed into a star, earning NL Most Valuable Player honors with the Brewers in 2011.

"I had never had a hitting lesson before," Braun told me one quiet spring training morning. "I had never thought about hitting in the terms he described it. He was like a mad scientist when it came to hitting, because I hadn't heard hitting dissected mechanically the way he was able to dissect it."

To the players who worked with him back then in the early days of the Ball Yard, the strangest part of hitting with Wallenbrock was his teaching setup. He had a large, boxy television connected to a VCR and a giant video camera set up by the batting cages.

"Craig videotaped every swing I ever took with him," Young said. "We would look at every single swing. We were popping in VHSs."

Today the idea of filming swings and analyzing the footage is so obvious that it seems weird to even mention it. But to young hitters like Braun and Young back when Wallenbrock was first doing it, this was something totally new and revolutionary.

It's hard to say for certain just how much of an impact Wallenbrock had on some of these players or whether they would have made the majors without him. For instance, Wallenbrock admitted that Braun didn't need to do too much. "He was a guy that I just had to polish," Wallenbrock said. "Braun could always hit." Braun concurred: "A lot of the things that he teaches were things that I was fortunate to naturally be doing already." With Young, Wallenbrock did a little bit more—helping him solidify his bat path, showing him how to keep his barrel in the hitting zone longer—but it was far from an overhaul. Both of these players already had the tools to be great.

But they also believed in Wallenbrock's method. When Young was hitting with Wallenbrock, he never told the Rangers, who might have been upset that he was working with an instructor whose ideas about the swing were almost certainly different from what the club's minor league hitting coaches taught. Looking back now, Young doesn't think the Rangers would have tried to stop him from going to Wallenbrock, but even if they had, it probably wouldn't have stopped him.

"I trusted my own instincts with Craig," Young said. "I wanted to be coachable with my organization, but at the same time, I'm taking control of my own career."

As for Braun, even though he hadn't hit with Wallenbrock since college, he told me in no uncertain terms that "almost everything I learned then is still applicable today," and that if he ever felt he needed to retool his swing, "Craig's the guy I would go to."

In the summer of 2018, Braun stayed true to those words. Mired in a dreadful slump, Braun reached out to Wallenbrock for the first time in years and sent him video of his swing. And then that winter Braun went to hit with Wallenbrock again in person. His swing needed another tune-up.

When Marlon Byrd first walked into the Ball Yard in the summer of 2012, he couldn't help but notice the pictures lining the walls. Chase Utley. Michael Young. Both of them had hit in the very cages Byrd was about to hit in, as had plenty of others. Byrd didn't know about the Ball Yard's illustrious client list when he found the place using a simple Google search. He also didn't know that those players came to the Ball Yard primarily because of Craig Wallenbrock, not the man who was now throwing to him.

Even if Byrd had known all of that, it wouldn't have mattered. He wasn't at the Ball Yard looking for a teacher. He just wanted a human being with a functioning arm. He told Latta he needed somebody to put balls on the tee, to flip underhand tosses to him and maybe throw light batting practice. Most important, he needed this person to be available to do those things as Byrd saw fit. He might have been cut and he might have been suspended, but Byrd still had what he described as "big league bravado."

Latta agreed to that arrangement without hesitation. He had created the Ball Yard to serve as a place of business for elite hitters, and if a major leaguer like Byrd needed a place to hit, he would make the Ball Yard—and himself—available to make that happen.

On their first day together, Latta asked Byrd what he thought he was trying to do when he swung. Byrd explained that he stayed on his back side, separated his hands from his torso, and let his back heel pop up. At that point, he would swing down and level out at the point of contact, bringing his barrel on a straight line to the ball. Latta listened quietly. When Byrd finished, he said, "Oh, okay," and had Byrd get into the cage. Before joining him, unbeknownst to Byrd, Latta switched on his trusty video camera. Then he watched Byrd swing.

"The swing he came in with was so jacked up and unathletic," Latta said. "It was a tribute to his athleticism that he could even compete at the big league level with that swing. It was that bad."

That might have been true, but Byrd didn't know it. Every few cuts, Latta would ask Byrd how he felt. Byrd invariably would say, "Oh, it feels great," and his mind would drift ahead to his eventual comeback. After his first round, Latta asked Byrd to sit down in front of the television monitor adjacent to the cage. He asked Byrd if he could share some thoughts about what he had just seen. Byrd agreed, admittedly with low expectations. Latta threw the video—video Byrd had no idea had been captured—onto the screen.

Byrd didn't know anything about Latta. They had spent very little time together. Never did he expect this man to offer him genuinely new and useful feedback. But Latta's confidence intrigued and impressed Byrd. He was respectful of Byrd's expertise but firm in his conviction that he had ideas that could help. It was enough to convince Byrd to listen with an open mind.

With the door open, Latta sprinted in, explaining to Byrd that instead of swinging down, perhaps he should consider working underneath the ball to generate power. He talked about the myth of "staying back" on the ball and the value of making an athletic move forward to attack it. He showed Byrd a different bat path, with the barrel moving backward before moving forward, the beautiful "lag position" that Craig Wallenbrock had seen decades earlier and was still fighting to bring to the mainstream.

Byrd was dumbfounded. He had never heard a coach describe a swing that way. He had spent the last six years of his major league career with the Rangers and Cubs working under Rudy Jaramillo, one of the most respected hitting coaches in the league. Jaramillo talked a lot about rhythm and timing, and he helped plenty of hitters in his career. This was something different. Byrd certainly wasn't sold, but he was intrigued enough to keep listening, even if only with one ear open.

Byrd and Latta headed back into the cage, but this time Byrd asked for some advice. Latta suggested that he narrow his stance and move his hands to a place that would allow him to work underneath and match the plane of the ball early to drive it into the air. Byrd started swinging. As he did before, after a few cuts,

Latta asked him how he felt. Byrd answered, "Amazing." This time, however, he truly meant it. The ball just sounded different coming off Byrd's bat than it had before. Latta will never forget the look on Byrd's face after those first few swings. It was "a smile of discovery," Latta said, "like, 'Yeah, I've got this.'"

"From that point on, it was just, 'That makes sense,' and I scrapped everything that I was doing—everything," Byrd said. "This is a guy I had just met!"

Byrd kept swinging, Latta offering minor tweaks after each round. Almost immediately, Byrd noticed something that amazed him: the bat he was using, the lighter bat that belonged to Dustin Pedroia to compensate for his decreasing bat speed, suddenly felt *too* light. He switched back to his old bat. The results only improved.

"So now, in one day working with Doug, I've changed my swing," Byrd said. "I'm feeling good, I'm getting confidence back. I'm realizing that I'm not over the hill in baseball."

For the next 87 days after that initial encounter, Byrd showed up at the Ball Yard to hit with Latta. He didn't miss a single session. Every morning when he woke up, he felt the itch. He needed to get back in the cage and experience that feeling again.

Over that time, Byrd started to learn more about Latta's background and the history of the Ball Yard. He asked some of the players from the pictures on the wall about their experience with Latta, only to learn that none of them had actually worked with him. They worked with Wallenbrock. Naturally, that piqued Byrd's interest, to the point that he had no choice but to meet Wallenbrock and see what he was all about. That led, at times, to Wallenbrock observing Byrd work with Latta, the way Latta used to observe Wallenbrock working with guys like Young and Utley.

But Marlon Byrd never got along with Craig Wallenbrock.

The clash came to a head one day when Wallenbrock started talking to Byrd about certain moves from Alex Rodriguez's swing and trying to add them to Byrd's. When Byrd tried to implement Wallenbrock's suggestions, however, something immediately felt off. He struggled at the plate that day, and the next. By the third day, Latta, back in the driver's seat, seemed perturbed.

"I felt bad, because I'm like, 'Am I letting you down? Are you mad at me?'" Byrd said. "And he was just upset that our flow got disrupted for a second, because we jumped too far ahead."

Byrd has plenty of respect for Wallenbrock's expertise and desire to make players better. He has no doubt that for a great many hitters over the decades his voice was the one that helped them achieve stardom. Byrd just wasn't going to be one of those players. In fact, later on in his work with Latta, Byrd said, he was able to install the exact moves into his swing that Wallenbrock was trying to teach him that day. He just hadn't been ready yet.

From that point on, however, Byrd wouldn't let Wallenbrock in on his work with Latta. "I said, 'Doug, look, it's you and me,'" Byrd said.

For Latta, this was a career-defining vote of confidence. It was the first time he had ever cultivated a major league client entirely on his own, earning his trust and playing a role in reshaping his swing. Before this, Latta had worked almost exclusively with amateurs, rarely getting a chance to emerge out of Wallenbrock's shadow. Now Marlon Byrd and Doug Latta were all in together, and there was no looking back.

A little more than a decade earlier, Doug Latta was building swimming pools for a living and the Ball Yard wasn't even a dream. It was a fantasy, an idea so far from the realm of reality that it hardly felt like a possibility. But now the Ball Yard was real. Very real. And he had a major league player who believed that Latta was a voice not just worth listening to but compelling enough to entrust with the fate of his career.

"We were doing our thing, you know?" Latta said. "It was definitely kind of a coming-out for me, where I'm unfettered. Nobody's sitting on me, nobody's telling me I'm wrong. Nobody's disrespecting me at this. I'm free."

UP, UP IS THE WAY

John Thorn is Major League Baseball's official historian. A cerebral man in his early seventies, with a bushy black mustache now speckled with gray, Thorn might know more about the roots of the national pastime than anybody on earth. A conversation with him is a walk through the very fabric of American culture. Visiting his home is like waking up in baseball heaven.

Thorn lives in Catskill, New York, a quaint little town about two hours north of Manhattan. His home is a veritable library, brimming with books not just about baseball but about the history of all the myriad subjects that interest him.

Thorn's home is the perfect place for a history lesson, and to fully appreciate the magnitude of Craig Wallenbrock's and Doug Latta's work with the baseball swing, a history lesson is in order. Where did all these ideas about "swinging down" originate? Why did people ever come up with jargon like "chop wood," "squish the bug," and "swing through the ball" in the first place? Why was everybody so wrong for so long—or were they wrong at all?

Here's the thing about longtime baseball fans: many of them want to believe that the sport they love has been exactly the same for the last hundred years or so. It's a romantic notion that understandably appeals to devotees of a sport so rooted in its past—that a game played by Babe Ruth, Ted Williams, Mike Schmidt, and Albert Pujols can remain consistent for over a century, connecting grandfathers to fathers, mothers to daughters.

But the reality is that baseball has changed dramatically. In fact, it's always changing. Sometimes gradually, other times very quickly. In the 2014 season, for instance, scoring dropped to 4.07 runs per game, the lowest in decades. By 2017, players had set a new home run record, a figure that was topped again in 2019, marking a sudden, radical, and fundamental shift in how the game is played.

Perhaps there was a perfectly plausible explanation for how coaches had taught their students to swing for so long. That's where Thorn comes in. He explained that there is a very simple reason the swing was long designed to bang the ball into the ground: in the early days of baseball it was incredibly valuable to do so. In the 1850s and '60s, Thorn said, in order to form club teams, people needed to invite inexperienced players to join up. To make the game easier for them, balls caught on one bounce were considered an out, greatly diminishing the return on balls hit in the air.

For a long time, gloves were not used. Even when they started to become commonplace, they didn't have webbing. Many pre-1920 ballparks had absurdly huge dimensions, if they had fences at all, making home runs nearly impossible to come by. Fields were rutted and poorly kept, leading to untrue bounces on the infield. The top 35 seasons for errors in MLB history all happened before 1918, with a large percentage of those miscues coming on balls hit on the ground. There's a reason baseball before 1920 was called the "dead-ball era:" it was hard to hit the ball far.

So, essentially, balls in the air, which weren't designed to travel very far in the first place, were easy outs. Balls on the ground were mishandled at shockingly high rates. Of course batters were taught to swing that way. Thorn described swings at that time as "choppy," without the high follow-throughs that are typical today.

Yet, while they were rare, home runs were an attraction from the very beginning. The ability to drive the ball far, to send it soaring high into the sky, was sexy. It was exciting. It was a sign of immense strength and power, of great masculinity and virility. Even back then, chicks dug the long ball.

An illustration of a hitter in *The Art of Batting and Base Running*, published by A. G. Spalding & Bros. in 1886.

Baseball "purists," however, did not. To them, the early stewards of the sport, baseball "was regarded as a game of strategy, a thinking man's game," Thorn said. Home runs were brutish. They were inelegant. They were unrefined.

As Hall of Fame baseball writer Henry Chadwick wrote in 1868, "Long hits are showy, but they do not pay in the long run. Sharp grounders insuring the first-base certain, and sometimes the second-base easily, are worth all the hits made for home-runs which players strive for."

Meanwhile, *The Art of Batting and Base Running*, a manual Chadwick wrote in 1886, was all but dedicated to the idea that fan and player fascination with the long ball was ruining the game—a position not unlike the one held by a certain segment of baseball fans today. The final words of the preface were: "The batsman who can the most easily earn a single base, and who is willing to sacrifice his record of total bases and a high average in faulty statistics in order to bring in a needed run, does work in batting in 'playing for the side' worth all that the most brilliant heavy hitting batsmen ever accomplished."

Less than 40 years later, however, a heavy-hitting batsman would come along who would change all of that forever.

The wildest thing about watching footage of George Herman Ruth today is just how *modern* it looks. Sure, the stuff around the periphery is different—why did people dress up to go to baseball games in the '20s anyway?—but that swing . . . the swing of the man called The Babe . . . looks eerily similar to the swings you'd see in major league stadiums nearly a century later. It was big. It was powerful. And it was up. This wasn't a swing designed to just make contact or to guide the ball through a hole. This was a swing whose sole mission was to pulverize the ball into another galaxy.

Babe Ruth had no interest in ground balls. They were boring. They didn't inspire tens of thousands of adoring fans to stand up and cheer his name. Home runs did that. So when Babe Ruth stepped up to the plate, his mission was simple: hit the ball as far as he possibly could.

"Babe Ruth swung large, ate large, lived large," Thorn said. "If the '20s were the age of excess, Babe Ruth was the embodiment of the age."

Ruth revolutionized baseball in ways that are almost inconceivable. When he hit 54 home runs for the Yankees in 1920, the first season of the live-ball era, no other American League team—no entire team—hit more than 50. His 714 career home

Babe Ruth, whose power stroke made him perhaps the first adopter of the fly-ball revolution.

runs stood as an all-time record for nearly 40 years. Nobody topped his single-season mark of 60 homers in 1927 for more than 30 years.

But changing a culture is difficult, especially in a game as hidebound as baseball. While Ruth was drawing crowds and thrilling the next generation of fans with his prodigious power, the old guard still clung to old ways.

Nobody embodied that idea better than Detroit Tigers legend Ty Cobb, the greatest ever at "hitting them where they ain't." In 24 major league seasons from 1905 through 1928, Cobb hit .367, the best batting average in history. He achieved that with a decidedly small-ball approach, wielding his bat with pinpoint precision to guide the ball wherever he wanted, then using his speed on the bases. He even used the unusual grip of separating his hands on the handle of the bat, a technique that would never be used today. Cobb finished his career with a mere 117 home runs— and 297 triples. By way of contrast, no active major leaguer today even has 100 three-baggers. Thorn calls Cobb "an artist."

As Ruth ascended, some traditionalists quickly grew nostalgic for Cobb's version of hitting. Former Red Sox owner Tom Yawkey, asked if he preferred Ruth or Cobb, said he would choose Cobb. "I like to see Ruth hit the long ones, but nothing has thrilled me more than the sight of Ty Cobb dashing around the bases, taking chances, outwitting the other side," he said in 1933, according to Charles Leerhsen's *Ty Cobb: A Terrible Beauty*.

Perhaps not surprisingly, Cobb resented Ruth, or at least he resented Ruth's popularity. He never embraced the live-ball style of baseball and remained a vociferous advocate for the pre-1920 game, which he considered less brutish, more refined and gentlemanly. Cobb's version of baseball involved strategy and thought, not sheer strength. And in May 1925, with the Tigers in St. Louis for a series against the Browns, Cobb set out to prove that Ruth and his newfangled style of hitting weren't so special.

Before the game on May 5, Cobb made a declaration: for the first time in his career, he would try to hit home runs. He could always do that, he insisted. He just chose not to, because homers weren't aesthetically pleasing. At least, that's how the legend goes. What Cobb said that day has been long debated and could be apocryphal. But what actually happened is not: Cobb hit three homers that game. The next day, he hit two more. Not even the great Ruth ever hit five home runs in two games. From there, Cobb went back to his old ways, finishing the season with just 12 dingers.

Ty Cobb, who holds the highest career batting average in MLB history, yet hit few home runs, except for one strange series in 1925.

Whether Cobb was actually making a statement or simply got lucky doesn't matter much. The reality is that Ruth had become the biggest attraction around, and his ability to slam balls over fences helped popularize baseball in a way Cobb never could. Ty Cobb might have been an artist, but like so many artists, his art eventually went out of style. Small ball was out. Power was in. For nearly the first century of baseball's existence, nobody had a greater influence on the swing than Babe Ruth.

"I think Ruth was a genius," Thorn said. "Ruth was a Leonardo, he was an Einstein."

Babe Ruth retired from Major League Baseball in 1935, after 28 largely forgotten games for the Boston Braves as a broken-down

40-year-old. His legacy was immense, as a horde of power hitters emerged after him. Lou Gehrig debuted with the Yankees in 1923. Jimmie Foxx showed up in 1925, and Mel Ott a year later in 1926. They felt like a natural follow-up to Ruth, forever cementing power as a viable strategy.

But it wouldn't be until 1939 that somebody came along and pushed the swing forward. In fact, this player would understand the mechanics of a baseball swing better than anybody to ever pick up the bat. That player was Theodore Samuel Williams. You probably know him as Ted.

Throughout his professional career, Ted Williams said that his goal was to have people see him and say, "There goes Ted Williams, the greatest hitter who ever lived." Nearly two decades after his death, it's safe to say that he very well might have accomplished it. In 19 seasons with the Red Sox, Williams posted a batting average of .344. He hit 521 home runs. His .482 lifetime on-base percentage (OBP) is still the best in history. Since he hit .406 in 1941, there still hasn't been a player to hit .400 in a single season. He did all that despite missing three seasons in the prime of his career to serve as an aviator in World War II, plus most of two more years during the Korean War. It was as if Williams was a wizard endowed with some sort of hitting magic that had never been seen before and hasn't been seen since.

Except it wasn't magic that made Ted Williams such a remarkable hitter. It was science. No, Williams didn't have high-speed video cameras, bat sensors, or sophisticated computer systems capable of tracking a hitter's every movement. But he studied and dissected the swing more than anybody, and a decade after the conclusion of his playing career, the Splendid Splinter decided to let the entire world in on his secrets.

In 1970, Williams and author John Underwood published *The Science of Hitting,* a roughly 70-page guide outlining what he had come to believe was the ideal way to swing a bat. He wrote it, at least in part, because it bothered him that hitting a golf ball had already been the subject of plenty of serious study, while the baseball swing had not. If hitting a baseball was the hardest thing to do in all of sports, a claim Williams made many times, why, he wondered, had the swing received "no such barrage of scholarly treatment"?

Williams was trying to do his part. In 1969, a year before the release of his book, he took a job as the manager of the Washington Senators, a gig he kept for four seasons, including the franchise's first as the Rangers. In his first year, he led this incarnation of the Senators, an expansion team that had started play in 1961, to their first winning season, going 86–76. The Associated Press named him American League Manager of the Year.

The rest of Williams's managerial career didn't go as well. His team's record got worse in each of the next three years, bottoming out with a 54–100 mark as the Texas Rangers in 1972. He would often become frustrated that his players couldn't do what he could do, couldn't see what he could see. It turns out that Williams was less interested in managing a team than in just talking hitting.

Something valuable did come out of his time managing, though: an honest-to-god protégé. Williams's first baseman from 1969 until the Senators traded him to the A's in May 1971 was a Berkeley grad named Mike Epstein. Before Williams arrived, Epstein wasn't much of a hitter by major league standards. He had a .229 batting average with 22 total home runs in 693 at-bats. In his first season under Williams, he broke out, hitting .278 and blasting 30 homers.

Epstein had a couple more strong seasons, and he wound up bouncing around the majors through 1974. He wouldn't reconnect with Williams until the early 1980s, when a journalist in Boston called for an interview and asked if they were still in touch. They weren't, but the question sparked a reunion, and they ultimately spent some time together in Florida chatting, reminiscing—and talking hitting, their favorite subject.

"Finally he says, 'You're a smart son of a bitch. You get this,'" Epstein said.

Those get-togethers continued annually for the next decade or so, with Epstein continuing to learn Williams's thoughts and ideas about the swing. Epstein went a step further, taking advantage of the improved technology of the time, adding video analysis to confirm—and refine—Williams's teachings. Sometimes Williams would argue with Epstein, but he never dismissed him. Coming from Ted Williams, that was the ultimate sign of respect. And in 1993, Williams wrote a reference letter endorsing Epstein as a hitting coach, saying in part, "I'm a tough guy to please and impress, but I believe Mike comprehends and teaches the science of proper hitting as skillfully as anyone I have run across in all my years in baseball." It is believed that it is the only such endorsement Williams ever gave out. Epstein has it saved in a bank vault.

"People would say, 'It'll be a cold day in hell when I teach that shit,'" said Mike's son, Jake, a former minor leaguer who now teaches his father's methods. "They teach it now. The cold day has happened. It's like my dad came in and said the earth was round."

Reading Ted Williams's book today, it's remarkable how contemporary it feels. He lamented the demise of the hitter and took aim at people who argued that batting averages were going down in the pursuit of power. With the right swing, he argued, there was no reason a hitter couldn't have both.

The Science of Hitting is filled with fascinating nuggets, from the value of waiting for the right pitch to how a batter should use his hips and hands. Williams offered his thoughts on what kind of bat to use, how to hit to the opposite field, and so much more.

But the most important part of Williams's book starts on page 47. The section is titled "Up, Up Is the Way." It's here where Williams upended conventional wisdom in the most dramatic way possible—and laid the groundwork for a revolution, even if it didn't arrive for nearly half a century.

"You have always heard," Williams wrote, "that the ideal swing is level or 'down.'"

Williams disagreed with that approach. He advocated for what he described as a "slight upswing" of about 10 degrees. His first reason for this was obvious: the only way to drive the ball, to hit a home run, is to hit the ball in the air. The other reason was a bit more subtle and insightful. Williams wrote that because pitchers are standing on a mound, by definition the flight of the ball will always be down. An upswing will put the bat "flush in line with the path of the ball for a longer period," essentially giving hitters more margin for error. Modern hitting coaches, the leaders of the revolution, would call this "matching the plane of the pitch"—in other words, getting the barrel of the bat behind the ball as quickly as possible and swinging up through it, rather than swinging down to meet the flight of the ball.

Williams's explanation of the upswing is accompanied by a diagram that shows the difference between the level stroke and the Williams stroke. It's a simple sketch—just a white box, with the outline of arms, bats, and baseballs showing the value of the upswing. But that little graphic, buried in the middle of Ted Williams's book, is perhaps the most significant visualization of the swing ever produced. It inspired a revolution.

Ted Williams was a craftsman of the swing, operating in an era before high-tech cameras and statistical modeling changed the game. But now we have the numbers to back up his approach.

According to Statcast, Major League Baseball's tracking

technology, players posted a .247 batting average and a .269 slugging percentage on balls hit on the ground from 2015 through 2019. On balls hit in the air? Those numbers jumped to .406 and .787, respectively. Of course, the quality of contact matters; infield pop-ups are bad, line drives are good. Yet the overall point remains: balls in the air are better than balls on the ground, especially when you consider that even when balls on the ground lead to a positive result, it's almost always a single. Nowadays, the rise of defensive shifts has only made slapping a ground ball through the infield more challenging.

Ted Williams knew all this intuitively. He recognized the value of hitting the ball in the air without any statistics to back him up. Hence, the upswing. As it turns out, science only confirms what Williams believed. Alan Nathan is a professor emeritus at the University of Illinois and one of the world's foremost experts on the physics of baseball. He was also part of two MLB commissioned studies that looked into the surge in home run rates. The second one, released in December 2019, concluded that decreased wind resistance on the baseballs themselves was responsible for about 60% of the spike. But the other 40%? That was attributed to "a change in player behavior"—specifically, the way batters were swinging the bat. All of this has only emboldened the practitioners of the Williams swing. Hitting the ball in the air has been the ideal outcome for most of baseball history. But in this particular moment in baseball history, the rewards for hitting the ball in the air have never been greater. This turbocharged baseball, coupled with a swing designed to keep balls off the ground, have emerged as a combination that has resulted in the shattering of home run records across the game.

In March 2019, at the Society for American Baseball Research analytics conference in Phoenix, Nathan presented one of his latest studies. It was called "Optimizing the Swing: A Physics-

Based Approach." Nathan made clear his debt to Williams, whom he called his "predecessor as the scientist of the swing." Now, with advanced physics modeling to simulate how the bat is moving when it collides with the baseball, Nathan has concluded that what Williams taught—matching the plane of the pitch—was exactly right. Not surprisingly, bat speed is also a crucial element of hitting the ball with authority.

The model showed that the most productive hitters are those who swing the bat in such a way that their maximum exit velocity—their hardest-hit balls—comes on balls that have an ideal launch angle for power. As an example, he compared Paul Goldschmidt, then the first baseman for the Diamondbacks, and Mark Trumbo of the Orioles. In 2018, Nathan concluded, Goldschmidt maximized his exit velocity on balls with a launch angle of about 24 degrees, compared to 12 degrees for Trumbo. Trumbo had a .764 OPS that season. Goldschmidt's was .922.

"The idea is if you're a home run hitter, you want your hardest-hit balls to come at a launch angle that is most conducive to getting long fly balls," Nathan told me.

Maybe Ted Williams really was a scientist.

There's an obvious question that comes from all this: if Ted Williams knew so much about the swing, why is the revolution only happening now, 50 years after he wrote *The Science of Hitting*? When Williams's book first came out, the trend in hitting couldn't have been more different from what he was preaching. Charley Lau—perhaps the best-known hitting coach in baseball history—was all the rage, along with his disciple, Walt Hriniak. They had loads of success in the 1970s espousing an older-school approach that didn't jibe with Williams's.

There are many reasons why, for decades, Lau's philosophy

won out. For starters, it *worked* for a lot of hitters at a time when contact took priority over power. The Lau swing made logical sense too. After all, the shortest distance between two points is a straight line, so naturally that maxim would apply to hitting. With no evidence empirically proving otherwise, there was no reason to do anything besides what had always been done.

Change, of course, is scary. Giant, monolithic industries—especially ones as deeply rooted in history as baseball—tend to embrace new ideas slowly. So even though Williams disagreed with Lau, Williams's alternative was easy to ignore or put aside. Lau represented conventional wisdom, and conventional wisdom is safe. It took decades for modern technology to evolve to the point where it could produce empirical data to back up Williams's claims, sparking the resurgence of the upswing.

There were other factors at play as well, like the "He's-a-Freak Syndrome": though the approach had propelled Williams, would it work for mere mortals? There was also the simple fact that times change. Just as Ty Cobb had to cede to Babe Ruth as the dead-ball era gave way to the live-ball era, the paradigm in which Lau and Hriniak thrived has passed, and it's Williams's approach that has climbed to the forefront.

And there's one other big reason it took so long for the upswing to catch on: being an amazing hitter doesn't by definition make Williams an amazing teacher. Lau, despite not being much of a hitter himself by major league standards, was a great teacher. Some of his philosophies have been debunked to an extent, but there's no doubt that he was an excellent communicator and teacher. Sometimes that's what matters even more than mechanics. Those who knew Williams say that he wasn't a particularly good instructor with the Senators at first, and that he'd quickly become frustrated when his pupils didn't comprehend his lessons.

"He'd get into the cage and swing and hit some line drives to right field, and then he'd say, 'See what I did? See what I did?'" Mike Epstein said. "No! Nobody saw what he did, because things happen really quickly in the swing. That's the way Ted taught."

That's why, Epstein said, Williams tended to focus on the (also crucial) mental side of hitting rather than the physical. Rarely did he dive into the in-depth mechanics of the swing, at least not during his time as a manager. It took somebody like Epstein to take Williams's ideas and figure out a way to explain them so that people could actually understand—to couple the upswing with the ability to pass it on to others.

And Epstein was far from the only one.

I met Mike Bryant in December 2018, at the indoor batting cage connected to his home in Las Vegas. I was there because I had heard he was a disciple of Ted Williams and had dedicated his life to teaching the upswing to anybody willing to listen, which, for most of his career, wasn't all that many people.

When I arrived, Bryant, now a muscular 61, immediately ran over to a nearby shelf. He had something to show me: a tattered book, the pages yellowed and wrinkled, the cover nearly detached, and the corners frayed from use. It was *The Science of Hitting*— and it was abundantly clear that he had read it a few times.

Bryant's mother had given him a copy of Williams's book when he was 14 years old. He's not sure what compelled her to bring it home that day. It wasn't Christmas, nor was it his birthday, and as a prototypical teenage jock, he generally detested reading. All he knows now is that picking up that book was among the most pivotal moments of his life.

Growing up outside of Boston, Bryant was born into loving the Red Sox. Carl Yastrzemski was in the prime of his career at

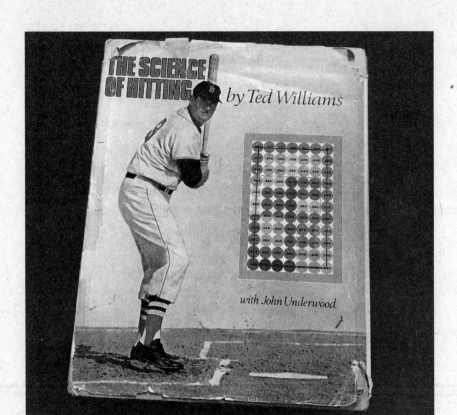

Mike Bryant's tattered copy of *The Science of Hitting.*

the time, so naturally he was Bryant's hero. But Williams always loomed large, hovering over him like some sort of mythical being who transcended all of time and space. Bryant was barely a year old when Williams retired, so he never had the chance to see him for himself. But as far as Bryant was concerned, Ted Williams was the greatest hitter who ever lived, so if he had something to say about hitting, Mike Bryant was going to listen—even if it meant cracking open a book.

Bryant plowed through *The Science of Hitting,* soaking up all of Williams's words like a boy who had just found an oasis after weeks of crawling through the desert. Then he reached page 47, and he stopped. He stared at the diagram of the pitcher throwing downhill, and the batter swinging up to match the trajectory, and suddenly, everything made sense. It was as if he had been nearsighted for the first 14 years of his life, and now somebody had given him a pair of glasses.

All through Little League, Bryant's coaches had told him to swing down. They instructed him to bring his knob to the ball and try to hit the top half of every pitch. They reminded him that grounders put pressure on fielders to make the play. Bryant didn't want to hit grounders. He wanted to hit the ball over an outfielder's head. Actually, he wanted to hit the ball over the fence. Hitting home runs was fun. It was exciting. It just *felt* better.

"What's the number-one thing that a six-year-old kid wants to do when he starts swinging a bat?" Bryant said. "He wants to hit a home run. Mighty Casey hit home runs. Babe Ruth hit home runs. They were trying to hit it hard, and they were trying to hit it in the air. That's Ted Williams."

From that point forward, Bryant didn't listen to his coaches very much. Ted Williams was now his coach, *The Science of Hitting* his bible. He brought that same copy with him wherever he went. It was with him through high school. It was with him in college at UMass-Lowell, where he developed into a fearsome slugger. He even took it with him after he was selected by his beloved Red Sox in the ninth round of the 1980 draft.

"I read the book a lot for inspiration," Bryant said. "When I was feeling down or having a run of 1-for-12, I'd go back to it. I'd think, *There has to be something in there, something that will pull me out of it.* It always came back to this: When I was slumping, I wasn't hitting the ball in the air. I was hitting the ball on the ground."

Professional baseball was a challenge for Bryant. He played 54 games for the Elmira Pioneers in 1980 and struggled mightily, hitting just .194 in 124 at-bats with two home runs. Playing time was scarce, and he had trouble adjusting to coming off the bench. He hoped that the next season, a full year that would include his first-ever spring training, would show what he could really do.

About a week after reporting to Winter Haven in 1981, Mike Bryant was called into an office. He had no idea why. Were the Red Sox giving up on him already? Had he been cut?

"Hey," he was told. "Ted wants to work with you. Be down at field 4 at 6:00 a.m."

Bryant couldn't believe what he was hearing. Ted Williams, a man who had practically become his god, wanted to work with him? It was unfathomable. He was going to learn the swing, live and in person, from the hitter whose book had taught him just about everything he knew. That night Bryant read *The Science of Hitting* three times.

Mike Bryant arrived at the field to hit with Ted Williams at 5:45 a.m., 15 minutes ahead of schedule. Nobody else was out there yet, besides Williams and the batting practice pitcher.

"Bryant!" a voice cried out. "You're fucking late!"

It was Williams.

"Sir?" Bryant responded, now officially woken up.

"If you're not half an hour early, you're late."

Over the next few minutes, a couple of other prospects arrived and were also chewed out by Williams. Then they went to work.

"We're going to learn to hit it hard, and we're going to learn to hit it in the air," Williams told his new students. "I want you on the barrel all the time, and I want you in the air all the time."

Bryant had roughly a dozen two-hour sessions with Williams that spring. By the end of it, Bryant was swinging up to the point that he wondered if he was swinging with *too much* of an upper-cut. He rarely spoke during their time together, until near the very end, when he asked Williams if he had any advice on how to handle the breaking ball, which continued to confound Bryant. Williams's advice was that Bryant should take the next 500 he saw, so he would get the feel for how they looked. This surprised Bryant, until he started parsing what Williams meant. The point, Bryant realized, was that he shouldn't swing at a curveball until he had two strikes, at least not until he felt more comfortable with them. Bryant asked if that's what Williams meant.

"Way to go, Bryant," Williams responded. "You must have been reading my book."

Bryant didn't react to the comment, not even with a smile. On the inside, however, he was so excited he wondered if he was shaking.

It turns out that not even lessons from Ted Williams himself were enough to turn Mike Bryant into a star. He appeared in 67 games at Single A Winter Haven in 1981 and hit .210 with two home runs. He returned for spring training in 1982 but was cut before camp broke, and that was that. Bryant's major league aspirations were dashed after 348 professional at-bats. For as good as he was, he wasn't quite good enough.

Bryant left baseball behind for a while after that. He joined a rock-and-roll band and worked as a laborer for a local pool and spa business. In 1988, he and his wife left the cold of New England behind for sunny Las Vegas, where he started a business of his own selling pools, patio furniture, grills, and the like. He didn't return to baseball until he had children and signed them up for Little League. His older son, Nick, turned into a strong high school player who was satisfied to end his career there. His younger son, well, he had bigger dreams when it came to baseball.

From the moment his boys picked up a baseball bat, Mike Bryant knew one thing: he was going to teach them to swing his way. Or, put more accurately, Ted Williams's way. They wouldn't be swinging down or chopping wood or looking to hit the top half of the ball. They weren't going to swing level. His kids were going to be indoctrinated, from birth, to swing up and hit the ball in the air. Even when they were too young to understand the nuances of swing mechanics, Bryant hung five-gallon buckets from string at the top of the batting cage and told his sons they'd win 100 points if they hit them.

Not all of the other parents understood what Coach Bryant was teaching Kris and his friends. But at least one dad was fascinated by Bryant's ideas. Tony Gallo, who had a brief minor league career, was now giving pitching lessons to local kids. He wanted Bryant to teach hitting to his two sons. Together, Mike Bryant and Tony Gallo put together the best club team in town. Bryant continued training the hitters to swing like Ted.

Looking back, Bryant can't help but wish he had been taught the upswing when he was younger. He's convinced that with a better understanding of the swing at a younger age, he could have reached the majors.

Mike Bryant with his son, Kris.

His track record as a coach might bear that out. Tony Gallo's younger son, who worked with Bryant from childhood, is Joey Gallo, a former first-round draft pick who hit 103 total home runs for the Rangers from 2017 through 2019.

"It's crazy, because growing up, everyone thought he was insane," Joey Gallo said of Bryant. "It was legit stuff, but people didn't understand that way of thinking yet."

And as for Bryant's younger son? He's done pretty well for himself after being taught to swing up from the moment he left the womb. His name is Kris Bryant—one of the best hitters on earth and living proof of the power of the upswing. Bryant was a star from the moment he arrived in the big leagues with the Cubs in 2015, winning Rookie of the Year and then following it up with an MVP campaign in 2016. He's only continued from there, and barring something unforeseen, he is in line to sign a massive nine-figure contract once he reaches free agency.

Kris Bryant didn't join the revolution. He was born into it. More than a decade after his death, Ted Williams had created a monster—with a bit of help from Mike Bryant, a devoted disciple.

"I knew I was teaching the right thing the whole time," Mike Bryant said. "But when Kris made it, it was so satisfying. It was vindication."

BOBBY TEWKSBARY, WITH AN A

On July 13, 2015, Bobby Tewksbary found himself living a dream he had long ago accepted would never come true: standing on the field at Cincinnati's Great American Ball Park, in front of more than 40,000 screaming baseball fans. Well, it wasn't exactly how he had dreamed it. First of all, none of those fans had any idea who he was or what he was doing there. Second of all, he wasn't playing.

This was the Home Run Derby, the night when a group of baseball's premier sluggers get together to slam as many baseballs over the fence as humanly possible. Some of the biggest names in the game were there: Albert Pujols and Kris Bryant, Manny Machado and Prince Fielder, not to mention the hometown hero, Todd Frazier. That's who the people had come to see. Tewksbary was, at best, an afterthought.

But while not everybody knew it, Tewksbary was quite possibly the most fascinating person in the stadium that night. His presence was a signal that baseball was on the verge of changing forever.

Three years had passed since Marlon Byrd first showed up at the Ball Yard and met Doug Latta. Now, Josh Donaldson, then the third baseman for the Toronto Blue Jays, was participating in the Derby. Not long before that, Donaldson was anonymous.

Though he was drafted with the 48th overall pick in 2007, by the time he had started advancing up the minor league ladder, he was far from a heralded prospect. Playing in Single A in 2008, he hit .267 with a .772 OPS. Promoted to Double A in 2009, he hit .270 with a .795 OPS. Between 2010 and 2012, he appeared in 89 major league games for the A's, posting a .232 batting average and a .666 OPS. Maybe Josh Donaldson could have forged a legitimate major league career doing what he was doing. Maybe he couldn't have. It almost definitely wouldn't have been a particularly memorable one.

And yet here he was, swatting home run after home run for a television audience of millions on one of baseball's most lavish stages. And this was the most interesting part: the man Donaldson had hand-selected to pitch to him at the Derby wasn't a Blue Jays coach, a relative, a childhood friend, or a mentor—the traditional picks. Donaldson's pitcher was Bobby Tewksbary, a man who until that night had never worn a major league—or minor league—uniform in his life.

Who in the world was Bobby Tewksbary?

Here's the first thing you need to know about Bobby Tewksbary: he is not Bob Tewksbury. Bob Tewksbury spent 13 seasons as a major league pitcher for the Yankees, Cubs, Cardinals, Rangers, Padres, and Twins. In 302 games, he went 110-102 with a 3.92 ERA. In 1992 he made his lone All-Star Game and finished third in the National League Cy Young race after going 16-5 with a 2.16 ERA for the Cardinals. Now a baseball mental skills coach, Bob Tewksbury also wrote a book about the game called *Ninety Percent Mental*.

Bobby Tewksbary has accomplished none of that. But considering he found himself on the pitcher's mound during the

2015 Home Run Derby, throwing batting practice to the player who would, remarkably, go on to win the AL Most Valuable Player award that year, it's safe to say he has achieved quite a bit.

Tewksbary was practically born with a bat in his hands. One of his earliest memories is of a family trip to SeaWorld. Tewksbary estimates he was four or five years old. The Tewksbarys were at the dolphin exhibit when one of the park employees asked for a volunteer to play baseball with one of the dolphins. The way his mother tells the story, she figured she should encourage little Bobby to raise his hand. By the time she looked down, he was already on the stage.

"They gave me a Wiffle ball bat, and the dolphin pitched Wiffle balls to me, with its tail," Tewksbary said. "And I was hitting Wiffle balls over the tank, into the stands."

Growing up in New Hampshire, Tewksbary never wanted to do anything but hit. He built a backstop in his backyard so he could hit off a tee and spent hours taking as many swings as he reasonably could. Nothing brought him more joy. Except here was the issue: he didn't really know much about hitting.

"I was definitely taught a linear swing path when I was growing up," Tewksbary said. "Take the knob to the ball, hands to the ball, squish the bug, all of those clichés."

For a long time, however, that didn't stop him. He became a star at Alvirne High School and was widely considered to be one of the best players in the state. Sure, that state was New Hampshire—which has produced less than three dozen major leaguers in the last century—but still.

Tewksbary could play. His high school coach, Mike Lee, called him "one of the two best hitters I ever had" in his nearly four decades at the helm. (The other was Kyle Jackson, who would ultimately advance to Double A as a pitcher in the Red Sox organization in the mid-2000s.) Tewksbary went on to play for the

University of Vermont. Again, not a baseball powerhouse—no major league position player has emerged directly from the Vermont program in more than 70 years, and barring a drastic change, no one ever will, since the school dropped baseball in 2009. But it was an opportunity to keep playing, and Tewksbary intended to make the most of it.

And he did. In his first season with the Catamounts in 2002, Tewksbary hit .325 and posted an OPS of .855, earning freshman All-American honors. He followed that up with an even better showing as a sophomore, when he hit .357 with an OPS of 1.002, buoyed by the first five home runs of his collegiate career. He was named the America East Conference Player of the Year. But even then, despite all of his success, Tewksbary realizes now that his swing mechanics were, as he put it, "a train wreck." He simply worked his way into being able to succeed against college pitching with a flawed swing, relying entirely on his athleticism, naturally superior hand-eye coordination, and a burning desire to be as great as he possibly could. By spending 45 minutes a day after practice hitting in the cage, he overcame an imperfect swing.

"I had to work really hard to make that swing work," Tewksbary said. "If you're going to race the Indianapolis 500, are you going to take out a Honda Civic and drive that around? That's what I was doing."

Eventually, as always happens, his deficiencies caught up with him. Tewksbary lasted longer than most, a testament to his skill and work ethic. No major league organization drafted Tewksbary, in part because of a torn ligament in his thumb that ruined his senior season at Vermont. He attended a pre-draft workout at Fenway Park in Boston and took off his brace to shake hands with Ben Cherington, then the Red Sox director of player development. Afterward, he overheard a scout saying, "Oh, yeah, I had his name on the board before he got hurt."

"Stabbed me in the heart," Tewksbary said.

Not ready to give up on his dream, Tewksbary played for the Worcester Tornadoes and North Shore Spirit of the Can-Am League for a couple of seasons but hit poorly and was released. That was that.

Somewhere deep in his soul, however, Tewksbary still believed there was more. He kept flashing back to times in his career when everything clicked, when he felt unstoppable with a bat in his hands. Normally, Tewksbary couldn't even hit a home run in batting practice, let alone in games—except in rare moments when baseballs would explode off his bat in ways he could barely describe, flying over trees well beyond the outfield wall. He called them his "blackout swings." When they happened, all he could do was wonder, *Where did this come from?*

At the time, Tewksbary made no real effort to figure out where the blackout swings came from. He chalked them up to random chance and continued swinging his usual way. It wasn't until after his playing career ended that Tewksbary came to realize that he could in fact learn what made his blackout swings so special. That realization was spurred by an old teammate from the Tornadoes—a teammate who would become a lifelong friend.

Chris Colabello was born into a baseball family. His father, Lou, played in Italy for seven years, even appearing as a pitcher in the 1984 Olympics in Los Angeles. Like Bobby Tewksbary, Chris Colabello never had any career plans that didn't involve playing baseball. Also like Tewksbary, he wasn't quite good enough to take the traditional path to get there. Colabello played at Assumption College, a Division II school in Worcester. He raked, putting up an OPS over .960 in each of his last three seasons. But it wasn't enough: no major league team drafted him. Hence his detour to the Tornadoes.

Colabello and Tewksbary already knew each other a little bit from the college summer circuit. On the Tornadoes, they solidified their friendship, even living together one off-season.

Colabello always believed he was too good for the Can-Am League. He wasn't being cocky either. His numbers backed him up: He hit .320 in 2005 and then .305 in 2006. In 2007 he hit .302, in 2008 he hit .336, and in 2009 ... well, you get the picture. Chris Colabello was an absolute stud in the independent leagues. And yet nobody seemed to notice.

Tewksbary had already officially given up on the dream. In 2007, he moved to New York and took a job as the general manager of a physiotherapy clinic. But the game kept calling, so two years later, with a childhood friend, he decided to open up a baseball training facility, driving from New York to New Hampshire on weekends to give lessons.

It wasn't much. Tewksbary would rent a couple of batting cages and work with high school kids on their swings while his partner helped them with weight training and conditioning. But by 2009 it had gotten big enough that Tewksbary decided he could make it a full-time job. He moved back to New Hampshire and began his life as a baseball coach, full stop.

He wasn't a particularly good one. Not at first. What he was, though, was curious. And he had the time to indulge that curiosity, especially during the school year, when his first clients wouldn't show up until late in the afternoon. So on those days, from the moment he woke up in the morning until his first hitter walked through the door, he would scour the internet in search of videos of the swing.

Tewksbary already understood the value of video analysis on some level. He had owned a camera since college, and in 2006 he purchased a two-camera system attached to a laptop. He knew video was the future. The problem was that he didn't know what he was looking at, so he used it totally wrong. Instead of watching video of great swings and drawing conclusions, he would use the video to confirm what he already believed, whether or not what he believed was actually on the video.

Everything changed in 2009. It started as an ordinary summer day. He had spent all morning in the cage working with hitters. He needed to hustle at that point if he wanted his fledgling business to survive. He and his partner were just scraping by, reinvesting virtually all of their earnings back into the facility. He didn't want to go back to the real world, with a real job, so he devoted just about every moment of his time to his clients.

In the late afternoon, Tewksbary returned to his apartment, still high on baseball adrenaline. Normally he might take a shower upon arriving home, but that day he wasn't ready to wash off the sweat. So he did what he always did when a free moment materialized: he bolted to his computer and started pulling up video, searching for any tidbit that could help him better understand the swing.

Most of these sessions were relatively fruitless, just noise and mindless screaming, because, well, it was the internet, so of course it was just noise and mindless screaming. Picture today's Twitter, only more insular and fanatical.

On this particular afternoon, however, Tewksbary stumbled across something that froze him in his tracks. It was on the website HS Baseball Web, which was mostly a collection of dads trying to help their middle school sons make the high school varsity. Somebody had posted a short clip of the slugger Albert Pujols, then with the Cardinals. Tewksbary was scrolling through a long thread, quickly perusing each clip before moving on to the next page. But the video of Pujols caused him to pause for a moment. Tewksbary watched it. Then he watched it again. Then again, this time going through it one frame at a time. And he kept watching it, over and over, because even though he had watched zillions of swings by that point, in this particular clip, in this particular moment in his life, he couldn't believe what he was seeing.

There came a point in the swing where Tewksbary was sure that Pujols's hands should be moving forward. That's what he was always taught: that as the front knee moves forward, so do the hands. That's what he taught his clients. That's what just about everybody taught. Except Pujols's hands weren't moving forward. They were actually moving backward, the exact opposite of everything Tewksbary had believed for his entire life. This was the epiphany. "If this was the best hitter on the planet," Tewksbary realized at that moment, "then what I think is right is actually wrong. The world is upside-down."

All these years later, Tewksbary thinks he understands why it took him so long to recognize what Pujols did. Tewksbary had a flawed swing for his entire life. But through sheer force of will, he had made it work. When he watched video, he wasn't looking for what made swings different from his. To the contrary, he was conditioned to look for the similarities, which only reinforced what he already believed. When he finally opened his mind to seeing the exact opposite, he said, "it was shattering."

Tewksbary immediately jumped to the forums. Was anybody else seeing what he was seeing? The reaction was not kind. Some people tried to let him down gently. Others were less concerned about decorum. One high-powered member of the message boards, a professional scout who worked for the Rockies, sent Tewksbary a private message that stated, in no uncertain terms, that he had no idea what he was talking about.

Nobody seemed to think Bobby Tewksbary had discovered

anything at all. But Tewksbary was convinced that this was a breakthrough. He just needed a test subject to try it out on. Fortunately, he had just the guy in mind.

"Hey," Tewksbary said when Chris Colabello answered the phone. "I think I've got something that I need to share with you."

Chris Colabello's career had reached a crossroad. He had broken his hand that summer of 2010, but still managed to hit over .300 for the sixth straight season in the independent leagues. He could pull home runs over the left-field fence, but struggled to hit for power into right-center, and when he watched the best hitters on television, he couldn't help but notice their swings didn't look quite like his. He knew there was a piece missing. "I'm getting to the point where it's like, shit or get off the pot with my career," he said.

Still, when Tewksbary called him up and said, "I think I figured out what the best hitters in the world do," Colabello laughed at him. But Tewksbary was one of his best friends, so he felt he at least owed it to him to listen. In Nashua, Tewksbary excitedly started showing him clips of what he had discovered. Colabello estimates that he was "90 percent of the way tuned out." ("He's being polite," Tewksbary said of that assessment.)

The 10 percent (or less) that was paying attention wasn't particularly impressed either. The second Tewksbary started talking about the barrel of the bat working backward instead of forward, Colabello interrupted him to say, "That's a long swing." It was what just about every hitter on the planet would have said at that time. Conventional wisdom had always preached the value of a short swing, a common maxim that typically led to hitters swinging down on the ball on a straight line. The idea of a "long swing" terrified hitters, because having a long swing opened the door for any batter's greatest embarrassment and fear: stepping into the box and being blown away by straight fastballs.

Now Tewksbary had Colabello's full attention, but not necessarily for the right reason. Colabello was dead set on proving Tewksbary wrong, if for no other reason than to shut him up. In their second session together, Colabello started arguing with his friend. By the third, Colabello lost his patience and told Tewksbary, bluntly, "Dude, you're fucking wrong." When that didn't stop Tewksbary, Colabello brought along Rich Gedman, his manager with the Worcester team, to offer his thoughts. Nothing worked.

At this point, Colabello was just popping by Tewksbary's facility to hang out with his friend. Occasionally he'd get into the cage. He had no real intention of changing anything. Until, that is, their eighth or ninth time together, about a month after Tewksbary's breathless phone call. Up to that point, Tewksbary was trying to convince Colabello about the barrel's rearward motion by showing him video of baseball's best hitters, an approach that wasn't going anywhere. Tewksbary could tell that Colabello had gone from 90 percent tuned out to 99 percent tuned out. He was running out of time to reach his friend. So at this get-together, Tewksbary decided to try something different: appeal to Colabello's professional-athlete-sized ego.

Worcester may have been a far cry from the major leagues, but every once in a while the Tornadoes' games were on TV. Colabello had earned the nickname "Red Light" from his teammates, because of his propensity to hit home runs in games where cameras were present. Tewksbary found a clip of Colabello on TV from the 2008 season stroking a home run that he hit on a high fastball. He sat Colabello down and begged him to watch the video. Colabello begrudgingly obliged. This time, watching himself, he finally saw it. His barrel was moving backward, his knee was driving down, and he certainly wasn't squishing any bugs. Colabello turned to Tewksbary in shock and said, "That's not what I would have told you I did."

For the first time since all of this started, Colabello was ready to listen. He finally agreed to let Tewksbary directly work with him in the cage. That didn't mean he had truly bought in, but, hey, it was a start.

"He was my best friend," Colabello said. "But in the back of my mind, I'm still thinking, *He hit fucking .230 in indie ball.*"

Colabello wondered if Tewksbary might be onto something, but he was scared to make such a radical adjustment to the way he had gone about his business for his entire life. He was a .310 hitter in Worcester, and he remained convinced that while it hadn't happened yet, he was a good enough hitter to attract attention from affiliated baseball. What if he overhauled everything and hit .200 the next year? It didn't help matters that the first time they got into the cage together, Tewksbary had Colabello doing what he described as "some funky shit," like holding his bat strangely in order to train his muscles to work backward with the barrel.

What kept him going was the same thing that convinced J. D. Martinez, Justin Turner, and every other swing-changer: desperation. While Colabello might have thought he should be in a major league organization, the industry was telling him otherwise. He was already in his midtwenties. Doing the same old thing wasn't magically going to lead to a different result one day. Anyway, he figured, if things went horribly wrong when the 2011 season started, he could always abandon ship.

Actually, that's almost what happened. Colabello spent the rest of the winter with Tewksbary fixing how his barrel moved, working it backward and more vertical, so he could drive the ball in the air with more frequency. The repair was done quickly and crudely; Colabello was, after all, Tewksbary's first true guinea pig in this realm. It was also quite rudimentary, not focusing much on hips or legs, all-important parts of an effective swing. So when Colabello didn't like the results after a few exhibition games, he was ready to put it aside for good. And he would have done just that if not for the fact that for the first time since Colabello joined the Worcester team, the organization was undergoing a regime change.

That winter, longtime manager Rich Gedman, a two-time All-Star with the Red Sox in the mid-1980s, had taken a job as the hitting coach for the Lowell Spinners, one of Boston's Single A affiliates. Worcester replaced him with Ed Riley. As one of his assistants, Riley tapped Chip Plante, a former college coach.

Plante was something of an outsider, and he reminded Colabello of his friend Tewksbary. That's why Colabello took an immediate liking to him, even as his teammates, some of his closest friends in the world, would say, "Why are you listening to Chip? He doesn't know shit." Well, Colabello thought Plante did know shit. Plante had already espoused views about the swing that lined up with Tewksbary's. Specifically, Colabello had been taught that when striding, he should first touch his toe, then plant his heel before swinging. Tewksbary had come to disavow that notion, arguing that many great hitters didn't follow that sequence. Plante agreed. For most of his career, Colabello didn't agree, and it was causing him to "double-load." By loading to swing, tapping his toe, and then loading again, he was slowing down his reaction time. Plante recommended a drill during batting practice of quietly humming when he started to move into his swing and, if he decided to stop swinging, to immediately stop humming. The idea was to help make Colabello's swing more fluid and streamlined, to better utilize the tweaks he had made with Tewksbary over the winter.

It was around that time that Tewksbary, still in search of

answers, published an article on his website about the changes José Bautista had made to his swing to turn into a slugger with the Blue Jays. From 2004 through 2009, Bautista was, at best, a journeyman, with 59 home runs to his name in 2,038 plate appearances. Then, with the Blue Jays in 2010, Bautista overhauled his entire swing to generate more lift and keep his barrel in the hitting zone longer. He hit 54 homers that year and went on to make 6 straight American League All-Star teams.

Tewksbary's piece featured GIFs of Bautista taking pitches before he changed his mechanics at the plate and then taking pitches after he changed them. The difference was clear: In the first clips, he would load with his body, then swing, generating speed by pushing his hands forward. In the second, everything happened simultaneously, creating bat speed as he loaded. Essentially, instead of loading then swinging, Bautista was always swinging—until he wasn't anymore. When Colabello saw the article, he immediately thought back to Plante's humming drill. A lightbulb went off.

The next day the Tornadoes were in Little Falls, New Jersey, to take on the New Jersey Jackals. On the mound was James Leverton, a hard-throwing left-hander who the year before had pitched in Double A in the Cubs organization. One of the best pitchers in the league, Leverton had a devastating cut fastball that broke in sharply to right-handed hitters like Colabello. Before the game, Colabello sought out Plante and asked to do the humming drill again. He had a plan.

Normally, Colabello liked to take the first pitch against somebody he had never faced before. But this time, when Colabello stepped up to the plate against Leverton, he vowed to attack the first good fastball he saw. In the past, Colabello would see a pitch and quickly determine whether to swing or not swing. But using Plante's humming drill, the mental cue was different. He had already decided to swing and would keep swinging—unless he decided to stop swinging. It was a key distinction.

Leverton delivered his first pitch, a cutter. Colabello hummed, quietly, but loud enough for the catcher to hear him.

Hmmmmmmmmmmm—THWACK—Colabello launched a home run.

Next at-bat, Leverton tried a sinker, moving down and away.

Hmmmmmmmmmmm—THWACK—Colabello smoked a double into the right-center-field gap.

Third at-bat, now facing a reliever who had long given him trouble, he saw a fastball.

Hmmmmmmmmmmm—THWACK—Colabello laced a line drive base hit.

After the game, he called Tewksbary right away. "Dude," he said, "I think we found something today."

That was the first breakthrough for Chris Colabello. The second came about two weeks later, during a game back in Worcester. Again, instead of resigning himself to taking the first pitch in his first at-bat, he decided to look to swing. The pitch came in. Colabello moved into his swing.

Hmmmmmmmmmmm—STOP—Colabello held up, recognizing a curveball that would end up out of the strike zone. He didn't flinch.

To an outside observer, it didn't look like much. It was ball one. But to Colabello, spitting on a pitch so easily and fluidly was proof that his swing was improving. One of the best ways to predict if a slumping hitter is about to break out is to watch how he takes pitches. When they're struggling, hitters often look awkward when they take pitches, their bodies misaligned and out of balance. Being able to take a pitch comfortably and confidently means that a hitter has eliminated unnecessary movement and that his body is organized, streamlined, and athletic. That's how

Colabello felt, and he said to himself, "Holy shit, what a fucking take." The catcher looked at him like he was crazy.

After the game, Colabello once again raced to call Tewksbary.

"Dude, you should have seen my take my first at-bat," Colabello said.

"Nice," Tewksbary responded. "How'd you do in the game?"

"I went 4-for-5 with a bomb and two doubles. But you should've seen my fucking take."

Chris Colabello felt different. Suddenly, his decision to put his trust in Bobby Tewksbary didn't seem quite so crazy after all.

Chris Colabello had a few things going for him when he finally started figuring out a better way to swing with Bobby Tewksbary. For one thing, he was a professional baseball player, a world-class athlete with superhuman strength and hand-eye coordination. For another, he had the time to spend his entire life working to refine his craft, and he worked for months before his first big breakthrough. But what about people who have . . . none of those things?

That's what I wanted to find out. Despite the legitimate journalistic reasons to pursue knowledge about the swing and how it works, I did have an ulterior motive. There's a long-standing tradition in New York, one that goes back decades: twice a year, the New York media squares off against the Boston media in a home-and-home series of honest-to-goodness baseball. One game is at Yankee Stadium. The other is at Fenway Park. Like, on the field. For real. Think of it as the journalism World Series.

Playing in these games was nothing short of a dream come true. I was playing baseball at Yankee Stadium! And Fenway Park! I was running the bases! My name was on the scoreboard (in Boston, at least. C'mon, Yankees!) If that ever stops being cool for a baseball writer, that person really should consider finding a new job.

I wasn't half bad either, relatively speaking. I was always a solid defensive first baseman, dating back to childhood—a perk of having a father who was willing and able to slam thousands (millions?) of ground balls at me basically every night when I was growing up. I had always been fearless in the field, comfortable staying in front of hot shots hit in my direction, even when a bad hop bounded up and hit me in the chest or face. I loved fielding grounders more than anything else in baseball as a kid. I always felt more at ease standing near first base with a glove on my right hand than in a batter's box.

My halfway decent defense earned me at least a modicum of respect from my teammates, many of whom were older and had been playing in this game for years. But in my 2016 debut in the Bronx, I made my mark. Late in the game, we were leading by a run. Team Boston had the bases loaded with one out. My good friend Ryan Hatch, formerly of NJ Advance Media, was on the mound.

The batter turned on the pitch and shot a rocket line drive straight down the right-field line. It seemed ticketed for the corner, which would have resulted in at least two runs and the evaporation of our lead. I read it off the bat and dived, snagging the ball out of the air. Then I crawled toward first base and slammed my glove on the bag to secure the double play. We wound up escaping the jam and winning the game. The final out, captured in exquisite video by my brother in the stands, consisted of me falling on the ground to scoop a throw from Ryan after he fielded a grounder and then scrambling around to find the bag to tag it just in time. It was glorious.

Here's the bad news: in my first three years playing in the game, I never got a hit. I had walked a few times and hit one decently far fly ball to the outfield. Still, no hits. But now I had access to some of the best and most innovative hitting minds on earth. If anybody could help me conquer the media game, it would be these people. With any luck, maybe I'd once again feel what I felt that incredible day at Dean Field when the ball exploded off my bat and, for a fleeting moment, I had mastered the swing.

Whenever I met a new guru over the course of researching this book, I made sure to tell him about the media game. Many of them were willing to give my swing a look, and I had the opportunity to get in the cage with a few coaches over the last two years. I got to see firsthand what some of the major league swing-changers experienced.

It was raining the first time Doug Latta and I connected for a hitting lesson. Well, it was raining where I was, at my apartment in Jersey City. In Southern California, where he was, it was another day of sun. This lesson was conducted over FaceTime, which is how Latta consults with his clients during the baseball season when they're unable to meet him in person.

The inclement weather presented a problem for me, because I needed to swing outside. I live in the New York metropolitan area. I am a journalist. My wife is a middle school teacher. Neither of us is a doctor, lawyer, Wall Street person, or mobster. So suffice it to say, I don't have a lot of extra space to swing a 34-inch bat at full speed without smashing something to pieces. Our building at the time did, however, have a back patio. Nobody ever used it, as it was more or less enveloped in mold. Perfect.

I trekked out into the rain, wielding an aluminum bat I "borrowed" from my parents' garage. It probably hadn't been used in almost a decade. I propped up my iPhone and sent a FaceTime request to Latta. Fortunately, the internet worked well enough to see him. "Let's get to it," I said.

The lesson, maybe not surprisingly in retrospect, wasn't what I expected. The first thing Latta asked me to do was simply swing with a bit of an uppercut, "to start getting the feeling," as he put it. I have to admit, right away it felt different than what I was used to. Like so many others, I had always learned to throw my hands at the ball, swinging down in a straight line led by my left hand—my top hand as a lefty hitter. Now I felt as if I was swinging under the ball, and I had no idea if I was doing it right, but, hey, this apparently worked for Marlon Byrd, so who was I to question it? Anyway, I was too worried about slipping on the slick ground and breaking all the bones in my body to think too hard about anything.

Next, Latta instructed me to "finish high," giving me the prompt of David Ortiz, the retired Red Sox slugger who followed through way up in the air. Again, it felt strange and exaggerated, like the way Popeye the Sailor might swing a bat in a cartoon after downing a couple of cans of spinach. The point of all this was simply to train my body to naturally swing this way, with the intention of driving the ball in the air.

Finally, after dozens of swings, I was given one final task: to swing while keeping my head down through the entire motion, my right cheek facing the pitcher. While this might sound weird, I quickly understood the purpose of this drill. My front shoulder was flying open on every swing, a problem that had plagued me all through high school. That habit resulted in an embarrassing number of weak ground balls to second base. I would eventually learn that the best hitters have strengthened their core so much that during their swings their hips open up, while their shoulder stays perfectly tucked in and closed. Doing this required a level of physicality I didn't possess. I became acutely aware that I was on the wrong side of 30—too old by baseball standards to command a giant free-agent contract. But keeping my head down as I swung forced my shoulder closed, even as I felt it trying to swing open. I was embarrassed by how difficult this was.

Fortunately, Latta was a patient and understanding teacher. As we prepared to sign off, he gave me homework: spend 10 minutes a day repeating the drills we worked on, particularly the last one. If I did that, he promised, my shoulder would become accustomed to staying closed, and I would be free of an issue that had haunted me for my entire life. He promised we'd FaceTime again the next week.

After he was gone, I looked at my hands. They were covered in sticky black soot. An enormous blister had formed underneath my right pointer finger, revealing a bright red layer of skin that clearly wasn't supposed to be exposed to the air. Before my next session with Latta, I bought a pair of batting gloves.

THE TEACHERMAN

Teachers Billiards describes itself as the premier billiard room in the St. Louis area. Located about 30 miles west of downtown in nearby St. Peters, in a strip mall near a Club Fitness and a physical therapy clinic, Teachers has been serving up beers, chicken wings, and games of pool for more than three decades, celebrating its 30th birthday in May 2019. It has a bar and grill, plenty of TVs, and 18 top-of-the-line Diamond billiards tables for patrons to rent by the hour in a 7,000-square-foot space. Teachers has welcomed countless people through its doors over the years and remains a popular and reliable part of the community.

But Teachers has a secret that would stun the average pool-playing customer, one given away only by the presence of a certain poster on one of the walls. The man who owns the establishment might have saved the career of one of the greatest sluggers in baseball. He goes by one name: Teacherman.

On the evening of January 18, 2018, at precisely 8:54 p.m. Eastern Standard Time, a tweet popped up on my timeline that upended the entire hitting world. It was from Aaron Judge, the burgeoning Yankees superstar whose thunderous bat had captivated the baseball universe the year before. An infrequent Twitter user, Judge posted a message featuring a photograph of himself standing next to a nondescript middle-aged man whose head barely reached Judge's shoulders. The caption glowingly endorsed somebody with the Twitter handle "Teacherman1986," thanking him for "all the hard work and dedication to transform my swing in 2017."

Judge called this Teacherman1986 "a career-changer." For more than a year, Aaron Judge kept it a secret that he had quietly remade his swing with an independent hitting guru, one so on the fringes of the hitting community that I had never heard of him. This was the equivalent of a paleontologist discovering a fully intact *Tyrannosaurus rex* fossil in her backyard sandbox.

Aaron Judge had just completed, almost indisputably, the greatest rookie season in the history of baseball in 2017. His 52 home runs set a record for a first-year player until Pete Alonso of the Mets hit 53 in 2019. Judge's OPS of 1.049 is the best of any rookie in more than a century. He finished second in the voting for AL MVP. Aaron Judge wasn't just a burgeoning star—he had emerged as a global sensation. In May, he appeared on the cover of *Sports Illustrated*. In July, halfway through his first season in the major leagues, Commissioner Rob Manfred said that Judge could become the face of the entire sport.

In New York, Judge first became a viral sensation during spring training in 2016. It was impossible not to be in awe of him: here was a young man, just 23 years old at that time, who stood six-foot-seven and weighed 282 pounds of pure muscle. During one particularly memorable batting practice session that February, Judge hit a ball that traveled nearly 500 feet, flying clear over the giant left-center field scoreboard at George M. Steinbrenner Field, the Yankees' facility in Tampa, Florida. Nobody had ever seen a baseball player who looked quite like him.

The fervor over Judge's arrival in New York extended through the summer, especially as the Yankees limped along, hovering around the .500 mark for much of the season. He finally debuted against the Tampa Bay Rays on August 13, 2016, a blistering 95-degree Saturday afternoon in the Bronx, and it didn't take long for him to show the world what he could do. On the fourth pitch he ever saw in the major leagues, a flat changeup by Matt Andriese, he blasted a 446-foot moonshot into straightaway center field. With the city buzzing with excitement, Judge homered again the next day. This one barely cleared the wall in right-center, but the message was clear: Aaron Judge had arrived.

At least, that's what it seemed like. But before long, Judge fell into a slump so dreadful that it was as if his first two games were a mirage conjured up by the ghosts of Mickey and the Babe. From August 22 through the end of the season, he hit a dismal .121 (7-for-58) with 33 strikeouts. During one particularly miserable stretch, he whiffed at least twice in nine consecutive games, the first player to do so in the previous 100 years.

For as impressed as I was with Judge's physicality, I wasn't sold by his abilities as a hitter. Even with my limited knowledge of the swing and what it should look like, it was clear to me that something about Judge's was . . . off. It was long and clunky, filled with unnecessary moving parts. And history suggested that his imposing frame might actually be a curse: there have been only three position players who were six-foot-seven or taller and had anything resembling a successful big league career. For sure, Judge's raw power was enormous. His strength alone would allow him to hit home runs in bunches. But to my admittedly untrained scouting eye, with a swing like his, Judge's ceiling was more along the lines of Dave Kingman: he'd be able to hit balls over the fence— but not much else.

So when Judge returned in 2017 and quickly set the baseball

world on fire, I took to Twitter and preached caution. He was prone to streakiness, I warned fans. Don't expect this to last. But then the season came and went, and his final numbers were beyond insane. I figured I was wrong about Judge, that his struggles in 2016 were simply a young slugger adjusting to major league pitching. Maybe his swing wasn't too long or too clunky after all.

But his swing *was* flawed when I first saw him in 2016. With help, he had fixed it. When I saw his tweet, acknowledging his work with an independent coach for the first time, everything about his transcendent 2017 campaign finally made sense.

Well, almost everything. Who was the mysterious Teacherman 1986?

Tracking down Teacherman1986 would prove more challenging than one might think. Clicking through to his Twitter profile uncovered his real name—Richard Schenck—but I couldn't find much else by way of details. His tweets consisted mostly of still photos pulled from Google Images, short, fuzzy animated GIFs of elite sluggers like Barry Bonds and Adrián González swinging, and bizarre half-thoughts that bordered on non sequiturs, as though fortune-cookie writers had suddenly discovered baseball: "He knew the snap was key. Whether consciously or not." Or "AGon's Oscillating Fan."

Combing the web didn't offer any help either. The website linked on his Twitter page, HittingIllustrated.com, had hardly been updated in a decade. A Google search for "Richard Schenck" revealed little other than some vague references on some obscure hitting message boards and websites, some dating as far back as 2002. Richard Schenck, as far as the internet was concerned, was nobody. *This* was the man who transformed Aaron Judge into an unstoppable juggernaut?

The first time I contacted Schenck, with a direct message on Twitter, he responded quickly with a 292-word wall of text explaining his unconventional background and how he came to believe that he had unlocked secrets of the swing that few others had ever recognized. In a way, Schenck's path was similar to that of his counterparts in the field of independent hitting gurus: he loved baseball but could never hit well enough to advance to the professional ranks. So he committed years of his life to studying video in an effort to figure out what he could never figure out as a player.

Something about Schenck was different, though. He used language to describe his theories that I hadn't heard from anybody else, words like "snap" and "stretch" and "tilt." He was adamant that his teachings were wildly different from those of his counterparts. "At the risk of sounding arrogant," he wrote in that first message, "none of the other independent coaches know what I know. The proof lies in the fact that their clients don't all do the same things, which means that their successful clients are doing something they don't know."

It isn't unusual for an independent coach to be critical of other independent coaches. This is a small, insular community where ego matters and reputations are staked on being the smartest, the best, the most innovative. But in reality, most of the gurus—the successful ones at least—are much more similar than different. Schenck, however, struck me as a true outlier. Suffice it to say, I was intrigued.

I first met Richard Schenck during spring training in 2018. He was working with a couple of minor leaguers and invited me to tag along for the session so I could get a sense of what he taught and how he operated. I still knew little about Schenck's background besides what little he had shared in his initial Twitter message to me. Ever since Aaron Judge announced that he had worked with an independent coach, Schenck had been inundated with requests from the hungry New York media, most of which he had declined at Judge's behest.

I was less interested in "Richard Schenck, the Aaron Judge whisperer," and more interested in Richard Schenck's philosophies on hitting and the swing. On that topic, he was thrilled to share: since our initial interaction on Twitter, Schenck had sent me dozens of video clips from his collection. I didn't really understand most of them—a memorable GIF of Manny Ramírez was accompanied by the caption "Manny's ferris wheel dropping into his merry-go-round"—but one video caught my eye: it was Schenck himself, his swing synced up with Adrián González's, and his hands were moving faster than seemed possible for a man who, to be perfectly frank, looked like he did.

Schenck told me he would be at a batting cage called the Florida Baseball Institute, an indoor hitting facility in Tampa. I pulled up at a quarter to six, 15 minutes earlier than he instructed, at what looked like . . . an empty building. I walked in the front door and found nobody waiting at the desk in the lobby. The lights were off, at least all the ones I could see. I wondered if I had gone to the wrong place, but after consulting with the text messages Schenck had sent me, I realized I hadn't. Then I started to wonder if this whole thing was a big ruse—maybe I had been baseball-catfished by a super-secret hitting guru trying to throw me off the scent.

I was about to turn around and walk back out the door when I heard a noise emanating from someplace deep in the building. The sound was unmistakable, that beautiful music of wood connecting with cowhide: *Crack! Crack! Crack!*

My ears now leading the way, I followed the sweet serenade

down a dark hallway until I discovered the source. There was Schenck, placing balls on a tee for Jake Holmes, then a 19-year-old infield prospect in the Phillies organization. Watching them, I hoped, Schenck would reveal his grand insight about hitting.

Instead, I was treated to what amounted to a real-life reenactment of Schenck's Twitter account. After one swing, he told Holmes to "think about tilt at launch," whatever that was supposed to mean. He said "snap it!" a lot. On occasion, he said that a swing looked "snappy," which I assumed was supposed to be a compliment, but I couldn't say for sure. All of this was like hearing a foreign language for the first time.

Right when I was about to give up and accept that this experience wouldn't explain the mysteries of hitting, I was saved. In walked an older man whose face I was sure I recognized but couldn't place. He had brought along Kevin Smith, a 21-year-old shortstop prospect from the Blue Jays, wanting him to learn from Schenck. As Smith ducked under the netting to join Holmes in the cage, the man introduced himself to me as Mark Newman.

Immediately, I realized why he looked so familiar. Newman was a longtime executive with the Yankees who had played a key role in the franchise's player development efforts for decades, helping to oversee the growth of the core players who would lead the franchise's dynasty in the late 1990s. Newman retired following the 2014 season and wound up opening this facility so he could remain in the business of developing athletes.

Newman didn't know Schenck well but was happy to let him use the cages free of charge. He just had one condition: Newman wanted to stand in and watch the lessons, so he could pick up whatever information he could about hitting. He wanted to stay on the cutting edge.

That desire, in itself, is unusual for a baseball lifer. The industry is littered with old-timers stuck in the past, too stubborn to even listen to new ideas, let alone accept them. Newman certainly didn't fit that stereotype. So while Schenck was hard at work with Holmes and Smith, I asked Newman why so much of this innovation in the realm of hitting was originating with coaches like Schenck, people who operate not just outside of the system, but so far out on the fringes that they hardly exist to many on the inside. Newman answered with two words that have stuck with me ever since.

"Cultural inertia," he said.

We settled in to watch the rest of the lesson. I still couldn't understand much of Schenck's instruction, but it quickly became clear to me that Holmes was seriously buying in. As we picked up all the baseballs he had slammed into the back of the cage, I heard him wonder aloud, "Why don't they teach this swing to kids?" Later, he relayed his frustration with some of his coaches in the Phillies organization, who saw the changes in his swing and immediately tried to change him back. At one point, he told Schenck, a coach had asked him, "Where are you learning that?" Schenck, clearly accustomed to coaches on the inside questioning his methods, responded, "That's when you pull out your phone and say, 'Look, Barry Bonds did it.'"

In a quiet moment later that evening, Holmes bemoaned the fact that his Phillies coaches seemed so uncomfortable with the work he was putting in with Schenck. I had heard stories like this before. Justin Turner went through them. Same with J. D. Martinez. In an industry as tradition-bound as baseball, people tend to reject what lies outside the status quo. The difference was that Turner and Martinez had already reached the major leagues; they had legs to stand on. Holmes was a teenager, more or less an interchangeable part in the giant machine of the minor leagues. Defying a coach could have dire consequences. Eventually, Holmes asked my opinion.

I couldn't vouch for Schenck, or for "snapping it," or any of that. "But if you believe in it," I told him, "keep doing it. You're the one responsible for your career, not them."

Later, I would wonder if I offered him worthwhile advice.

Once Holmes and Smith wrapped up for the evening, breathing hard and dripping with sweat, it was finally my turn to be educated by Schenck. Well, it was Mark Newman's grandchild's turn to be educated by Schenck. The way I figured it, he and I were at roughly an equal skill level.

While Schenck's young pupil settled into the cage, I grabbed a bat so I could follow along.

Snap it! Snap it! Snap it!

At that moment, I vowed to myself that I would figure out how, no matter how much pain it caused me. Only then did I realize that a massive blister had broken out on my thumb and started to bleed, the bright red drops dripping down my wrist. I guess something had snapped—my skin.

Richard Schenck was born and raised in rural Iowa. He always loved baseball, inheriting a passion for the sport from his father, a pastor who played in a local amateur league in the small towns nearby. He received no coaching or formal instruction in hitting. "Our high school coach didn't teach anything," he said. "You just picked up a bat, swung it, and tried to hit it as good as you could."

Schenck didn't typically hit it so good, but that didn't matter much. He faced little competition where he grew up—his high school had about 400 kids—and his defensive skills as a catcher were enough to get by. "I was a good ballplayer," Schenck said. "I wasn't a very good hitter. I was never real athletic."

That didn't stop Schenck from wanting to keep playing after high school, so he went out for the team at Iowa State, where he attended college his freshman year. The second day of the tryout conflicted with his sister's wedding. Schenck chose the wedding. He didn't make the team.

Still not ready to hang up his spikes, Schenck pursued other opportunities, eventually latching on at Northeast Missouri State, a small Division II program in Kirksville. (The school is now known as Truman State.) Even in college, Schenck received virtually no coaching about how to swing. "The guy would hit ground balls to us, we'd take infield, and he'd get mad if we threw the ball away or kicked a ground ball," Schenck recalled. "I didn't even know there were hitting mechanics."

When Schenck graduated in 1977, he had no intentions of making baseball his life. He became a social studies teacher at a small high school in Missouri, serving as an assistant coach for the football and basketball teams. He eventually left teaching and went into the insurance industry. In 1989, he opened up Teachers, the bar devoted to his second-favorite sport. It's located less than 10 miles from where Craig Wallenbrock was born.

Schenck earned his nickname in the world of billiards. "I played in pool tournaments and pool leagues, and nobody could remember my name, but they knew I was a teacher," Schenck said. "Everybody called me 'Teacher,' and then it became 'Teacherman' as I started teaching pool." The moniker stuck. (More than one fellow hitting instructor, in our conversations over the past two years, cited Schenck being a pool hall proprietor as proof that he's a "hustler" and a "con man.")

Through it all, Schenck continued to play fast-pitch softball, ultimately earning a spot on some pretty competitive teams. "I got recruited because I was so skilled defensively," he said. "And I'd bat ninth. I still sucked. I always sucked." As Schenck, the man who would one day retool Aaron Judge's swing, entered middle age, he not only had not yet started coaching hitting—he still had almost no knowledge of the swing at all.

Then he had kids. Like their dad, they loved baseball. Also like their dad, they weren't particularly good hitters. But unlike during his own childhood, Schenck now had a resource: the internet. And as he would quickly find out, even in the late '90s it was filled with people sharing information. "I started doing everything I could, just like any dad would do, to help his kids," Schenck said. "I read every site. We tried everything. I wanted someone to grab a hold of me and teach me, so I could teach my sons."

And by "everything" he meant everything. Schenck scoured every online forum he could find, some run by ex-major leaguers, places like BatSpeed.com, SetPro.com, BaseballDebate.com. In the early days of the internet, before the rise of social media, these were the hotbeds of discussion about hitting, because suddenly almost anybody had access to video of swings and a platform to share their observations, philosophies, and theories. Most of them were wrong, but at least people were searching for breakthroughs and challenging the status quo. Nobody challenged the status quo more than Schenck. He started posting on these websites and quickly became a legend on all of them—but for all the wrong reasons.

Even before I had met Schenck, I had heard quite a bit about his internet presence. None of it was positive. I could hardly get through a single interview without the subject mentioning Schenck's inappropriate behavior online. Fairly early in the process, one major league hitting coach interrupted my line of questioning and said, "Hold on, I have a question for you: What's the deal with that guy Teacherman? Is he as big of an asshole as everybody says?"

That question is more complicated than it sounds. In person, Richard Schenck is nothing short of a sweetheart. He's unassuming and gentle and funny in a self-deprecating way. He spends a lot of time talking about how much he looks forward to seeing his grandchildren.

But online everything changes. It is fair to say that in the world of hitting Richard Schenck is the most controversial person on the internet. Schenck has been banned by every major hitting website. When he would resurface with alternative accounts, those would be banned as well. Internet Schenck was hostile. There's no other way to put it. He attacked other forum members personally when he didn't agree with their ideas about hitting. Those on the receiving end of those attacks say they came with a level of online harassment and trolling that some say crossed over into straight-up abuse. Anybody who dared question Schenck's methods was immediately subject to his wrath.

This post from April 2014 on the website DiscussFastpitch .com by a user called "Cannonball" sums up Schenck's reputation online: "I consider Schenck to be an enemy. I despise him and will pay someday when I meet my maker because I bear deep hatred for the—I can't call him a man."

Schenck seemed to take pride in his reputation. The first time I asked him about his internet persona, he beamed as he told me, "I've been kicked off all these forums." "Why?" I asked. "Because," he responded, "I'm . . . aggressive."

Then Schenck discovered Twitter, which quickly became the dominant place to discuss ideas about the swing. In his earliest forays into this new medium, Schenk was no better behaved than he'd been on message boards. He called people liars and frauds and idiots. Every video of a swing anybody else posted was wrong. In his mind, he had discovered inarguable truths about the swing, and anyone who believed there was a place for nuance and healthy conversation was personally indicting him. He would relentlessly and ferociously attack anybody who dared question him, earning Twitter infamy in the process.

But offline, Richard Schenck was still a nobody. He was still far away from meeting the hitter who would turn him into a somebody and shine a light on his rantings and ravings. He was just another internet troll without a platform, a man lurking behind the safety of a computer screen and screaming into an empty void.

SEARCHING FOR ACCEPTANCE

In April 1986, *Sports Illustrated* published a conversation between three brilliant baseball minds: Ted Williams, Wade Boggs, and Don Mattingly. The topic, naturally, was hitting.

At that time, Mattingly and Boggs were two of baseball's brightest stars. Mattingly was the reigning AL MVP. Boggs had just won the batting title, hitting .368. Williams was unimpressed. Almost immediately in their chat, as Mattingly explains that he hits by transferring his weight from back to front, just like Charley Lau and his disciple Walt Hriniak preached, Williams interjects.

"I don't think what you're telling me is right," he says. "My impression is that, even with all your great success, you don't really realize what you're doing."

Williams never agreed with Lau, and he wasn't the only one. Hall of Fame slugger Hank Greenberg reportedly once said, "Lau screwed up more hitters than anyone." Williams believed that Lau's teachings set hitting back 25 years. He was beyond adamant that Lau was wrong, and he never relented in that opinion.

After questioning Mattingly's technique, Williams doesn't hold back with Boggs either, criticizing him for his lack of power. Boggs was a spectacular hitter, winning five batting titles, compiling 3,010 hits, and posting a .328 lifetime batting average. He is in the Hall of Fame. But it's true that he lacked power: Boggs hit only 118 home runs in 18 major league seasons, mostly with Williams's Red Sox. To Williams, this was unacceptable.

"Everyone tells me that in batting practice you're hitting them out of sight, that you're pulling the ball and getting it in the air and going to hit 30 home runs," Williams says. "Why not in a game?"

In Williams's mind, the answer was that in the game Boggs followed Lau's teachings and swung down on the ball. After all, Hriniak was Boston's hitting coach and Boggs's mentor, much to Williams's dismay. As the conversation goes on, Boggs becomes frustrated. He points out to Williams that he read his book in high school and considers it sacred. He insists that he has "pictures at home that people have taken at the point of contact where I almost look like you." Williams isn't having it.

Their conversation becomes more technical and nerdier as it goes on. They talk about subtle moves they make with their hands, hips, and legs while swinging. They discuss their approach against certain pitchers. They even talk about the value of hitting the ball in the air.

"I tried to hit every ball I ever hit in the air," Williams says. At one point, Mattingly says, "I want to make more outs on the ground, I think I've got a better chance of getting a hit." Williams jumps all over that, asking Mattingly how many extra-base hits he had in the season before and then reminding him that he didn't get them by hitting the ball on the ground. Nevertheless, by the end of the conversation Mattingly and Boggs are still skeptical.

This conversation appeared in *SI* more than three decades ago, well before anything Williams was saying became mainstream. But now? His remarks are almost word-for-word what a Craig Wallenbrock would say. Or later a Mike Bryant. Or a Doug

Latta. It wasn't, however, what Charley Lau would say, and that was Williams's problem.

It's safe to say that Lau has now fallen out of favor. Some contemporary gurus even say that he didn't know what he was talking about and that his fame was unwarranted. But that's not entirely fair.

Lau's theories rose to popularity in the 1970s and 1980s, when baseball was a different game. Giant multipurpose stadiums with pitcher-friendly dimensions were all the rage. Many of them had AstroTurf, a relatively new technology that was becoming increasingly popular and changing the way baseball was played. In these ballparks, home runs were difficult to come by. There were hits on the ground, however, even extra-base hits, because of how quickly balls rolled on the artificial surface compared to grass.

"Baseball is prone to fashion, trends, just as Seventh Avenue is," said John Thorn, the official MLB historian. "As hemlines go up and hemlines go down, there are some designers whose edicts will transform the marketplace. If Dior says, 'We're going to wear a pillbox hat,' next year everybody's wearing a pillbox hat. In baseball, if the Royals and then the Cardinals make a success with a lineup of whippets on AstroTurf, everybody wants to do the same things."

Lau was operating under that paradigm, one in which teaching hitters to make solid contact consistently, often on the ground, would result in loads of success at the plate. There's a reason why George Brett and Wade Boggs believed in what Lau had to say. It worked—then. These days, it probably wouldn't. No big league stadiums have the hard, carpet-like turf anymore, and the artificial surface that does exist much more closely resembles grass. Defensive shifts in the infield are the new normal, brought about by more sophisticated data, which has made ground-ball singles increasingly rare. With closer fences and a more aerodynamic baseball, balls hit in the air are more likely than ever to be a home run. Things have changed.

What Charley Lau would have thought about all this, we'll never know. He died of cancer in 1984, at the age of 50. Greg Walker, a former major leaguer who had Lau as his hitting coach, still wonders.

"Charley was very controversial, but had the curiosity it takes to be somebody like Craig Wallenbrock," Walker told me. "What would he have done if he had the video we have now?"

Walker worked with Lau early in his career as a first baseman for the White Sox. Near the end of his tenure, Hriniak was his hitting coach. So he had plenty of experience with different ways of thinking about the swing. They worked fairly well for Walker. In his nine major league seasons, he hit .260 with 113 homers, including 27 in 1987. After retiring in 1990, Walker left baseball for a while, but eventually returned to the White Sox organization in 2002. That year he was the hitting coach for Triple A Charlotte, where he planned to teach Lau's and Hriniak's style of hitting. That was what he was hired to do.

But one of Walker's players in Charlotte had different ideas. After hitting .346 in three seasons at Stanford, Joe Borchard was taken by the White Sox with the 12th overall pick in the 2000 draft. It turned out that when it came to hitting, Borchard knew a guy.

That guy was Craig Wallenbrock.

Coming up through the minors, Borchard never shared that he was working with Wallenbrock. Back then, nobody did. The potential for negative fallout was too great, especially for young, often interchangeable minor leaguers with no leverage. Wallenbrock told some of his early pro clients that it would be "dangerous" to admit they worked with him—even though keeping the relationship secret meant that Wallenbrock would receive no credit for his work.

That's how it went for years. Wallenbrock operated in the shadows, relying only on players whispering among themselves about his magic. Talking about Wallenbrock risked alienating your hitting coach, your manager, and ultimately the entire organization. In fact, going to hit with Wallenbrock was a lot like joining a fight club: the first rule of hitting with Craig Wallenbrock is you don't talk about hitting with Craig Wallenbrock.

"He made a point to tell us, 'If you're talking to reporters after a game, make sure you don't mention you're working with me, because what it's going to do is create a political battle,'" Borchard said. "'They won't like the fact that you're working with me.'"

In Walker, however, Borchard believed he had an ally. Walker seemed open to new ideas. He appeared to genuinely care about his players. Which explains why one afternoon over lunch Borchard decided to take a big risk and spill his guts.

"He kept talking about this independent hitting coach back in California that he had worked with," Walker recalled. "He was very respectful of me, but he started bringing up things he and this coach had talked about."

Walker was intrigued. He didn't know of Wallenbrock, and he was far from an expert on Wallenbrock's ideas about hitting, but what Borchard was saying fascinated him. Walker decided to meet the guy. Nowadays, that seems like a perfectly normal and reasonable reaction. Back in the early 2000s, Walker's willingness to sit down with somebody like Wallenbrock was nothing short of radical.

"Professional baseball looked at independent hitting coaches as evil," Walker said.

But Walker, despite being a Lau disciple, saw value in seeking out information from unusual sources. His curiosity came not from baseball at first, but from another sport altogether. During his time away from baseball, Walker, like so many retired ball-players, had resolved to take up golf. He never had much success in the game, but as he met golf swing coaches, he couldn't help but pick their brains about the baseball swing, looking for similarities in how athletes use their body to produce power.

In many ways, golf has long been ahead of baseball when it comes to accepting outsiders as potential sources of knowledge. Butch Harmon, a renowned swing coach who worked with Tiger Woods and Phil Mickelson, played only briefly on the PGA Tour. Hank Haney, another coach for Woods and many other top pros, never played professional golf himself, but has been considered a heralded swing doctor for top players for decades.

"You go to a small town in South Georgia, you go to a driving range there, somebody knows the golf swing pretty doggone good," Walker said. "With hitting, that wasn't the case."

The way Walker saw it, if Hank Haney could teach Tiger Woods how to swing a golf club, this Craig Wallenbrock fellow could teach somebody how to swing a baseball bat. So in the winter between the 2002 and 2003 seasons, he trekked out to Southern California to meet the man himself.

For three or four days, they hung out at Wallenbrock's home, mostly around the batting cage, talking about hitting and the swing. That turned into phone conversations once Walker went home, starting a relationship that reintroduced Wallenbrock to professional baseball—not as a scout this time, but as a hitting expert.

"The combination of talking to him and realizing that baseball was behind golf, I just knew," Walker said.

The more Walker talked with his new friend, the more he was convinced Wallenbrock was onto something. Why did hitters want to hit the ball on the ground? Of course they should want

Craig Wallenbrock, the Oracle of Santa Clarita.

to hit it in the air. Why wasn't anybody else talking about this?

"It was all because Greg Walker was a good enough guy to have a methodology that entailed meeting a guy who didn't play a day past high school," said Borchard, overlooking Wallenbrock's junior-college career for effect. "Imagine the humility of that person."

Their time in California wasn't a one-time thing. For years, Wallenbrock and Walker would meet in the winter, gathering interesting people together to discuss their favorite subject: the swing. Walker described it as a "think tank" for the hitting community. Wallenbrock called it "a meeting of the minds." Eventually it became known as the Ball Yard Hitting Summit.

One of the regulars at these get-togethers was Don Slaught. Slaught played 16 seasons in the major leagues, from 1982 through 1997, spending time with the Royals, Rangers, Yankees, Pirates, Angels, White Sox, and Padres. He was a pretty good hitter too, retiring with a lifetime batting average of .283 in more than 4,000 at-bats. He didn't, however, hit for much power, finishing with just 77 total home runs. As his career reached its end, Slaught began to wonder: Why wasn't he even better?

That question sparked a quest that ultimately led Slaught to Wallenbrock. Around the year 2000, Wallenbrock was working with Area Code Baseball, an elite tournament for top amateurs around the country. He needed a manager for the Southern California team. Slaught put his name in the hat.

"And so Don started talking to me about hitting, and I told him my views on hitting," Wallenbrock said. Before long, "we started talking the same language. Sometimes we used different expressions, but as we talked to each other, we were saying the same thing."

Slaught turned into a regular at Wallenbrock's annual get-togethers. A few years later, Walker joined the crew, and from there the meetings grew. Scott Fletcher, a former teammate of Walker's with the White Sox, frequently showed up. So did Ron Roenicke, the manager of the Brewers from 2011 to 2015. Mike Scioscia, the longtime Angels manager, even participated a few times starting in 2007 or 2008. Tim Laker, a retired catcher who before the 2019 season was hired as the Mariners' hitting coach, was in the club, as was Brant Brown, a major league outfielder who is now the hitting strategist for the Dodgers.

It wasn't just former major leaguers at the gatherings either. Wallenbrock brought in a sports psychologist one year, as well as Marcus Elliott, the Harvard-trained physician who specializes in studying the performance and development of elite athletes. Charley Lau Jr. was a part of it. The summits at some point grew to include Sue Enquist, the legendary former softball coach at UCLA. These meetings were mostly friendly, but intense, open only to serious minds committed to discussing cutting-edge ideas about hitting and the swing.

Sometimes the conversation became heated. Slaught recalled a fiery argument one year between Laker and Charley Lau Jr. about a certain move that hitters should or shouldn't make with their bottom hand while swinging. At one point, Enquist spoke up and said she agreed with Laker's position. Lau, frustrated over the fact that he appeared to be losing, said, "How many books have you written, Sue?" Enquist snapped back, "How many national championships have you won, Charley?"

Wallenbrock ran these little seminars until about 2012, when he stopped organizing them in large part because they weren't so little anymore. What started as a roundtable discussion of five or six people had grown to close to 50. "It was costing me money all the time," Wallenbrock said. "I would have sandwiches brought in."

To this day Wallenbrock hears from old friends and coaches he knows asking if he plans on ever restarting the Ball Yard Hitting Summit, now that his ideas have entered the mainstream and he has achieved a level of recognition in the baseball world. He doesn't plan to. But the spirit of the event Wallenbrock created lives on. Others have taken up the mantle with a singular goal: to bring the most cutting-edge hitting minds together to keep pushing the swing into the future.

One Saturday in August 2018, I found myself sitting in the Orchid Ballroom of the Hilton Garden Inn in Irvine, California. Just outside was a table filled with the same mediocre bagels, stale pastries, and bland coffee that one might expect would be served at the Orchid Ballroom of the Hilton Garden Inn in Irvine, California. Inside sat a collection of men—exclusively, as far as I could tell—dressed like guys who spend most of their lives on baseball fields.

This was the "Bridge the Gap" seminar, a conference devoted to discussing the future of hitting—a successor to Craig Wallenbrock's get-togethers. Bridge the Gap is run by a man named Eugene Bleecker. Though he never played baseball beyond college, Bleecker went on to open 108 Performance Academy, a high-level training facility in Southern California dedicated to using science to advance baseball training.

Bleecker grew up on Long Island as a baseball junkie. When he was around seven, his mother sent him to summer camp at Buckley Country Day School, a fancy-pants private school in Roslyn. After the first day, he came home and laid down the law with his mom.

"I never want to sing or do arts and crafts ever again," he told her.

"What do you want to do?" she responded.

"I want to play baseball."

And so he did, signing on at the New York Baseball Academy at nearby Hofstra University. He spent every summer there for the next decade, ultimately developing into a good high school ballplayer. He even had a scholarship offer on the table to play baseball at Fordham, but he lost it when he failed to raise his GPA over 2.7. Telling his grandfather that his scholarship had been pulled remains one of the most difficult moments of his life. "I was only interested in studying baseball," he said. "That's where I put all my chips."

With Fordham off the table, Bleecker began a wild college baseball journey, from junior college to NAIA to NCAA Division II. After several failed attempts to earn a professional contract, he turned his attention to coaching, initially parroting the coaches he'd had growing up. He also had an idea: a specialized grip for the handles of baseball bats designed to teach people the best way to hold the bat. He filed for two patents, built a prototype, and even took it to market, selling it at the American Baseball Coaches Association annual convention in 2010.

It was there, at the Hilton Anatole in Dallas, that Eugene Bleecker had his epiphany. At a nearby booth, he met Don Slaught, who was showcasing a swing analysis tool he had invented. Slaught showed Bleecker a slow-motion video of Derek Jeter's swing. He wasn't swinging down. Why was this so revelatory? Because one of Jeter's hitting coaches with the Yankees was Rick Down—someone Bleecker himself had worked with many times at the New York Baseball Academy.

"When I saw that something that I thought I knew like the back of my hand was wrong, I thought, 'What else do I think I know that's wrong?" Bleecker said.

Eugene Bleecker was determined to do everything he could to find out. In 2014, he opened 108 Performance. The name stems from a line in his favorite movie of all time, *Bull Durham*, which features a speech from Annie Savoy, as portrayed by Susan Sarandon.

"I believe in the Church of Baseball. I've tried all the major religions and most of the minor ones. I've worshiped Buddha, Allah, Brahma, Vishnu, Shiva, trees, mushrooms, and Isadora Duncan. I know things. For instance: there are 108 beads in a Catholic rosary, and there are 108 stitches in a baseball. When I learned that, I gave Jesus a chance."

By the off-season before the 2017 season, Bleecker's facility had started to make a name for itself, to the point where that winter he had the opportunity to work extensively with two major leaguers: Austin Barnes and Jake Marisnick, former teammates at Riverside Polytechnic High School. That year, after retooling their swings with Bleecker, Barnes, a Dodgers catcher, hit .289

with an .895 OPS in 102 games; and Marisnick, after hitting 18 total home runs and posting a .607 OPS in 956 at-bats from 2013 through 2016, enjoyed a renaissance with the Astros, blasting 16 home runs and compiling an .815 OPS. In October 2017, their teams met in the World Series.

Now Bleecker was running Bridge the Gap. Speakers on hitting for this modern meeting of the minds included Rick Strickland, a former minor leaguer turned independent hitting instructor who consulted for the Cardinals; Andy McKay, the Seattle Mariners' director of player development; and Jason Ochart, the director of hitting at Driveline, a well-known baseball development center in Kent, Washington, that was founded in 2008.

Driveline is the creation of Kyle Boddy, a former amateur pitcher whose arm always hurt, and he was determined to find out why. Boddy spent the early part of his professional life bouncing around in various data-science jobs. He worked for an online poker platform helping identify security flaws and was a professional gambler himself.

But Boddy's passion remained baseball. After reading *Moneyball* in his early twenties, he came to a realization: that book was all about finding unrecognized talent—it didn't discuss how to *develop* talent. That was what Boddy aspired to do: to make players better than they already were. He used his background in engineering to build a biomechanics laboratory in service of that goal. His mission, at first, was to understand pitching mechanics better than anybody, so he could keep pitchers healthy and help them improve their velocity. Today more than 500 pitchers a year train with Driveline, including major leaguers like Trevor Bauer, a data-obsessed right-hander who has become the poster child for what Boddy's facility can do.

"We want to be the best player development company in the

world," Boddy told me. "We want to be better than the Red Sox and Yankees at developing players, better at developing than any MLB team. That bar is low. We can do that in the next five years."

For most of Driveline's history, the focus was almost entirely on pitching. It's what Boddy knew and was passionate about. But as Driveline's reputation grew, so did its scope, and in 2016 Boddy hired Jason Ochart, a little-known coach at Menlo College in Atherton, California, to be the company's first director of hitting.

Ochart grew up in Southern California and describes himself as a "very average college baseball player." He graduated from high school in 2008, spent a couple of years at Glendale Community College, and then transferred to San Francisco State, where he hit so poorly that the coaches there converted him into a pitcher.

His interest in coaching had started even earlier—about a year after he finished high school. When his brother Adam, just a year younger than him, asked him to help him improve his swing, Ochart bought a video camera and went to work, analyzing Adam's swings and offering his advice. He saw that Adam, a naturally strong hitter, had a slight upswing—something Ochart had been taught was bad. In fact, Ochart remembered, coaches on some of the teams he played for told him that if he hit a ball in the air in batting practice, his round was immediately over, an incentive to get him to use his speed and hit the ball on the ground. Ochart coached Adam out of his upswing, flattening his swing and imploring him to hit more ground balls. The results were . . . predictable.

"We spent the entire summer trying to fix these quote-unquote flaws, and by the time he was practicing with his college team, the poor kid couldn't hit the ball out of the infield," Ochart said.

The coach at Glendale Community College, who had coached

Ochart and had now brought Adam aboard, called Ochart in shock. He wondered whether Adam was injured or was having problems at home. He had been hitting home runs with ease when he visited the school. Now he could barely reach the out-field grass. That fall, Adam was cut from the team.

"I will never forget that phone call," Ochart said. "Here's my first-ever client, somebody who trusted me completely, and I made him worse."

Haunted by his brother's failure, Ochart turned to the inter-net, devouring hitting content wherever he could find it—online forums, YouTube, whatever he could uncover. He quickly dis-covered what so many modern-day hitting coaches have discov-ered: "My idea of a good swing was completely the opposite," he said. One video of Manny Ramírez especially stands out. Watch-ing it, the swing looked eerily familiar. The barrel of his bat was traveling slightly up, his back foot was off the ground, his shoul-ders were moving a particular way. It was Adam's swing—his original swing.

"Your stomach sinks," Ochart said. "You get nauseous."

In school, Ochart studied kinesiology and exercise science and spent some time working as a personal trainer. Meanwhile, Adam Ochart rebounded. After being cut at Glendale, he regained his stroke and wound up transferring to Menlo College, where he hit so well that he landed a scholarship. He also did something else while at Menlo: help his brother Jason secure a job as an assistant coach on the team. It certainly wasn't a high-profile job, and it didn't pay much—Menlo competes at the NAIA level, rather than the NCAA. But it was a way to stay around baseball, and it was a job so that Ochart didn't have to take out more student loans and keep going to school. By the 2015 season, Jason Ochart was Menlo's hitting coach. His reputation quickly grew. He taught his players to hit the ball in the air at a time when that way of thinking was still far removed from the mainstream. To most of his players, the concept was foreign, and Ochart faced skepticism.

That all went away when the players saw the results. The season before Ochart became the hitting coach, Menlo's players hit 31 home runs, or one in every 60 at-bats. After Ochart took over, they bashed 58 homers—one in every 33 at-bats. In his second season as hitting coach, 2016, Menlo hit a ridiculous 80 home runs. That June the Brewers selected one of Ochart's hitters, Lucas Erceg, in the second round of the draft. The White Sox followed that seven rounds later by taking Max Dutto, another Menlo product.

Because this was all happening at Menlo, not too many people noticed. But Ochart had started posting videos of his hitters' at-bats on his Twitter account, and they were gaining traction in the online hitting community. That ultimately led to Boddy following him. He needed to learn more about this kid in California. In September 2016, Boddy hired Ochart to head up Driveline's hitting initiatives. Ochart had come a long way from nearly ruining his brother's career.

"He was developing these losers from junior college, guys who had switched schools three times with no results and then hit 20 home runs," Boddy said. "He had guys hitting home runs that I had never heard of. Who is this guy? How did he get the best out of these guys when no other coach could?"

All of this made Ochart the perfect presenter at Bridge the Gap, which had drawn the attention of people in high places. About two dozen representatives from major league organizations attended that year. Craig Wallenbrock wasn't there, but his presence was felt, with many attendees speaking about him with great reverence. They knew that without Wallenbrock these conversations probably wouldn't be happening.

"He paved the way," Bleecker said.

* * *

On May 18, 2003, the White Sox made a decision that indirectly changed Craig Wallenbrock's life. They had just lost, 3–2, to the Twins, dropping their record on the season to 20-23. With their offense foundering, general manager Ken Williams fired hitting coach Gary Ward. At the time, Williams said, "We felt the need for a change." White Sox manager Jerry Manuel said, "You need a new voice."

The new voice turned out to be Greg Walker, who earned the call-up from Triple A to fix what ailed the White Sox. His first project was an important one: first baseman Paul Konerko, viewed by the organization as a crucial part of its future. After bouncing around from the Dodgers to the Reds to the White Sox, the former 13th overall draft pick had finally broken out in 2002. He hit .304 with 27 home runs, 104 RBIs, and an .857 OPS, a showing that earned him a spot on the AL All-Star roster.

But in 2003, everything was going wrong. On the day Ward was fired, Konerko was batting just .221, with an OBP that had dipped to a dreadful .296. "I got the hitting coach fired I was doing so bad," Konerko told me. He was kidding, but only sort of.

Enter Greg Walker—and by extension, Craig Wallenbrock.

Konerko knew almost nothing about Walker or his philosophy. He just knew he needed to snap out of what had developed into a two-month slump. So when Walker sat him down one early afternoon in the dugout before a game at Chicago's U.S. Cellular Field, Konerko listened.

"We were having a heart-to-heart, and he said, 'Listen, I know what you have going on. I see all the mistakes and flaws you have going on, and I think I can help and fix that. I can help you here,'" Konerko said. "'But you have to totally buy into this. It's going to be different stuff and different ways of thinking. You have to be committed to this.'"

He didn't know it yet, but Craig Wallenbrock was about to have his first real major league reclamation project. Sure, Michael Young was already in the big leagues. So was Brad Fullmer, a former second-rounder from the Southern California circuit. But Wallenbrock had started working with Young and Fullmer before they reached the majors and helped them maximize the potential that allowed them to get there. This was different. Maybe, after all these decades preaching what he believed to be the gospel, the establishment was ready to hear what Craig Wallenbrock had to say.

Walker started with the basics. He worked with Konerko to develop a bat path that would keep his barrel in the hitting zone longer, allowing him to launch fly balls with authority on a consistent basis. He showed Konerko how to drop his barrel into the slot, how to reach Wallenbrock's famous "lag position," instead of slashing his hands down through the zone. Konerko described it as "a clear-cut break from what I had done."

Before they started working together, Walker warned Konerko that things would probably get worse before they got better. In trying to retool his swing in the middle of a major league season, Konerko would be asking his body to do things it had never done before. Even for an elite athlete like Konerko, there would be a period of adjustment. And lo and behold, Walker's prediction came true. In his first 37 games after Walker's arrival as hitting coach, Konerko hit .165 (16-for-97) with just four extra-base hits. He went into the 2003 All-Star break batting a miserable .197.

If there was a moment when Konerko could have lost hope, could have given up and gone back to what he was doing before, this was it. The year before, Konerko spent his All-Star break in Milwaukee, where he doubled in consecutive at-bats in his Midsummer Classic debut. On the television broadcast, announcers

Joe Buck and Tim McCarver said that if the game had ended in an AL victory instead of a tie—yeah, it was *that* All-Star Game—Konerko would've been the game's MVP. All of that had happened just the year before. This season, with Konerko's home ballpark hosting the All-Star Game, he was watching at home.

But Konerko didn't quit. He was determined to give the new swing a fair shake.

"I was at such a rock-bottom place," Konerko said. "It was a broken place, so I was like, 'Okay, let's do this. I have nothing to lose here.'"

Konerko's patience and dedication paid dividends. When he returned from the break, things started to improve. In 61 second-half games, Konerko hit .275 with 13 home runs and a very respectable .853 OPS. Right away, Konerko realized it wasn't a coincidence or a fluke. This felt . . . different. For the first time in his life, he had power not just to left—as expected for a right-handed swinger—but to the opposite field as well. He was rapping singles up the middle on pitches he couldn't handle before. Konerko said he was "seeing a different me."

At that point, Konerko hadn't met Craig Wallenbrock in person. All he knew about the swing whisperer was what he had heard from Walker. In September 2004, when the White Sox visited Anaheim, he decided to finally meet the man who had helped restart his career from afar.

Throughout that season, Konerko was a dominant force. He hit 41 homers and drove in 117 runs. As terrible as he was at the start of '03, that's how locked in he was in '04. Now it was time to meet the master.

The conversation between Wallenbrock, Walker, and Konerko grew sophisticated and ongoing. As time passed, they'd often meet when the White Sox came through Anaheim, sometimes at Wallenbrock's batting cage. Walker would occasionally fly

Wallenbrock to Chicago to work with Konerko and others. Later on, Wallenbrock would even go to Arizona during spring training to hit with Konerko "at oddball hours," Wallenbrock said, to work around the team's busy workout schedule.

Konerko was nothing short of a teacher's dream, and not just because he was motivated: Konerko aspired to learn not only the technique but also the theories behind it. He wanted to advance to the point where he could self-diagnose the issues with his swing and correct them with no assistance, without needing to run out to California to have Wallenbrock fix the problem. If he could do that, Konerko thought, he would be slump-proof—or at least able to snap out of slumps quicker than most.

During one session, Wallenbrock was talking to Konerko about how to make some subtle moves with his elbows and hands. Wallenbrock instructed Konerko to think about revving a motorcycle or wringing a towel to feel what he wanted him to feel. By the next time they were together, Konerko had taken a piece of PVC pipe, cut it down the middle, and attached it to his bat with tape. He positioned the pipe in a way that forced his hands, when he swung the bat, to move the way Wallenbrock had shown him. Wallenbrock told him it was brilliant: not only had Konerko done it on his own, but he'd created a drill that even Wallenbrock himself hadn't devised.

"I gave him the concept, and he figured out a way to advance that concept," Wallenbrock said.

Ultimately, that's what Wallenbrock wanted—a pupil who surpassed him in knowledge, who didn't need a teacher anymore. He was inspired by an interview he once saw with Michael Phelps, the Olympic swimmer, talking about Bob Bowman, his longtime coach. Phelps started working with Bowman when he was 11 years old and stuck with him for his entire competitive career. When the interviewer asked Phelps how he had managed to stay with one coach for so long, Phelps responded that it was because their relationship had developed to where they could argue with each other. In Konerko, Wallenbrock saw someone who could become his Michael Phelps—a hitter he could teach and who would eventually teach him.

As time passed, Konerko spoke with Wallenbrock less and less. He no longer needed to. That dismal slump at the start of 2003—the slump that precipitated Walker's arrival and his eventual relationship with Wallenbrock—was the last brutal slump Konerko ever went through. He retired after the 2014 season with 439 home runs, all but seven of which came with the White Sox—the second most in franchise history, trailing only Hall of Famer Frank Thomas. Konerko's 1,383 RBIs with Chicago also rank second in the team's history, and he earned nearly $130 million in salary with the White Sox. His number 14 has been retired.

For all of that, Konerko thanks two people more than just about anybody else: Greg Walker and Craig Wallenbrock. Reflecting on the moment of crisis that led him to them, Konerko sounds like he's even absorbed Wallenbrock's bent toward Eastern philosophy.

"A teacher," Konerko reflected, "will appear when the student is ready."

In Greg Walker's mind, Craig Wallenbrock had nothing left to prove. In helping Paul Konerko regain his swing and embark on what would turn into a brilliant career with the White Sox, Wallenbrock had shown that he could benefit major league hitters. The way Walker figured it, if Wallenbrock could do that for Konerko, he could do it for others: Craig Wallenbrock, he decided, should work for the White Sox.

So, before the 2005 season, Walker approached White Sox owner Jerry Reinsdorf and suggested that he hire Wallenbrock as an exclusive consultant during spring training. Wallenbrock would work not just with the major league team but also with the minor leaguers and, most important, the minor league coaches, to help install a hitting philosophy throughout the entire organization, so that when prospects reached Chicago, they would already be on the Wallenbrock-Walker program.

Reinsdorf was open to the idea, but Ken Williams, the White Sox general manager at the time, felt differently. "Our GM didn't appreciate anybody outside of the game," Walker said. (Williams declined to comment on the situation for this book.)

Ultimately, Wallenbrock spent about one week working with White Sox hitters in Tucson, Arizona, during that spring training. It didn't go well. Though Walker wanted him there, Williams very much did not. Wallenbrock eventually heard from another member of the White Sox front office that Williams didn't feel comfortable with an outsider he didn't know working with the hitters, even with Walker's stamp of approval. So they paid him for the week, and Wallenbrock hopped in his car and left.

But Walker didn't give up. He pitched the idea of having Wallenbrock travel around the organization's minor league affiliates and work only with prospects, but that didn't fly either. The baseball establishment was not ready for Craig Wallenbrock.

Through all of this, Wallenbrock continued his relationship with Walker. He kept working privately with individual hitters on the team, like Paul Konerko, not in any official capacity as an employee of the Chicago White Sox but as an independent hitting instructor.

That October, mere months after Wallenbrock's brief stint at spring training, the White Sox won the World Series, completing a four-game sweep of the Astros. It marked the franchise's first championship since 1917, a stretch of failure that was actually longer than the much more famous drought that the Red Sox had snapped the year before. Wallenbrock wasn't a part of it.

THE ROAD TO J.D.

Joe Borchard wasn't the best baseball player Craig Wallenbrock ever worked with. Not even close. But in many ways, Borchard was the single most important client Wallenbrock ever had. It was Borchard who led The Oracle of Santa Clarita to Greg Walker, paving the way for Wallenbrock to bring his knowledge of the swing inside professional baseball. And it was Borchard who ultimately led Wallenbrock to J. D. Martinez, the player who would make sure that nobody in the baseball world ever forgot his name.

Borchard first met the Oracle as a high school sophomore. This was in the mid-1990s, when Wallenbrock was working as a scout for the Indians, driving the Southern California freeways in search of Cleveland's next big star. When he arrived in Camarillo, Wallenbrock was sure he had found him.

Borchard was a natural athlete, blessed with physical gifts most ballplayers could only dream about. He was tall and strong, eventually growing to six-foot-four and 230 pounds. He could fly around the bases. He had a cannon for a right arm. He could do just about everything on a baseball field. There was just one itsy-bitsy problem: his swing was—to put it nicely—flawed.

Wallenbrock didn't put it nicely. He walked right up to Borchard and delivered the cold, hard truth.

"Your swing just sucks," Wallenbrock told Borchard. "If you learn to do a few things, you can be a decent baseball player. I'd like to meet with you and teach you some of the things I teach guys."

Other prospects might have leapt at the opportunity. Sure, Wallenbrock didn't yet have the reputation he would ultimately develop, but this was a professional scout offering to help Borchard improve his swing. Borchard, in all his infinite wisdom, blew him off. At that point, football was Borchard's first love, the sport he aspired to play at the next level. Baseball was just something he did to pass the time in the spring. As the months passed Borchard didn't think much about the unusual offer he had received from the mysterious scout. But then his junior baseball season started, and for the first time in his life nothing was going right at the plate. The natural athletic ability that had compensated for his poor swing mechanics was no longer enough. That's when, at a tournament, the Oracle approached Borchard again.

"Look, I can really help you," Wallenbrock told him. "Let's sit down and meet to figure out how to get you on the right track."

This time Borchard took him up on it.

When Joe Borchard first started working with Craig Wallenbrock, the idea of watching footage of his swings was life-changing. Until that point, nobody had ever even discussed mechanics with him, let alone analyzed his swing on video. In his senior year of high school, he said, after extensive work with Wallenbrock, he raised his home run output from 2 his junior year to 11 or 12. "I was a completely different player," Borchard said.

That level of success continued as Borchard graduated from

high school and moved on to Stanford, opting to attend college to play baseball and football after declining to sign with the Orioles, who drafted him in the 20th round in 1997.

Borchard was nothing short of a monster for the Cardinal, racking up numbers that placed him among the best players in the history of Stanford's storied baseball program. In three years there, he hit .346 with an OPS of 1.040. In June of his junior season, the White Sox made him an offer difficult to refuse: they drafted him in the first round, 12th overall, three slots before the Phillies picked up UCLA infielder Chase Utley, another Wallenbrock product.

But football called too. Some scouts projected Borchard as a first-or second-round pick in the NFL draft if he stayed in school and played quarterback for Stanford for his senior season. To entice him away, the White Sox awarded him a $5.3 million signing bonus, then the biggest minor league contract ever. White Sox scouting director Duane Shaffer, the man who had hired Wallenbrock as a scout for the A's years earlier, told the *Chicago Tribune* that Borchard had "the best power from a college player since Mark McGwire."

And Craig Wallenbrock was a major reason why.

The path for Joe Borchard seemed preordained: he would soar through the minor leagues and quickly join the White Sox, where he would enter a lineup already populated with Frank Thomas, Magglio Ordóñez, and a rising star named Paul Konerko. In the wildly unpredictable world of evaluating baseball prospects, Borchard seemed close to a sure thing.

The summer he was drafted, he quickly rose through the ranks from rookie ball to advanced Class A to Double A. In 2001, his first full season as a professional baseball player, he hit .295

with 27 home runs, 98 RBIs, and an .892 OPS for Double A Birmingham. He started 2002 with Triple A Charlotte, hit a respectable .272 with 20 homers in 117 games, and on September 2, 2002, on the artificial turf at the SkyDome in Toronto, Joe Borchard made his major league debut. (Chase Utley wouldn't join the Phillies until 2003.)

Borchard's first encounter with major league pitching went about as one would expect for a prospect of his caliber. After popping out in his first at-bat, Borchard stepped up to the plate in the fourth inning against Corey Thurman of the Blue Jays and smacked a home run. It was a storybook moment for Borchard—and for Craig Wallenbrock, whose protégé had truly made it.

It would be nice to think that Joe Borchard followed up that homer in Toronto with a long and successful major league career, replete with All-Star Game appearances and prestigious awards. It would be nice to think that, once he established himself as a bona fide superstar, a reporter would ask Borchard for his secret, and he would publicly acknowledge the swing doctor in California who showed him the way. It would be nice to be able to say that Borchard's professional success was what gained Wallenbrock, and his theories, mainstream acceptance.

But baseball is a cruel game. Borchard, against all odds, never panned out. He played just 16 games for the White Sox in 2003, went 9-for-49 (.184), and spent most of the season back in Triple A. He didn't fare much better in 2004, playing in 63 major league games and hitting .174 with nine home runs. (One of those homers traveled an estimated 504 feet, a monumental blast that only served as a tantalizing reminder of the talent hidden inside.) The White Sox gave up on Borchard in 2006, trading him that March to the Mariners. Borchard's last major league game came as a member of the Florida Marlins on August 5, 2007, at the age of 28. He finished with a lifetime batting average of .205 and an OPS of .636. He was, undeniably, a bust.

Of course, he has regrets. Borchard was destined for greatness, and greatness never arrived. Why things didn't work out, he'll never know for sure. There is a lot more to succeeding at the highest level of professional baseball than just swing mechanics. The reasons why some players thrive and others falter are often impossible to pin down.

But for years he also carried with him the burden of guilt. By the time Wallenbrock had gotten his hands on Borchard, he had spent decades on the margins, ignored by the baseball mainstream and told that his ideas were crazy. Borchard was going to be the one to change all of that. He was going to prove, once and for all, that Wallenbrock did in fact know what he was talking about. Instead, he only validated the critics.

"I was afraid I would be a black mark on Craig," Borchard said. "I wanted to do well for myself and give him a good name."

He didn't know it yet, but Borchard was far from a black mark. Though he fell far short of expectations on the field, he remains one of the most important hitters Wallenbrock ever worked with. Because while Borchard might not have talked about Wallenbrock in public, players talk to each other. And one of the people he had mentioned Wallenbrock's name to over the years was listening.

Robert Cord Phelps was never big enough, never strong enough, never talented enough to play professional baseball. Scouts didn't pay attention to him during his time at Santa Barbara High School. Colleges barely noticed him. Phelps was destined to be like the millions of other dreamers who loved baseball more than anything else in the world and were too blind to see that it was unrequited.

Until, that is, he met a certain batting coach a little farther down the coast.

One of Phelps's older brothers had worked as a student-manager for Stanford's baseball team a few years before. Joe Borchard was on that team. He passed Wallenbrock's number along to Phelps's brother, who passed it along to Cord. At the time, Phelps was just a sophomore in high school, but he could already see the writing on the wall. If he had any chance of ful-filling his dream and advancing to the next level, he needed help. If this guy helped Joe Borchard, surely he could help Cord Phelps too.

The way Wallenbrock remembers it, the first time he met Phelps, the young man looked like he was about 11 years old. Wallenbrock knew some 11-year-olds with better swings too. "I went, 'Oh my God, what did I get myself into?'" he said.

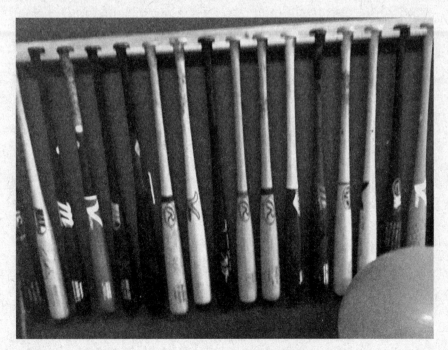

A row of bats at Craig Wallenbrock's facility in Santa Clarita, California.

Phelps was smart, though, and coachable, willing to throw out everything he had ever done before and remake his swing under Wallenbrock's guidance. After all, like so many of Wallenbrock's early clients, Phelps knew nothing about proper mechanics. Everything he knew to that point he had learned from his Little League coaches, well-meaning dads who regurgitated the same wrong information that well-meaning dads had been teaching for decades.

But not Wallenbrock, of course. By the time Phelps arrived, Wallenbrock had taken a step into the 21st century: he would show Phelps DVD clips of Barry Bonds, Manny Ramírez, and Larry Walker. It was with those DVDs that Wallenbrock made the first big change to Phelps's swing: he stopped him from rotating on his back foot, the technique known as "squishing the bug."

Just about everybody who played Little League in the 1990s and 2000s at some point heard the virtues of squishing the bug, the well-worn teaching maxim that at some point became accepted practice in youth baseball. The idea behind it seemed to be to teach young hitters how to better rotate their hips while swinging. High-level swing coaches today reject that terminology, arguing that most kids, told to "squish the bug," simply spin on their foot rather than truly rotate their hips while swinging. While this explosive hip rotation does lead some elite hitters to finish their swing with their foot turned in a "squish the bug" position, for most it does not. Phelps pointed at Astros star George Springer as the perfect example of a hitter who fully rotated his hips while swinging, even though his back heel barely moved.

Wallenbrock quickly beat "squish the bug" out of Phelps. That was only the beginning.

"He was the guy who really helped me to start to understand what you're trying to accomplish in the swing and dispel a lot of myths as a younger baseball player," Phelps said. "There are a lot of people who don't know what they're talking about, and you pick up a lot of bad habits."

Phelps trained under Wallenbrock about once a month through the rest of high school, and his performance improved. He got bigger too, eventually growing to around six feet tall. Still, as he approached graduation, he hadn't gotten his scholarship, even with Wallenbrock making plenty of phone calls on his behalf. The best offer he received was an opportunity to be a walk-on with the team at Stanford, an option made possible by his sterling academic record in high school. It was far from a guarantee, and he'd have to pay his own way, but it was a chance. It was all Cord Phelps could have asked for.

Cord Phelps's transition to college baseball didn't go smoothly at first. He had made the team at Stanford, but when he arrived on campus for his freshman season in 2006, he quickly realized that when it came to raw talent, he didn't quite fit in with his teammates. The fastballs were faster and the curveballs were curvier. Almost everybody was bigger and stronger than him. They ran faster, too. Some of them had been drafted out of high school and were considered legitimate professional prospects at age 18. Phelps was not.

Still, thanks to some injuries to established starters and his effort in practice, Phelps wound up playing in 38 games that season. He went 18-for-92, for a .196 batting average. All 18 of his hits were singles. Working with Craig Wallenbrock might have put Phelps on a college baseball roster, but if he wanted to thrive on one, there was a lot more work left to do.

"I had a big learning curve," Phelps said. "The step for me in college was pretty big."

So Phelps went back to the drawing board. He wanted to be

better. That meant more sessions with Wallenbrock, all through the summer and then again over Christmas break that winter. It showed in the results. By 2007 Phelps had cracked Stanford's everyday lineup, appearing in 55 games, tied for the most on the team. He hit .301 in 186 at-bats, with 19 of his 56 hits going for extra bases—15 doubles and four triples.

By now Phelps had grown past six feet and was building muscle. He was no longer the little pipsqueak that Wallenbrock had mistaken for a sixth-grader just a few years earlier. More important, Phelps had started to show that he could play at the collegiate level after all, that the coaches who had ignored him were wrong. For Wallenbrock, that meant it was time to put the final touches on Phelps's swing.

In the summer between Phelps's sophomore and junior years, Wallenbrock helped him implement a leg kick. The thought behind it was that Phelps had proven he could hit college pitching, but power production remained a problem. After 93 games at Stanford, he still hadn't managed to a hit a home run, a fact that more or less precluded professional scouts' interest in him. But a leg kick, Wallenbrock believed, coupled with the high-level bat path they had started working on years before, would allow Phelps to send balls flying over the fence. The bat path would result in more balls in the air. The leg kick would shore up his timing.

When he returned that fall, Phelps was pleased with his progress. An exaggerated leg kick was new to him and made him different from his peers, but it seemed to work, and he couldn't wait to unleash his newfound power stroke on the pitchers of the Pacific-10 Conference. There was just one problem: Phelps may have believed in his swing, but the powers-that-be at Stanford weren't exactly on board. The Cardinal's head coach, Mark Marquess, was a legend in the world of college baseball. He played baseball and football at Stanford in the 1960s—even rooming with former presidential candidate Mitt Romney for a year—before returning to the school as an assistant baseball coach in 1972. By 1977, Marquess was the head coach, and he wouldn't relinquish that job for the next four decades, going on to amass 1,627 wins and lead Stanford to consecutive College World Series championships in 1987 and 1988.

All of this is a long way of saying that as long as Marquess was coaching, Stanford would do things a certain old-school way—the way Marquess had learned to do things during his professional career, which had fizzled out in 1973 in Triple A. That meant sticking to a traditional line-drive and ground-ball approach that didn't lend itself to power production. Swinging with an exaggerated leg kick, a move clearly designed to maximize power, certainly wasn't part of the game plan.

"Stanford at the time wanted everybody to swing the same way," Phelps said. "I had this big-ass leg kick, and it was clear I was doing something different."

Almost everybody who has worked with Wallenbrock eventually arrives at a moment when he has to decide whether to trust in Wallenbrock's radical ideas, and risk alienating coaches, or go back to the old way of swinging. Now, before his junior season at Stanford, it was Phelps's turn to make that critical choice.

Phelps decided to put his faith in Wallenbrock.

"The reason I made it as far as I did was that I was pretty stubborn," Phelps said. "People said, 'Don't go to Stanford, go to City College, because you'll play at City College.' They were telling me, 'These are your limitations.' I never listened to that."

To that end, he didn't listen when coaches at Stanford wanted him to ditch the leg kick and fit in with the team's hitting philosophies, and he was rewarded. Phelps's junior season was nothing short of magical: He hit .351, the second-best batting average on the team, only behind the team's catcher, Jason Castro, a future big league All Star. Most impressively, despite failing to hit a home run in his first two years of college, he utilized his newly installed leg kick to blast 13 homers, contributing to a team that advanced to the College World Series. "I was stubborn enough not to change," he said.

It was an incredible performance, one that few had seen coming. But once it happened, people noticed—important people, people with the power to help Phelps achieve his lifelong dream. That June, as Phelps's remarkable season was winding down, the Indians selected him in the third round of the draft. That is how much Phelps's stock had risen. With Wallenbrock's help, this unrecruited nobody had climbed the ladder all the way to professional baseball.

For Wallenbrock, Phelps getting drafted was validation of his methods. Phelps may have represented Wallenbrock's greatest accomplishment yet, given his undeniable athletic limitations. Phelps was also a living, breathing advertisement for what Wallenbrock could offer a developing hitter. Naturally, Phelps's teammates at Stanford wanted to know where he suddenly learned to slam baseballs over fences. Phelps told them about the Oracle of Santa Clarita. Most players promptly forgot about it and went on with their lives and careers. But one player committed Craig Wallenbrock's name to memory.

During their time at Stanford, Jason Castro was more or less the opposite of Cord Phelps. Unlike Phelps, he had been drafted out of high school and heavily recruited by other top colleges. As a junior for the Cardinal in 2008, he hit .376 with 14 home runs, 73 RBIs, and a whopping 1.042 OPS. The Astros that summer took him with the 10th overall pick of the draft, 97 spots before the Indians selected Phelps.

Castro knew about Craig Wallenbrock from Phelps. Wallenbrock would come watch Phelps play whenever Stanford visited UCLA or USC. At one of those games, Phelps's dad introduced Wallenbrock to Castro's dad. At the time, however, Castro didn't feel like he needed outside help, and the numbers showed why. He soared through the minor leagues, advancing all the way to Triple A in his second full professional season. He made his big league debut on June 22, 2010, and picked up a single off Tim Lincecum in his first game.

The rest of that season, however, turned out to be a struggle unlike any Castro had experienced to that point. He wound up playing in 67 games for the Astros that year, mustering a measly .205 batting average and a .573 OPS. Among National League players with at least 200 plate appearances, only five had a worse slugging percentage than Castro's .287.

For the first time maybe in his entire life, Castro felt genuinely overmatched. The swing that had always come naturally to him, the one that had carried him all the way to the major leagues, was failing.

"I realized after my first season that if I wanted to try to stick at this level, I probably needed to make some changes that would allow me to handle the type of pitching you see in the big leagues," Castro said.

Castro had never before sought out instruction for his swing. Now that he was ready to, he knew who he would call. He had watched Phelps tinker with his swing and suddenly start blasting home runs a couple of years earlier. "Seeing the success he had," Castro said, "you couldn't help but think he was on the right track swing-wise." So naturally, Castro reached out to the Oracle. He needed help, and in the off-season before the 2011 season, he was ready to hand over the keys to his swing to a man who had barely played baseball after high school.

In Castro's mind, he picked the perfect moment to go outside the organization for swing help. At the All-Star break in 2010, with their offense ranking among the worst in the sport, the Astros fired their hitting coach, Sean Berry, and replaced him on an interim basis with Jeff Bagwell, a franchise legend who had been involved with Houston's front office. Bagwell announced that October that he wouldn't return to the role, leaving the Astros searching for somebody new. It was a rare chance to work with Wallenbrock without offending anybody.

Castro says he made "some drastic changes" that first winter as Wallenbrock showed him how to get his bat on plane earlier in order to consistently hit line drives and fly balls rather than grounders. They spent hours watching the swings of the best hitters throughout baseball history, searching for common traits and trying to emulate them.

Wallenbrock's teaching methods immediately impressed Castro. For every flaw in Castro's swing, Wallenbrock would immediately have a video queued up of an elite hitter doing it correctly, followed by a drill in the batting cage that would allow Castro to fix the issue himself. Wallenbrock didn't teach Castro to hit the ball in the air. He simply showed him what the great hitters did. It just so happened that the great hitters, the hitters who produced runs, tended to hit the ball in the air. It was a subtle distinction, but a meaningful one.

"Saying guys are trying to hit the ball in the air is wrong," Castro said. "That's looking at the outcome instead of the beginning. It's looking at it backward."

Castro hoped to showcase his new swing in 2011. He realized it was still a work in progress, but he thought he had done enough to demonstrate real improvement in his first full major league season. The baseball gods had other plans. In a Grapefruit League contest that March, Castro blew out his knee running to first base. His season ended before it had even begun. There was an unexpected benefit, though: once he healed enough to swing, Castro returned to Southern California to continue working with Wallenbrock.

"It let me refine the major changes I was trying to make instead of doing them all in just one off-season. I had a much longer timeline to get comfortable with them," Castro said. "It might have been a blessing in disguise."

As Jason Castro, now a catcher with a few months of major league service time to his name, was beginning his rehab from knee surgery, Cord Phelps was reporting to the Columbus Clippers, the Indians' Triple A affiliate. Phelps had finished 2010 there and had hit quite well: in 66 games, he put up a .317 batting average and an .892 OPS, with 30 of his 77 hits going for extra bases. Actually, Phelps had hit quite well everywhere he had been to that point, including a strong showing that autumn in the Arizona Fall League, a showcase for highly touted prospects across the game. Phelps, the player who needed to walk on at Stanford just to play college baseball, was on the doorstep of the major leagues.

In early June, the call arrived. On June 8, 2011, Phelps played second base for the Indians against the Twins. He batted seventh. Twice, he grounded out. Once, he struck out. In his final at-bat, he flew out to deep left-center, taking an 0-for-4 in his major league debut. He didn't mind too much. He had beaten the odds. He had made it.

Phelps played again on June 10, in the Bronx against the Yankees. This time he served as the designated hitter. In his second at-bat, he singled, grounding a ball into right field off Iván Nova. He added a bases-loaded walk in the eighth inning off Kevin Whelan, picking up his first career RBI. On June 19, he blasted a three-run walk-off home run off Tim Wood of the Pirates. The homer came on Father's Day. Afterward, he gave the ball to his dad.

These memories stand out to Phelps because they represent some of the best moments of his life in professional baseball. For everything Phelps accomplished—and he accomplished an incredible amount, considering where he started—he never turned into a major league star. He wouldn't be the one to launch Craig Wallenbrock to mainstream prominence, even though Wallenbrock continues to view him as one of his most profound successes.

Phelps wound up playing in 56 major league games from 2011 through 2014. He finished with a batting average of .155. His final professional season came in 2015 for the Lehigh Valley IronPigs, the Triple A affiliate of the Phillies. At some point, talent wins out even over the best possible technique. When I asked Wallenbrock why he thought Phelps didn't quite pan out, he gave a simple answer: "Some guys have more in there, and they're not getting it out," he said. "But do you think you could put 16 ounces of water into an eight-ounce cup?"

Wallenbrock meant this not as a criticism but as the ultimate compliment. From Little League on, Cord Phelps had never been the most talented player on any baseball team. He had gone as far as he possibly could, realizing every last ounce of potential in his body. How many people in any profession could say that?

After he stopped playing, Phelps returned to Stanford to finish his bachelor's degree in human biology and mechanical engineering before going on to earn a master's in communications and media studies. As of late 2019, he was working as a business analyst for Deloitte Consulting. Before that, he was a Major League Baseball player—and he helped bring Craig Wallenbrock one step closer to the hitter who would validate his life's work.

His knee seemingly healed from the surgery that cost him the entire 2011 season, Jason Castro returned to the Astros in 2012 finally ready to show off what he had spent the last 18 months working on with Craig Wallenbrock. It started . . . poorly. On the Astros' first homestand, he went 0-for-11.

Like Phelps, Castro now faced his moment of truth. He knew he could abandon ship. Part of what had made him comfortable enough to go train with Wallenbrock in the first place, he said, was knowing that he could always go back to how he swung before "if I found it didn't work."

But by now Castro believed in Wallenbrock. Working with him had taught Castro not just a series of moves that created the swing but the underlying mechanical reasons for why those moves resulted in an ideal bat path. And the theory was borne out by so many of the best hitters through the ages. He resolved to keep going. It paid off. In the top of the second inning against the Marlins on April 13, Castro shot a single up the middle, before smoking another single into deep right-center two frames later that plated J. D. Martinez from second base. From that day through the end of April, Castro hit .293. Maybe this stuff worked after all.

Castro battled with his health for the rest of the 2012 season, dealing with residual discomfort in his knee. He spent more than a month on the disabled list in the middle of the summer when the soreness became too severe to manage. By the end of the year, he had appeared in just 87 games, batting .257 with six home runs and a .735 OPS, essentially league average. He hadn't established himself as a star by any means, but he had proven that he could cut it in the major leagues, something that hadn't seemed so certain in 2010. He went into the winter this time not looking to remake his swing or recover from a significant injury, but to tune up for what would turn into a crucial year—and not just for Castro.

A BYRD LEARNS TO FLY

Marlon Byrd was a free agent before the 2013 season. He had completely remade his swing with Doug Latta at the Ball Yard and looked like an entirely different hitter, but at that point nobody else knew that. No major league team was going to give him a job because he had spent some time hitting with a dude at a little batting cage in Chatsworth. And no major league team was rushing to sign a 35-year-old who had hit .210 the year before and was coming off a PED suspension.

So Byrd had to resort to drastic measures: he went to Mexico, where he latched on with the Tomateros de Culiacán. Before he left, Latta gave him a simple piece of advice: "You're going to feel weird," he told him. "Stay with it."

Mexico was a humbling experience for Byrd, a far cry from the life of luxury he had led ever since he broke into the major leagues in 2002. At one point during the season there, his team took an 18-hour bus ride to play in Tijuana. After the game, there was a food spread waiting for the team, but the tortillas and carne asada for tacos were covered with flies.

On another occasion, the team arrived at its hotel in Puerto Peñasco at two o'clock in the morning. His uniform was still wet with sweat and covered in dirt and mud. There was no clubhouse attendant who handled the laundry. It was his responsibility. As he sat in his room washing his jersey with a bar of soap, he thought to himself, *If I ever complain about anything else in baseball, I need to be slapped.*

"I didn't know what was going to come of this Mexican league," Byrd said. "But it was not going to get worse than this."

For Marlon Byrd, Mexico was a step backward. But for Doug Latta, it was unlike anything he had ever seen before, a window into the world of professional baseball. He was with Byrd as much as possible in Mexico, visiting him in Culiacán and meeting him for games in Mexicali so they could keep working. He still felt like Byrd needed the reinforcement, especially because his teammates in Mexico didn't exactly support his new mechanics. In Mexico, Byrd said, coaches teach to swing down. Latta's presence—not to mention his trusty video camera—ensured that he would stay on track.

When Byrd first arrived in Mexico, he couldn't shake the doubt. As much as he trusted his new swing, he had yet to test it against high-level pitching. He kept thinking to himself, *All right, when am I going to slip? When am I going to go back to that .210-with-one-homer swing?* The answer, it turns out, was that he wouldn't. In 57 games in Mexico, Byrd hit .318 with 16 home runs. Team Mexico invited him to return for the Caribbean Series, the most prestigious tournament in Latin American baseball. Byrd quickly accepted, under one condition: he had to be allowed to bring his hitting coach with him.

By this point, after working together day after day after day, Byrd's relationship with Latta had deepened beyond player and coach. "We were like this," Byrd said, linking his hands together. "We're boys." So it was appropriate that Latta was with Byrd in Mexico when the phone call arrived: the Mets wanted to sign him to a minor league contract with an invitation to spring training, which was about to start. Byrd jumped on it. Sure, it wasn't a major league deal, but considering his baggage, that wasn't happening. With his new swing clicking, he just wanted an opportunity to show what he could do, and the Mets had given that to him. His trip to Mexico had been an unbridled success. Now it was time for the real test.

Byrd arrived at the Mets' facility in Port St. Lucie, Florida, that winter with no fanfare. His signing barely made a ripple in the local media. In mid-February, I wrote an article for the *Wall Street Journal* with the headline, "Heading into Camp, the Mets' Outfield Isn't Very Amazin'."

"Everyone assumed I was going to get released," Byrd said.

He wasn't kidding. Early in camp, even as Byrd was slamming balls over the fence during batting practice, Mets coaches told him that if he "kept swinging like that, they were going to be lazy fly balls at Citi Field," one of the toughest ballparks in the majors for hitters. Byrd would politely respond, "I disagree." Nothing could shake his conviction.

Still, Byrd understood his place in the baseball landscape at that point. That's why he had accepted the Mets' deal in the first place, even though it didn't offer guaranteed money—he had no better options. All he wanted was a chance, and fortunately, he had one important ally in the organization: Mets manager Terry Collins, an old-school skipper who valued the presence of veterans in a clubhouse and in a lineup. Collins liked the idea of keeping Byrd around, so he would offer him a chance to prove he deserved the roster spot. That was the opening Byrd needed. He had just left Mexico, and his new swing was as sharp as it ever was. When the Grapefruit League season began, Byrd didn't miss a beat: in his first at-bat against Washington Nationals right-hander Stephen Strasburg, he laced a double.

"From that point on, everybody started paying attention," Byrd said.

Granted, it wasn't all positive attention. His teammates

couldn't help but ask about Byrd's approach, the path of his barrel, his desire to work underneath the ball. Byrd remembers outfielder Kirk Nieuwenhuis, after hearing his explanation, saying simply, "I would never do that." Daniel Murphy, already one of baseball's most obsessive students of hitting, said, "You're an idiot," and walked away. Byrd just nodded along. He wanted to let his bat speak for itself. Divulging the specifics of his swing was too risky—most players just wouldn't get it.

"If I was sitting there, walking around saying, 'I'm working underneath the ball, guys,' I probably would have gotten released," Byrd said.

This is a strange reality of the culture of professional baseball. Saying that you are doing something different, something against the status quo or conventional wisdom, is immediately met not just with skepticism but with ferocious pushback. But have success on the field doing something different? Nobody says a word. So Byrd largely kept his mouth shut. When camp broke and the Mets prepared to head back to New York to open the regular season, they had no choice but to bring Byrd with them: he had gone 20-for-56 in spring training (.357), with nine doubles and a home run.

"I was so happy for him," Doug Latta said. "He earned it."

So had Latta.

What happened next should come as no real surprise. Armed with the revamped swing he had learned from Doug Latta, Marlon Byrd had a spectacular 2013 season. By the end of May, he had taken over the cleanup spot in the Mets' lineup, never mind that just a couple of months earlier he had been on a minor league contract. He played so well that other teams started taking notice. In late August, the Mets, well out of contention,

traded him along with catcher John Buck to the Pirates for mi-
nor league infielder Dilson Herrera, then a top-10 prospect in
Pittsburgh's organization, and hard-throwing relief pitcher Vic
Black.

It seemed like a remarkable haul for somebody like Byrd, a
player the Mets had signed with zero expectations. He finished
the year with a .291 batting average in 532 at-bats, with 24 home
runs, 88 RBIs, and an .847 OPS. He even helped lead the Pirates
to the playoffs for the first time since 1992, going 8-for-22 (.364)
with three extra-base hits in October. His ground-ball rate,
which in his career was nearly 49 percent, dropped to around 40
percent as his performance shot up with a swing that led to more
balls in the air. Byrd played 15 major league seasons, and 2013,
his first after meeting Latta, was undoubtedly his best.

But this isn't a story about Marlon Byrd. Not entirely anyway.
This is the story of what Marlon Byrd meant to the revolution.
Byrd wasn't the first person to remake his career after learning a better way to swing from an outside hitting coach. Plenty
of others had trained, mostly in secret, with Craig Wallenbrock
a decade before and seen incredible results. Byrd, however, was
one of the first players to bring these ideas into the mainstream.
In many ways, the modern-day "fly-ball revolution" started
because Byrd willed it into existence.

For a long time, Byrd stayed quiet about the changes he had
made. The early negativity and skepticism from his teammates,
coupled with Latta's desire to remain anonymous, stopped him
from broadcasting his newfound ideas about the swing. But once
he had numbers to back up his words, Byrd no longer cared about
what people might say. In September 2013, he opened up to journalist Travis Sawchik, then of the *Pittsburgh Tribune-Review*,
about his work with Latta. The secret was out.

"It was time for me to start being honest, so I started talking about 'ball in the air,'" Byrd said. "I was quiet, and quiet, and quiet, and I'm not going to sit there and say, 'Oh, yeah. I did it all myself.' I mean, without Doug . . ." His voice trailed off. He didn't have to finish the thought for the meaning to come across.

The world was starting to listen. Other players on the Mets were increasingly curious, trying to understand how Byrd—just six feet tall, relatively small by baseball standards—was able to generate so much power. The first thing Byrd needed to explain, he said, was that "hit the ball in the air" didn't necessarily mean trying to hit high fly balls.

"A line drive is a ball in the air," Byrd explained. "You're trying to hit the outfield grass. That's it."

It came to a head in the middle of August, when the Mets traveled to Los Angeles for a series against the Dodgers. Byrd brought Latta to the ballpark as a thank-you for everything he had done. There, Byrd introduced Latta to Daniel Murphy.

"Oh, you're Marlon's guy!" Murphy said, mimicking a swing with a slight uppercut. "Well, I'm this guy." He then showed off his swing, a classic, short bat path straight out of a hitting textbook.

Latta smiled. "You'll be this guy someday," he said to Murphy, now imitating an upward swing himself, the one he had taught Byrd and the one he was sure Murphy would one day adopt. It was a bold statement for an unknown like Latta, but it revealed his confidence in the swing he was espousing, and now he had Byrd as proof that it worked.

And here's the amazing part: Latta wasn't wrong.

Daniel Murphy was never a coveted prospect. By professional baseball standards, he isn't fast or strong. For years, he struggled to find a defensive position where he wasn't a liability. Murphy is, however, a notorious cage rat, the ultimate student of hitting. As a freshman at Jacksonville University, when asked to introduce himself and name his position, Murphy famously responded, "I'm Daniel Murphy from Englewood High School, and I bat third." He was referring not to defense, in the spirit of the question, but to the most prestigious spot in the batting order.

That obsession with his craft made Murphy a far better hitter than anybody would have ever expected looking at him. From 2008 through the end of the regular season in 2015 with the Mets, he hit .288 with an OPS of .755, about 10 percent better than the league average. He consistently made contact, mostly grounders and low line drives. He didn't hit for much power. By that point, the kind of player he was seemed clear. He was good, but he'd never be a star.

But in the 2015 postseason, something miraculous happened: Daniel Murphy learned how to hit the ball in the air. He delivered a performance forever etched into Mets lore, slamming seven home runs in his first nine playoff games, setting a major league postseason record by homering in six straight contests. Murphy earned NLCS MVP honors and led the Mets to the World Series, the franchise's first pennant since 2000. It was nothing short of amazing.

"I wish I could explain it," Murphy said then. "I would have done it like six years ago."

Naturally, doubts about Murphy's insane turnaround persisted. Teams called Murphy's magical October a fluke and chalked it up to the random variance inherent to baseball. The Mets let Murphy walk in free agency, unconvinced he would be able to carry over the hot streak into the next season, and the Nationals scooped him up for $37.5 million over three years. It was the kind of contract that the old Daniel Murphy would have received, the Daniel Murphy who hit for a solid batting average and not much else. It wasn't the kind of contract given to a player expected to bash home runs.

It didn't take long for Murphy to prove the skeptics wrong. He put up a dominant 2016 campaign, setting career highs with a .347 batting average, 25 home runs, 104 RBIs, and a .390 on-base percentage. He finished second behind Kris Bryant in the National League MVP voting, leading the league in doubles (47), slugging percentage (.595), and OPS (.985). He led the NL in doubles again in 2017, to go along with his .322 batting average and .928 OPS—a worthy encore to a breakout season.

Murphy didn't work with Doug Latta, Craig Wallenbrock, or any other independent hitting coach. His experience with Marlon Byrd got him thinking, opening his mind to different ideas in spite of his initial resistance. It started there. The next step happened in 2015, when the Mets hired Kevin Long as their hitting coach. That winter, a few weeks before reporting to Port St. Lucie for spring training, Long was hanging out on vacation at his uncle's pool in Hawaii. He received a message from Murphy, asking for a detailed assessment of his swing and how he could improve. Long had some thoughts, but he wasn't sure how to convey them. He knew about Murphy's reputation as a swing-obsessed cage rat. He didn't want to make a bad impression. But after staring at his phone for a while, Long mustered up the courage to press "Send."

Long believed that Murphy had untapped power potential. He just needed to bring it out. So Long helped Murphy change his mind-set and approach. With Long's help, Murphy moved closer to the plate in an effort to pull the ball more often. Previously, he looked to slap balls around the field, often to the opposite field. Adhering to an oft-cited tenet of the old-fashioned hitting philosophy that people like Latta are desperately trying to destroy, he would make contact very deep in the hitting zone. Murphy changed his stance, going from standing upright in the box to crouching about six inches lower than previously. That helped him adjust his swing path to hit more balls in the air. He altered his approach, looking to drive balls in the air to his pull side that he used to fist the other way.

"Instead of just hunting hits, was there a way by changing his swing, by changing his mechanics, by changing his intent, to pursue a chance for this guy to blossom into one of the best hitters in the game?" Long told me. "It made sense to him, he understood it, and he was all in."

This wasn't a radical overhaul, as Doug Latta had done with Marlon Byrd. Long was suggesting more subtle tweaks designed to help Murphy be his best self. Murphy took care of the rest from there. He became obsessed with data and analytics, adding them to his never-ending pursuit of the perfect swing.

Numbers proved to him that his previous approach, focusing on singles up the middle and to the opposite field, wasn't ideal. In interviews, he frequently cites the statistic that only 7 percent of ground balls go for extra-base hits as evidence that ground balls are not a desirable result. In the dugout, when a player does manage to hit a grounder for a double, he's been known to say something to the effect of, "That's a seven-percenter right there." He has cited that figure so often and with so much conviction that it almost doesn't matter if it's completely accurate. The point remains. And a deeper look at his numbers shows what has made the new Murphy so special: With the Mets from 2008 through 2015, his ground ball rate was 44.7 percent. From 2016 through 2019, it was 37.4 percent.

Daniel Murphy remade himself into one of the premier hitters in all of baseball. Just as Doug Latta had predicted.

ON THE VERGE

Chris Colabello finished the 2011 season—the season after he reshaped his swing with Bobby Tewksbary—with the best numbers of his career. He hit .348 with 20 home runs and a 1.010 OPS in 412 plate appearances. *Baseball America,* one of the industry's premier scouting publications, named Colabello the Independent League Player of the Year.

Colabello was hooked. All he ever wanted to do was spend time in the cage with Tewksbary. "It was like a drug," he said. Meanwhile, Tewksbary's stock was starting to rise. Buoyed by Colabello's success, he started posting articles and videos of some of their training together online, and people started noticing. Not only did the new swing appear to help Colabello, but the experience of working with him helped Tewksbary understand it and devise better ways to teach it to the younger hitters who came by his facility. "It was validation," Tewksbary said. "A low level, but validation."

Skepticism still abounded. Tewksbary would frequently hear from other coaches and parents, and the conversation usually started with them asking, "What the hell are you talking about?" Tewksbary would respond by requesting that the skeptic "just put in a couple hours of objective video study. Look at what the barrel's doing, look at what the body's doing. What I'm telling you is not wrong. You might not love the way I'm saying it, but it's not wrong."

As spring training drew closer, Colabello had started to re-sign himself to another year in Worcester. Then his agent called with news: the Twins had expressed interest. They sent a scout to watch him work out before offering him an opportunity to attend spring training. There were no promises made, no commitments, no guarantees. But for the first time, Colabello had a foot in the door. After toiling away in the independent leagues for seven long seasons, he finally had a shot.

That said, the Twins weren't necessarily the best fit. Led by old-school general manager Terry Ryan and his equally old-school manager Ron Gardenhire, the Twins weren't exactly receptive to new ideas about how to swing the bat. Tewksbary called them "anti-progressive." True to form, Colabello said that within one week of his arrival in Fort Myers, Twins coaches were trying to change his swing. They wanted to eliminate the high leg kick he had developed with Tewksbary, along with the rearward barrel movement that Tewksbary had helped him perfect. They told him, "This isn't going to work in Double A." For Colabello, who had about as little leverage as anybody in camp, failing to appear coachable would be a quick ticket back to Worcester.

Colabello called Tewksbary for advice. "What do I do?" he asked his friend. "Don't listen to them," Tewksbary responded. "Just be yourself." For the rest of camp, Colabello did his best balancing act, giving the appearance that he was listening and internalizing the information in the cage, but using the swing he had worked on with Tewksbary in games and hoping his performance would get the coaches off his back.

It turned out that was easier said than done. Colabello wound up limping into the season when camp broke and he took his place on the roster of the New Britain Rock Cats, the Twins' Double A affiliate. The beginning of the season didn't go much better. Colabello finished the month of May with a batting average of just .224. Almost everything had gone wrong. He felt pulled in multiple directions as he struggled to trust his swing while dealing with coaches every day who told him he needed to change. He wondered if the Twins were right all along, that his new swing simply wouldn't cut it in Double A. Maybe he'd never be anything more than an indie ball player. Maybe he just wasn't good enough.

Colabello was having a crisis. He was miserable. He wasn't having fun playing baseball for the first time he could remember. At his lowest point, he thought to himself, *I hope they release me*. He knew Worcester would always have a spot open for him.

On June 18, with everything falling apart, the Rock Cats had a day off before a road trip to Altoona. Colabello's batting average was sitting at .226. Typically, he would spend the day in his hometown of Milford, Massachusetts, about a 90-minute drive from New Britain. But this time Colabello drove to Milford and kept on driving, not stopping until he arrived in Nashua. He badly missed his girlfriend and didn't know when he would see her next. He couldn't say for sure what passing up an opportunity to spend a day together would mean for their relationship. But on this day Colabello needed a different kind of comfort.

When Colabello arrived at Tewksbary's facility, he immediately jumped into the cage, somehow seeming both depressed and enraged. "My swing is broken," he told Tewksbary. He needed to hit. So they did—but not for long. After four swings, Tewksbary stopped him. "What the fuck are you doing?" Tewksbary asked him. "Your swing is disgusting right now."

Colabello's mechanics were a mess, but his mental state also needed an overhaul. Tewksbary told Colabello to put the bat away and step out of the cage. They went outside and sat on the curb. At first, they just sat there. Then they started talking. An hour passed. Then a second hour. Then a third. The conversation bobbed and weaved from baseball to any other topic imaginable and back to baseball again. "I just unloaded every fucking little bit of shit that was in my brain," Colabello said.

For the most part, Tewksbary listened. He knew his friend needed to vent more than he needed advice. Only after Colabello finished did Tewksbary speak up.

"Be yourself," Tewksbary said. "If you're going to go out, if you're going to get released, don't do what they're telling you to do. Go out on your terms."

All these years later, that conversation still resonates with Colabello, both for its simplicity and its poignancy. Six words in particular stood out for him: "Fail doing what you think works."

And with that, Colabello headed back to New Britain to prepare for the road trip. He never did see his girlfriend that day, a grudge that she simply couldn't let go of, no matter how hard she tried.

That girlfriend, Ali, is now his wife.

Chris Colabello arrived at Peoples Natural Gas Field in Altoona, Pennsylvania, after his heart-to-heart with Bobby Tewksbary, with a new outlook on life. The opposing pitcher was Jeff Karstens, an established big leaguer on a rehab assignment. Before the game, Colabello said to himself, "Fuck it, I'm going to have a good time today."

His very first at-bat put that vow to the test. With two strikes, Karstens flipped in a big looping curveball that started up around Colabello's eyes. *It can't be a strike, it can't be a strike, it can't be a strike,* he thought to himself. Except it was. Good-bye, thanks for playing.

A few days earlier, this would have sent Colabello spiraling into a whirlpool of misery and self-doubt. Today he returned to the dugout and declared to his teammates, "If that mother-fucker throws me that again, I'm going deep." In Colabello's next at-bat, Karstens obliged. So did Colabello. He sent one soaring deep to the fence, a ball ticketed for a home run—until Altoona left fielder Quincy Latimore jumped over the wall and brought it back. "I told you guys I was going to hit that shit out!" Colabello yelled as he got back to the bench. "I didn't know he was going to fucking catch it, though!"

Colabello went 0-for-4 that day, but he fell into his hotel bed afterward feeling better about himself than he had in months. In his next game, New Britain was facing Gerrit Cole, who had been the number-one overall draft pick the year before and would de-velop into a star major league pitcher. Colabello picked up two hits. He had a hit in his next game. Then two more. And then another two. And then three. It never stopped. From June 20 through the end of the season, a span of 74 games and 319 plate appearances, Colabello hit .332 with a .922 OPS. Despite his miserable start, he finished with a respectable batting average of .284 to go along with 19 homers and a team-leading 98 RBIs.

Chris Colabello had put everything together. His work with Bobby Tewksbary the winter before resulted in the best swing he had ever had, one built for consistency and power. His moment of crisis in June and his subsequent conversation with Tewksbary cleared his mind so he could go out and play without getting in his own way. That winter, after his first year in affiliated base-ball, he went to Mexico to play for the Algodoneros de Guasave to stay in shape and keep his stock climbing. He hit .332 with 17 homers and a 1.043 OPS in 57 games. In March, he played with

Team Italy in the World Baseball Classic. He went 6-for-18 with a couple of homers. By this point, his approach looked even more nontraditional to old-school baseball people, with an even bigger leg kick and more exaggerated movements. "But I'm bangin'," he said, "so they can't say shit."

As he prepared for his second spring training with the Twins, Chris Colabello was right on the cusp of making it. As it turns out, so was Bobby Tewksbary, the man who had brought him there.

By the 2012 season, Bobby Tewksbary had two professional clients other than Chris Colabello: Mark Hamilton and Adam Heether, friends from the minor leagues who had found Tewksbary's writings about the swing online. Hamilton appeared in 47 games for the Cardinals in 2010 and 2011. Heether never made it to the big leagues. But he did introduce Tewksbary to Josh Donaldson.

Donaldson first met Adam Heether during the 2010 season. Donaldson was a catcher for the Sacramento River Cats, Oakland's Triple A affiliate. Heether was a jack-of-all-trades for the Nashville Sounds, the Brewers' Triple A outpost. In a game in May of that year, Heether took a cartoonishly aggressive cut at a pitch, only to come up empty. Donaldson mocked him from behind the plate, much to Heether's amusement. The banter between the two continued for the rest of the game. The A's claimed Heether on waivers about a week later. Suddenly, Heether and Donaldson were roommates. They quickly became close friends. It was a meet-cute straight out of a Julia Roberts movie.

When 2012 came along, Heether was reaching the end of his rope. While Donaldson was shuttling back and forth between Sacramento and Oakland, trying to establish a foothold in the major leagues, Heether was bouncing between Double A and Triple A in the Angels organization.

One late night toward the end of the season, after Tewksbary had wrapped up one of his regular marathon video study sessions, his phone buzzed with a text message from Heether. Josh Donaldson was curious about his friend's mysterious hitting instructor and wanted Tewksbary to look at his swing. Tewksbary was about ready to go to sleep. He had already put his computer away for the night and figured he would answer in the morning. Heether fired back.

"I remember Adam was like, 'Yeah, he said you wouldn't, because you're a little bitch,'" Tewksbary said.

Never one to shy away from a challenge, Tewksbary jumped out of bed and whipped open his laptop to watch Donaldson's swing and offer his feedback. That continued for the rest of the season and into the winter, Donaldson and Tewksbary sending video back and forth.

Donaldson had already gone a long way into the process of retooling his swing. He was a notorious workaholic, and his obsession with honing his craft was always impressive. Before he met Tewksbary, he had worked extensively with Hunter Bledsoe, his former agent, who had similarly modern ideas about the swing. (Bledsoe also worked with Justin Smoak, who hit 38 home runs for the Blue Jays in 2017.) Having laid the groundwork with Bledsoe, Donaldson was already a believer. In a piece that appeared on MLB Network in 2017, Donaldson relayed a story from the 2012 season: A coach from the Oakland organization approached him and asked what he wanted to work on. Donaldson responded, "You and me aren't working on anything. I'm working on what I'm going to work on."

The point is, when Donaldson first started talking to Tewksbary, he was already on the road of discovery and had even started to see results: in his final 51 games with the A's in 2012, he hit .286 with an .822 OPS. Tewksbary helped him push his progress even further through frequent text messages, phone calls, and video reviews, refining the moves he had worked on with Colabello—especially the rearward barrel movement, which allowed him to get on plane as early as possible.

By the 2013 season, Josh Donaldson already looked like a different hitter. He had added a leg kick, whereas in the past he had appeared to simply push his hands and body forward to swing. His barrel started rearward, generating the bat speed that leads to power. His bat path was up, not down.

In May of that year, Tewksbary published an article on his website titled "Josh Donaldson: Swing Changes over Time and Adjusting to Off-Speed Pitches," featuring exclusive comments from the man himself. In it, Donaldson said his favorite contemporary hitters were José Bautista, Miguel Cabrera, and Allen Craig. By the end of the year, Donaldson had emerged from nowhere to become a star. He hit .301 with 24 homers, 93 RBIs, and an .883 OPS, finishing fourth in the AL MVP vote.

And it wasn't just a big year for Donaldson. After a red-hot start, when Chris Colabello hit .358 in his first 46 games at Triple A, the Twins promoted him to the major leagues. He made his debut on May 22. On May 25, he picked up his first hit, a ground-ball single up the middle. His first home run came on July 26, a game-winner in the top of the 13th inning off Seattle's Yoervis Medina.

Colabello wasn't nearly as great for the Twins that year as Donaldson was for the A's. He went just 31-for-160 (.194) with a .631 OPS. Still, in the same year, two of Bobby Tewksbary's players had arrived at the pinnacle of the baseball world. In September, the trio was united in person for the first time when Colabello flew Tewksbary out to Oakland for a Twins series against the A's. A few months after that, Tewksbary joined Donaldson and Mark Hamilton at the Big Easy Sportsplex in New Orleans to keep working. For Bobby Tewksbary, who had dreamed his entire life of making it to the major leagues, it felt like a beginning.

The winter before the 2013 season was also a time of transition for Craig Wallenbrock. He had been working out of Doug Latta's facility in Chatsworth, the Ball Yard, for more than a decade. Though they were more like roommates than partners for much of that time, Wallenbrock and Latta did some amazing things together.

But both parties were ready for a change. Latta wanted an opportunity to escape from Wallenbrock's shadow and prove his mettle on his own, especially now with Marlon Byrd taking off. Wallenbrock felt he could pay less rent if he worked out of a different facility. It was a business relationship, and it had run its course. It wasn't personal, even if there was some disappointment on both sides. With the passage of time, any hard feelings between the two men have dissipated and been replaced with respect and nostalgic memories.

Wallenbrock found a new facility in Santa Clarita. It wasn't exactly high-tech. Actually, it still isn't. It's a warehouse that he converted into a makeshift hitting facility—a batting cage, a computer, and not much else. "It's a hole in the wall. It's pretty unimpressive," said Dodgers outfielder A. J. Pollock, one of the many players who have spent time under the tutelage of the Oracle. "But I love it. When you get in there, it's a great baseball place. You drive to the middle of nowhere, and there are some incredible players who walk through that door every day."

When Wallenbrock left for Santa Clarita, he wasn't alone. Over the previous few years, Wallenbrock had taken on a young apprentice, who was quickly establishing himself as much more than just a mentee or intern. He was becoming a true partner.

Robert Van Scoyoc grew up in Southern California and attended William S. Hart High School in Santa Clarita. He wasn't an elite baseball player, but he did love hitting, and he desperately wanted to be better. He just didn't know how.

At some point during his high school career, one of his teammates, Steve Susdorf, suddenly got a lot better. Susdorf had never been much of a hitter, Van Scoyoc remembers, but now he was cranking out home runs with ease. Naturally, Van Scoyoc was intrigued.

"I was like, 'Dude, what are you doing?'" Van Scoyoc said. "'Tell me.'"

The answer was that he had started working with Craig Wallenbrock, as had his brother, Billy, who at the time was playing at UCLA. Billy Susdorf played three seasons of minor league ball, advancing to High A. Steve Susdorf did even better, appearing in three games for the Phillies in 2013, even collecting a double during his brief stint.

Van Scoyoc sought out Wallenbrock, who at the time was working closely with major league outfielder Brant Brown. Immediately, Van Scoyoc's eyes were opened to a whole new way of thinking. In high school, he couldn't help but feel that nobody in his life really understood what made a swing good or bad. When he hit a ball hard, he was told his swing was good. When he didn't, he heard that his swing was bad and needed tweaking. But Van Scoyoc thought a good swing was a good swing, even if the result on a particular batted ball wasn't good. Wallenbrock was the first person he had ever met who understood that. Instead of focusing on the results, Wallenbrock was fixated on the process. He talked about what Van Scoyoc's back elbow should be doing when he swung, how to get his barrel to match the plane of the pitch, the importance of his famous "lag position." It all felt so scientific. It felt real.

Did it turn Van Scoyoc into a great hitter? Not exactly. He wasn't cut out to be a slugger himself. After graduating from high school in 2005 and playing two undistinguished seasons at Cuesta College, a junior college in San Luis Obispo, his playing career reached its end.

"I would rate myself as a mediocre player," Van Scoyoc said. "I had a natural curiosity and was constantly tinkering with myself. I treated myself as a guinea pig. I was just very interested in the swing."

Van Scoyoc thought about transferring to a four-year college and continuing his education. But what he really wanted to do was continue to learn about the swing. He helped out at nearby Valencia High School and gave some private hitting lessons, even though he realized he was far from an expert. He did, however, know somebody he considered to be one. So one day he called Craig Wallenbrock with a proposition: could he hang out around the cage and watch him work with hitters? He'd do anything Wallenbrock needed—flip soft toss, pick up balls, whatever. Just as long as he could watch the Oracle at work.

Wallenbrock remembered Van Scoyoc and liked him. He was happy to have him come aboard. There was just one problem: he couldn't afford to pay him.

"And he said, 'No, this is like going to college. I'd pay for college, so I should be paying you,'" Wallenbrock said.

From that point on, Robert Van Scoyoc, barely 20 years old, was a regular at the Ball Yard. At first, he was seen and not heard. He watched and listened, quietly observing how Wallenbrock went about teaching the swing, and he soaked up information like a sponge.

Van Scoyoc arrived at the right time. Wallenbrock, then in his sixties, was starting to slow down a bit physically. He was having trouble with his hip, a condition that would ultimately lead to a full replacement. Van Scoyoc, young and energetic, was able to pick up some of the slack by spending more and more time in the batting cage, allowing Wallenbrock to focus on analyzing video and offering advice. As time went on, Wallenbrock began to ask Van Scoyoc for his own thoughts and observations as they worked with hitters.

In the 2013 season, Wallenbrock had an opportunity to do some consulting work for the Astros. To make time for it, he had to step away a bit from working with amateur hitters and put his focus on pros. It was Van Scoyoc's chance to shine. To these players, he wasn't Craig Wallenbrock's protégé. He was Robert Van Scoyoc, the Craig Wallenbrock–approved hitting coach. That's when his relationship with Wallenbrock became more permanent: the two formed an official business partnership. At first, Wallenbrock took two-thirds of the payments from clients, with Van Scoyoc taking the rest. Over time the cut became 50–50.

Something else happened that year: the long chain of players, from Joe Borchard to Cord Phelps to Jason Castro, finally brought them to the doorstep of the player who would launch them into the baseball consciousness forever. The Astros were in town, squaring off against the Angels in Anaheim. Through a connection of Wallenbrock's in the Houston organization, he and Van Scoyoc were invited onto the field for batting practice. There an Astros coach asked them casually if there was anybody on the team they thought they could help with a swing adjustment. Wallenbrock and Van Scoyoc barely had to think to come up with an answer.

"We said J.D. has a ton of talent but has a bad swing," Van Scoyoc said. "We thought we could help him, make a big impact with him."

A few months later, they would have that chance.

By 2013, J. D. Martinez was more or less an established major league outfielder. Not a particularly good one, mind you, but like his teammate Jason Castro, one who had earned the right to stick around. As a 24-year-old in 2012, he hit 11 home runs in 395 at-bats, enough to make him think that if he just kept working against elite pitching, he would find a way to improve and develop into a top player. The notion that his swing was fundamentally broken and would ultimately fail him hadn't even crossed his mind. Yet.

"J.D. thought his swing was beautiful. He loved his swing," said Greg Brown, the former Astros scout who signed Martinez and the current minor-league hitting coordinator for the Rays. "I would tease him all the time about it—'Man, your swing is ugly.'"

Martinez possessed a swing that traveled on a steep downward angle. His barrel finished low, rather than high. He relied on his hands more than his body. He would load twice, tapping his foot, stopping, and then starting again. He had a hitch in his elbows, seeming to bring them back behind his face before beginning his swing. He started with his hands low, only to raise them as the pitch arrived. It all looked uncomfortable and unnatural and generally weird, to the point that Martinez looks back now and wonders, "How the fuck did I hit that way?"

The answer was pure athleticism and an undying devotion to his craft. Martinez was nothing short of obsessed with hitting, spending hours and hours in the cage every night. His hand-eye coordination was elite, and he used those inborn abilities to find ways to put the barrel on the ball, even with a swing that could be best described as "suboptimal."

In Martinez's case, it turns out that even with an inefficient swing, practice really does make perfect—he found a way to make it work for him. Few people with a swing like Martinez's could've had success, not even in high school. But Martinez isn't a normal person, and that's what enabled him to thrive all the way up into the minor leagues.

People who have bad swings—in other words, almost everybody—tend to fizzle out pretty quickly. It's hard enough to have success at the plate with a good swing, and plenty of people with flawless mechanics still fail. With a bad swing, it's practically impossible. That's what made J. D. Martinez so special: he had a terrible swing, and it didn't matter even against people who were being paid money to get him out.

Given that, it makes sense that Martinez would be so enamored with his own swing. For one thing, he had been a monster at the plate wherever he went, including professional baseball. He was getting promotions and earning accolades. Of course he never would have considered the possibility that everything he was doing was wrong.

"What are you going to tell a guy that was hitting .330 in the minor leagues? I would have told him to kick rocks," Martinez said. "I would've said, 'This isn't wrong. This can't be wrong.'"

Martinez's first inkling that maybe he didn't know as much about the swing as he thought he did came early in 2013—the season Jason Castro officially arrived. In the first 154 games of Castro's career with the Astros, a span of 452 at-bats, he had hit eight home runs. It took him just 185 at-bats to match that total in 2013 alone. By the end of June, his homer total had ballooned to 11, tied for second on the team. He had 22 doubles, seven more than the next-closest Astro, a young second baseman by the name of José Altuve. Castro's .805 OPS was the best on the Astros among anybody with at least 100 at-bats. These were strong numbers for anybody. For a catcher, they were superb, and a few days later he was rewarded for his performance by being named to the American League All-Star Game roster as Houston's lone representative.

During all this, Martinez watched Castro's ascendance with nothing short of perplexed amazement. None of it made the slightest bit of sense. Starting in spring training, Martinez had seen Castro in the batting cage working on his swing. To his eyes, it looked . . . terrible. Disgusting. Ugly. Insert any negative adjective here. Martinez figured there was no way this bizarre uppercut swing could work in the major leagues. It went against every rule of hitting. So at the beginning, Martinez chalked up Castro's performance to luck.

"I'm thinking, 'What the heck is all of this?'" Martinez told the *Detroit Free Press* in 2015. "I'm like, 'That's not going to work.' So I just left it at that."

Except Castro didn't cool down. If anything, his performance kept improving, while Martinez continued to flounder, hitting just .248 with a .676 OPS through the end of June. His hitting coach with the Astros, John Mallee, leveled with him, pulling him aside one day after a session in the batting cage and telling him, more bluntly than anybody ever had before, that if Martinez was going to turn into the player he wanted to be, he needed to make a change.

That pep talk angered Martinez. Of course it did. His first instinct was to just forget about it and keep pushing forward. Mallee would just be another doubter in an ever-growing club of people who didn't believe in him. And yet . . . Castro kept hitting. Homer after homer. Double after double. The more Castro hit, the more it bothered Martinez, nagging at him because he didn't understand it. Seeing Castro succeed with that swing was like seeing a hippopotamus ambling through Times Square—it was theoretically possible, but surely there was more to the story, right?

Perhaps. But Martinez figured he needed to find out. He needed to start paying attention to that weird swing, the one that shouldn't work, but miraculously did.

RICH FROM THE BASEMENT

Richard Schenck had initially gotten interested in hitting to help his two sons become better baseball players. But for years Schenck would read advice about hitting on the internet, pass it on to his sons, and nothing would happen. "They weren't getting better. They weren't getting the jump they needed," Schenck said. "They both wanted to play in college, and I needed the information now."

For his older son, Brad, the information didn't come fast enough. He didn't wind up playing baseball in college. He did, however, play fast-pitch softball, ultimately joining a team with his father. This led to what Schenck described as his "first big aha moment." Now Schenck wasn't just reading things online and reciting them back to his son—he was trying to implement the techniques himself. One night, in his basement, where he would practice swinging against a machine called a Personal Pitcher that shot out Wiffle balls, Schenck had a breakthrough, his biggest one yet. It wasn't that Schenck had figured something out. To the contrary: he figured out, for the first time, that everything he had been trying, all the methods he had relayed to his kids over the years, didn't work.

"As soon as I got in the batter's box, all of this stuff I was teaching my son that I thought would work, I could tell instantly, 'This has no chance,'" Schenck said. "It convinced me that nobody knew what they were talking about."

This was in 2004. Schenck was approaching 50 years old. He still didn't know how to improve his sons' swings—but for the first time he knew that what he was seeing online wasn't the answer.

"That's when I went to my basement and threw everything out the window," he said. "It took being in the batter's box before I was convinced that when my son was telling me, 'This doesn't work,' it really wasn't working. I thought he was just not doing it right. And I apologized to him."

From that point on, Schenck was no longer open-minded in search of information. He was frustrated, he was angry, and he was ready to burn everything down.

"I was getting well-meaning advice from people that didn't really know anything," Schenck said. "I was convinced, after reading all of these websites, that was the case."

This is when the aggressive side of Schenck's internet persona emerged. He started lobbing grenades at the people he had once believed were on the cutting edge of progressive baseball training. On every forum, whenever somebody posted a thought, Schenck immediately went on the offensive, "badgering the advice-givers to prove what they're telling me," he said. "And none of them could do it." Whatever goodwill he had built up on the forums was quickly gone. He didn't care.

"I've got one rule: show me yourself or someone you taught swinging a bat and it produces a match of Barry Bonds or Albert Pujols or some Hall of Fame hitter," Schenck told me. "If you can do that, I'll tell you that you're right and I'm wrong."

To Richard Schenck, the way the ideal swing should work, and the best ways to teach it, weren't subject to interpretation or analysis. He didn't engage in conversation or good-natured debate. His thoughts and concepts were rarely influenced by those of anybody else, and he was prepared to fight anybody who disagreed with him. He was rigid and unyielding in an industry where most of his peers were willing to admit they might not have all the answers. Most of the hitting world online despised Schenck, not because he was incompetent or didn't have some meaningful ideas, but because of how he treated people.

"Rich's Twitter posts are inexcusable, and there are some things he teaches that I'd do differently," said one major league hitting coach, who requested anonymity so as not to appear associated with Schenck. "But he has a guy who got better. Most guru types have never been anywhere near a big leaguer. You have to pay attention to that and see if there's anything you can learn from it."

It was 2004 when Schenck decided to take matters into his own hands. The best hitter on planet earth at that time was Barry Bonds. Maybe you've heard of him. He hit 762 home runs, the most in history, a record mired in controversy because of his alleged use of performance-enhancing drugs. But no matter. Whatever Bonds did or didn't put in his body, one thing is undeniable: he had, quite possibly, the prettiest swing in the history of baseball.

"So the theory was, if I could make my arms and my body and my feet and everything in the same position Barry Bonds's was in, I would feel what he feels," Schenck said. "I'm not saying I can hit like him, because there is an athletic element to hitting. It's not just the swing. But if I could swing like him, I believed my sons would be the best hitters they could be, because they'd be doing exactly what he's doing."

From that point forward, Barry Bonds became Richard Schenck's obsession. As many as five nights a week, Schenck

would hole up in his basement to study every video
of Bonds he could find and
then try to replicate the
swing himself, movement by
movement.

There were a lot of false
starts. So back to the tape he
went. He watched the swings
in slow motion. He watched
them at regular speed. He

Richard Schenck, in his basement,
trying to match the swing of Barry
Bonds.

watched Bonds's feet and his legs and his hips and his arms and
his hands. Somewhere, he would find the key.

And one day, two years after he began to devote his entire life
to the Church of Barry, he did. He still remembers, as clearly
as he remembers any other moment of his life, the moment it
clicked. "It was a Friday night in September of '06," he said. "I'm
watching the Cardinals play the Giants." (The San Francisco
Giants, in fact, played in St. Louis on Friday, September 15,
2006. The Cardinals won, 14–4. Bonds went 1-for-3 at the plate.)

What he saw that night changed Schenck's life. As Bonds
swung, the barrel of his bat blurred behind his head. Schenck
had never noticed that before, and he couldn't figure out how or
why it was happening.

At first, he assumed Bonds was flattening his barrel and
pushing forward, but with far superior hand speed, causing the
blur. But upon further consideration, Schenck realized it wasn't
that at all. Bonds wasn't flattening his barrel—his first move
wasn't forward, but back. He was launching into his swing with
a rearward move, "snapping it into an arc," as Schenck put it.
He was creating bat speed not when he started moving forward,
but when his bat went backward. "It's creating an arc, a fan, if

Richard Schenck learning to *snap it!*

you will," Schenck said. "It's like he's throwing a wad of paper into it, and it shoots it out.

"I don't know why it took me two years," he continued. "I wish it wouldn't have."

But he had found it. To Schenck, the discovery was a miracle. He hustled down to the basement and loaded up the pitching machine. Usually, he had trouble hitting the Wiffle balls with any authority. That night, after about 20 minutes of tinkering, Schenck started snapping his barrel rearward—the very first time Mr. "Snap It!" snapped it.

After working on the *snap* for a few more days, he picked up the phone to call his younger son, Brandon. When Schenck began his quest to unlock the mysteries of the swing, Brandon was in the eighth grade. Now he was a sophomore in college, struggling to earn playing time at Millikin University, a Division III school in Illinois. Brandon answered.

"Brandon, I'm coming over. I'm driving two hours Tuesday, and I'm going to pitch you batting practice," Schenck remembers saying. "I have found what we're looking for."

David Matranga was born to be a baseball star. He was a slick-fielding shortstop, he could run, and he could hit. He could always hit. Nobody ever really taught him how. He just picked up a bat, started swinging it, and the ball started flying. He didn't know much about swing mechanics. He didn't need to. "I was doing what my body was telling me to do," Matranga said. "And it was right."

Matranga was a good enough hitter to play baseball at Pepperdine, a top college program in Malibu, California. He hit well enough there for the Astros to select him in the sixth round of the draft in 1998.

In the pros, Matranga essentially picked up where he left off. He made his minor league debut for the Auburn Doubledays, the Astros' short-season affiliate in the New York–Penn League. He hit .306 with 18 extra-base hits and a .916 OPS in 40 games, production sure to put him on the fast track to the major leagues and the realization of his lifelong dream.

But Matranga never could have imagined what would happen next. When he returned for spring training in 1999, he met the obstacle that would derail his career: professional coaching. Early in camp, a man Matranga had never met approached him and delivered a stern message.

"I was in the cage taking swings the way I did before," Matranga recalled. "He stopped me cold turkey and said, 'You will never hit like that. You need to swing down on the ball. You have to stay on top of the ball.'"

Matranga didn't know how to respond. Never before had somebody told him that his way of swinging—mechanics that came naturally to him as a child, mechanics that carried him into pro baseball, mechanics that had afforded him nothing but success—wouldn't work.

"Being a really young guy, I'm saying, 'Oh, shit,'" Matranga said. "This guy is at the top of the organization, and if I don't listen, what's going to happen? He could go to management and say, 'This guy is uncoachable.' Now I'm changing what I'm doing, taking it into games, and I was completely lost."

The next two seasons, Matranga was a mess. He hit .231 in 1999 for the Kissimmee Cobras, the Astros' High A affiliate. In 2000, he hit .233 for Double A Round Rock. His swing had betrayed him, his power was gone, and whatever status he'd had as a prospect was all but lost.

Looking back now, Matranga understands that he faced a familiar—but frustrating—problem: he simply didn't look the part. He was under six feet tall and weighed about 170 pounds. That's not the typical body type of a slugger. Professional coaches saw him as a slap hitter, not a player who should be worrying about driving the ball. That was for real sluggers like Barry Bonds or Manny Ramírez. Matranga wanted to hit like those players, but when he tried, he was told, "You can't hit like them. You have to keep the ball out of the air."

When he arrived for spring training in 2001, after two disastrous seasons, Matranga decided that something needed to change. For inspiration, he looked to another player in the Astros' farm system: Keith Ginter. Like Matranga, Ginter was small, listed at just five-foot-10. Like Matranga, he didn't look like a power hitter.

But Matranga and Ginter differed in one major way: Ginter, Matranga said, never listened to anybody. He knew his swing was effective and never doubted it, no matter what anybody said. "Keith believed in what Keith believed in and wasn't going to let anybody change him," Matranga said.

Ginter had also been drafted by the Astros in 1998, 120 picks after they took Matranga. As with Matranga, somebody had also pulled Ginter aside and told him he "couldn't swing like that" and expect to survive in professional baseball.

Not wanting to appear unprofessional or uncoachable, Ginter smiled and went along with it. But inside, he already knew he wouldn't change. He believed in his swing.

"It was my career, and I was going to go down the way I felt comfortable," Ginter said. "My comment was, 'Until I don't hit .300, just let me be.'"

That confidence and conviction was rewarded. Ginter blasted 14 home runs in the minor leagues in 1999 and 26 more in 2000, soaring past Matranga in the eyes of the Astros. And on September 20, 2000, a few weeks after Matranga finished a disappointing campaign in Double A, Ginter made his major league debut at Busch Stadium in St. Louis.

Ginter went on to enjoy a relatively modest, but not unsubstantial, major league career, playing for the Astros, Brewers, and A's from 2000 through 2005. He hit 19 home runs for Milwaukee in 2004, second on the team behind outfielder Geoff Jenkins. He was far from a star. He wasn't even a household name. But Keith Ginter had a decent little career at the highest level of baseball, and he earned more than a million dollars in the process.

Watching Ginter ascend to the majors so quickly stuck with Matranga. So in 2001, Matranga vowed to stop listening, to stop trying to appease his coaches, to stop worrying about the consequences. He would swing the way he had always swung, no matter what anybody said. After all, he figured, things couldn't get much worse. The strategy worked to perfection. In 107 games at Double A and Triple A, Matranga hit .303 with 11 homers and an .870 OPS, a long-awaited return to form that put him back on the Astros' radar. It was then that Matranga reached the conclusion that would affect the rest of his life.

"The guys who really make it either get to the major leagues quickly without being influenced by anybody who could ruin their swings," Matranga said, "or they just never listen to anybody and hit the way they want to hit and don't care what anybody says."

Matranga did ultimately make the major leagues—with

a bang. He stepped up to the plate for the first time as a major leaguer on June 27, 2003, pinch-hitting for pitcher Nate Bland at Houston's Minute Maid Park. Facing Joaquin Benoit of the Rangers, he smoked the third pitch he saw, a 90-mile-per-hour fastball, over the left-field fence, becoming the 86th player ever to hit a home run in his first at-bat.

"It was a very emotional moment," Matranga said. "A lot of trial and tribulation, hard work and sweat, wrapped up in one moment."

That, however, didn't stop coaches from trying to change him. Even in the major leagues. Even after he had just shown what he could do swinging his way.

"I'm in the show, and the first thing I heard was, 'Hit that ball out front, kid,'" Matranga said. "I was being told to swing down on it."

Matranga never recaptured the magic from that first at-bat. He appeared in five more games for the Astros that summer and then one more for the Angels in 2005. He finished his major league career 1-for-6.

Looking back, Matranga was careful not to criticize any specific coach by name. He stressed, repeatedly, that he didn't want to come off as if he were blaming anybody for his failures besides himself. The reality, however, is that Matranga was coached out of a good swing. It's impossible to say for certain that this alone prevented him from making it as a big leaguer. There is much more to hitting than mechanics. But pro coaching definitely didn't help him. What if he had stuck to his convictions from the beginning, the way Ginter did?

By 2006, Matranga was approaching his 30th birthday. He knew he might never make it back to the major leagues. (Indeed, he would not.) His window, which once seemed wide open, had slammed shut.

But he was still curious about hitting. He read everything:

the forums, the hitting websites, all the crackpot theories and wild ramblings. Most of it, not surprisingly, was ridiculous, he quickly concluded. But one particular person kept catching his eye: Teacherman1986.

"He was very controversial, very passionate, and people didn't like him," Matranga said. "But I was looking at his content and watched him take his kids from dog crap swings to all of a sudden taking it to a level of trying to re-create Barry Bonds's swing, and I thought, *This is awesome*."

With nothing to lose, Matranga reached out to the Teacherman.

When Richard Schenck first connected with David Matranga, he was finally starting to believe. Days after his epiphany while watching Barry Bonds, Schenck kept his promise to his son to drive to see him and bring him into the batting cage.

"He's raking, and we're both thrilled," Schenck said. "We've been looking for this for eight years."

As his son continued to progress, Schenck went back to the internet, back to all of the people on all of the forums he had alienated and antagonized and wrote what he described as a "mea culpa." Admitting that "all this stuff I've been promoting is wrong," he announced his "new discovery."

That went about as well as you might expect. Ostracized by the online hitting community, Schenck ventured out and created his own website. Slowly, he generated a small but devoted audience, attracting open-minded people from around the web, mostly other dads who wanted Schenck to critique videos of their children's swings. Suddenly, Schenck had an explicitly 21st-century business: online baseball coaching.

He had some success too. One of his first clients was Patrick Kirby, a former college player who, like Schenck initially, had turned to the internet for advice in teaching hitting to his

11-year-old son, Ryan. From 2006 through 2011, he visited all the same websites as Schenck, spending two or three hours every night watching video and reading discussion forums on the swing. When he learned something new, he went to the batting cage in his backyard and swung, testing the latest theories. Anything that he thought worked, he then imparted to Ryan.

Naturally, he couldn't avoid the Teacherman.

"He's a dick on the internet," Kirby told me. "Richard wouldn't hold anything back. He would tell you if he liked it and he would tell you if he didn't like it. A lot of people on those boards would take offense to his approach. He was brutal."

Kirby didn't mind Schenck's abrasiveness. Or at least, he tolerated it, mainly because the more time passed, the more convinced he was that Schenck knew what he was talking about. Then he saw a video clip of Schenck's son Brandon. From that point on, he was sold.

"His swing as a freshman in high school was not very good at all. It was bad. It was a bad swing," Kirby said. "His son is not an athletic, gifted person body-type-wise. But he made some amazing progress. What Richard was able to do with him when they started working, to me, was amazing."

Kirby became one of Schenck's earliest disciples. He sent constant video updates of Ryan's swing, asking for Schenck's perspective and critiques and then passing those comments along to his son. The lessons didn't work as planned right away. Ryan Kirby says that, for the first year he was trying to apply Schenck's philosophies, "I was terrible. I didn't know why we were trying to change my swing."

Patrick Kirby pressed on, telling Ryan that he believed swinging this way would help him drive the ball and hit for power. Ryan listened, mainly because he was a just a child and children tend to listen to their dads and he didn't know any better. At the age of 12, he hit the first home run of his life. At age 14, he hit a home run on a regulation-size field, at a time when few kids his age could hit the ball that far.

That led to a scholarship to play baseball at the University of San Diego and ultimately a place in the professional ranks. Ryan Kirby was selected in the 12th round of the 2016 draft by the Giants. He advanced to High-A before retiring in 2019.

"Shoot, once I started to change my swing when I was 11, it was crazy the amount of success I had growing up," Ryan Kirby told me. "I don't think I would have had that success if my dad hadn't found Rich."

Around the same time Schenck met the Kirbys, he also connected with Mike Nagle, who was looking for help for his young son, Ryan. Schenck and Nagle worked together in person, and Nagle was ultimately drafted by the Pirates in the 27th round in 2015.

For Schenck, Ryan Nagle and Ryan Kirby were validation, players he could say he helped make it to professional baseball. Now Ryan Kirby's father runs a baseball training facility in Tracy, California, about 50 miles east of Oakland. Much of what he teaches derives from what he learned from Schenck, that crazy dude he met on the internet.

For a while, Schenck figured that would be the extent of his contribution to the hitting world. He would work with kids whose dads were curious enough to find his website, and maybe he could help them get better. The idea of working with a major leaguer with as much hype as Judge was incomprehensible.

Fortunately for Schenck, one person who was paying attention to his internet rantings and ravings was David Matranga.

David Matranga, in his search for internet hitting knowledge, had come across Schenck's theories, and he liked them. The two began to correspond over email. That turned into Matranga sending Schenck videos of his swing for review, and eventually that turned into in-person meetings.

At this point, Matranga was nothing more than depth for organizations in Triple A, and he had bounced around the Pacific Coast League—Portland in 2006, Oklahoma in 2007, Omaha in 2008, New Orleans in 2009—before he finally decided to step away from playing professional baseball at the age of 32. But make no mistake: after starting his conversations with Schenck, Matranga improved.

Playing in the Padres organization in '06, he hit just .219 with a dismal .658 OPS. He raised that OPS more than 100 points in 2007 and 2008, to .798 and .786, respectively. In his final professional season as a player, Matranga had 21 extra-base hits in 232 at-bats. His OPS of .835 was his best since 2001.

"I brought some of what I was doing to a hitting instructor in 2009, tried to show some of it, show them up-close video of what my hands were doing in slow motion," Matranga said. "He wouldn't believe what his eyes were seeing. I'd show them what a superstar in the major leagues was doing, and he'd say, 'That's not what he's doing.'"

Matranga was undeterred. He believed in what Schenck was saying. It reminded him of how he swung as a kid, before coaches messed with his mechanics and, more important, messed with his head. So when Matranga retired as a player and started his second career as a player agent, he vowed to protect his clients from what had happened to him—and Schenck would be a part of it.

In the mainstream baseball world, Schenck was more than just an outsider. He was a complete unknown. Although his ideas about the swing had gotten some traction—and hate—in dark corners of the internet, professional baseball was another planet. Besides Matranga, Schenck had worked with just two other pros at this point.

One was a player named Jose Vargas. He was a standout at Ventura College for two seasons, highlighted by a sophomore year when he hit .411 with an OPS of 1.266. He was selected by the White Sox in the 22nd round of the 2008 draft. In the minors, however, Vargas immediately struggled. He hit .232 in 42 games in '08 for the Bristol White Sox, a rookie ball affiliate. In 31 games at Single A Kannapolis in 2009, he hit .191. The more he foundered, the more coaches would try to change his swing, encouraging him to hit the ball to the opposite field rather than pull it for power. After three seasons in the White Sox organization, Vargas was done, relegated to the indie leagues, with nothing but lofty dreams of major league glory left.

Vargas played well there, latching on with a team called the Traverse City Beach Bums, but he knew his chances of returning to affiliated baseball were shrinking every season. So in 2016, after reading about the success that Josh Donaldson enjoyed after changing his swing with an independent coach, Vargas, at age 28, took to the internet in search of help. Enter Richard Schenck.

Vargas began lurking on Schenck's Twitter, where, he recalled, "he had 20–25 followers, and he was bashing a whole lot of guys." But Vargas wasn't turned off by Schenck's brashness. At that point in his career, he just wanted to learn and improve. Despite Schenck's abrasive online persona, what he was saying about the swing made sense.

Vargas had liked some of Schenck's tweets, and eventually Schenck made the first move—a bold step that was the hitting equivalent of asking somebody out on a first date: he sent Vargas a direct message asking if he wanted to Skype. Vargas said yes.

In late August, before a scheduled doubleheader against an opponent called the Washington Wild Things, Schenck and Vargas spoke for the first time. Schenck was in his backyard in St. Louis, bat in hand, ready to give advice to a baseball player who had accomplished exponentially more than he ever had in the game. Vargas was preparing for the game in the visiting clubhouse.

For 40 minutes over the internet, Schenck demonstrated his ideas about the barrel generating speed rearward, about the swing path resembling a Ferris wheel and not a merry-go-round, and about *snapping it!* Vargas distinctly remembered Schenck at one point using the term "torsion spring" to describe how his hips should rotate while swinging, whatever that meant.

"He's looking at me like, 'Man, you are fricking crazy,'" Schenck recalled.

Following that Skype session, Schenck figured that was the end of his relationship with Vargas, who didn't seem to be buying in. But unbeknownst to Schenck, Vargas had already bought in—or at least was willing to experiment. Right after hanging up with Schenck, Vargas went into the cage to hit off the tee, focusing on working the barrel of his bat rearward and up rather than forward and down.

At first, for every good swing, there were two or three bad ones. He thought to himself, *Man, I don't know if I can do this in the game*. And at first, he didn't. In the first game of the double-header, Vargas wasn't comfortable enough to trust Schenck's methods when the results counted, and so he more or less stuck with his original swing. Vargas went 1-for-6 with two strikeouts in that game.

So when Vargas came up again in the third inning of Game 2, now 1-for-7 on the day, he stepped into the batter's box and thought, *Why not?*

"I was struggling anyway, and I had nothing to lose," Vargas said, "It was toward the end of the season, and I figured trying it two or three at-bats wouldn't hurt anything."

"I guess he said, 'You know what? I'm just going to try what that old man said,'" Schenck said.

Vargas was in a slump, struggling particularly with inside fastballs. He was having trouble whipping his barrel—or *snapping it,* as Schenck would probably describe it—fast enough to connect on those pitches. And now here he was, about to swing with mechanics he had learned just a few hours earlier . . . over Skype . . . from a random middle-aged man he had found on the internet. Against all odds, Vargas singled on an inside heater, a hard shot back up the middle.

"It felt so effortless," Vargas said. "My swing felt 100 times better."

He came up to bat again in the fourth. Again, Vargas received an inside fastball. Again, he smoked the ball, banging it down the left-field line for another single.

"I hit it, and as I was running down the line I was like, *Holy crap, how did I do that?*" Vargas said. "Rich says, 'Snap it!' and it was just that I felt, the snap and the barrel working behind me. It was just a new feeling for me."

Vargas had bought in. He stuck with Schenck's swing for the rest of the season. He had two more two-hit games, followed by his first three-hit game in a month. When the season ended, he decided to dedicate his time to learning from Schenck. He had discovered the Teacherman at the best possible time: he was about to be part of something big.

MEETING THE GURUS

Justin Turner started at shortstop for the Mets on August 28, 2013, his first time playing since Marlon Byrd had been traded to the Pirates. He batted seventh. On the mound for the opposing Phillies was Cole Hamels, one of the top left-handed pitchers in the National League.

Turner came up to bat in the bottom of the second inning with two outs and nobody on base. As he stood in the right-handed batter's box, nobody watching the game would have guessed that anything about him had changed.

But it had. Before his at-bat, SNY's cameras had briefly turned to the on-deck circle, where Turner was swinging the way Doug Latta would teach, clearly focusing on working underneath the ball, on hitting it in the air, as opposed to the flat, level swing he had used before.

The results were different too. After taking a changeup for a strike and then a fastball high for ball one, Turner pounced on a 93-mile-per-hour heater from Hamels up in the zone, between the belt and the letters, blasting a rocket deep into straightaway center field. Roger Bernadina, positioned shallow and shaded toward right-center, had no chance. The ball soared over his head and one-hopped off the fence, 408 feet away. Turner cruised into second base with a double, just his seventh extra-base hit since the beginning of June. Two innings later, Turner came up again. This time he stayed with a 1-2 curveball from Hamels and lined it into left field for a single, another well-struck ball in the air. Turner finished that game, a 6–2 Mets loss in an already lost season, 2-for-4.

And it didn't stop there. Turner never cooled down, only stopping at all because the season ended. From August 28 through the last day of the season, 17 of Turner's 50 at-bats ended with a hit, for a .340 batting average. He had four doubles, two home runs, and a .905 OPS. Before September 2013, Turner had hit only six home runs in his entire major league career. Now he had hit two in a month.

"I got a small taste of it. I got a taste of driving some balls, and I was like, 'Holy cow, I can drive balls out of the park,'" Turner said. "And I wanted more of it."

To get it, he needed a teacher. He knew who it would be. He would join Marlon Byrd on the Doug Latta Plan.

The first week after the end of the 2013 season, Turner made the pilgrimage to hit at the Ball Yard. Byrd was there too, of course.

"It was all Marlon's word, saying, 'This guy knows what he's talking about, this guy knows what he's doing,'" Turner said. "I loved it. I loved the language he was speaking. I loved the video system that he had. I loved how he broke down literally every single swing. And he believed it."

Right away, Latta could see the potential in Turner. It was his hands. They were quick and strong, and he had the rare ability to consistently put the bat on the ball. But his swing needed an overhaul. By this point in Turner's life, he had swung a baseball bat hundreds of thousands of times, if not more. The pattern of movement that went into that swing was imprinted on him. Now he needed to change it all.

Will Wu is an associate professor at Long Beach State and the director of the Center for Sport Training and Research. He's an expert on motor control, motor learning, and biomechanics. Wu studies "schema theory," which divides movement into different generalized motor programs, or GMPs. Every distinct movement is controlled by different GMPs embedded in our brains, and they are divided into subsets known as "parameters." To walk, we access a GMP. To run, we access a different GMP. But if we go from running slowly to running quickly, we are simply accessing a different parameter of the running GMP.

From a scientific standpoint, the biggest question about how easy it would be for Turner to remake his swing was whether his new swing would simply be a different parameter of his old one or a new GMP altogether. "Schema theory tells us that if it's a new swing GMP, that would take more time than if it's a parameter change of the old one," Wu said.

Wu outlined three primary characteristics of a new GMP for any movement, including a baseball swing: the sequence of events of the swing changes, the relative timing characteristics change, or the relative force characteristic changes. Any one of these changes would create a new GMP and an entirely new swing.

Another school in the field of motor control, "dynamical systems theory," would say that Turner over the span of his life had adopted a preferred motion for how he swung a bat, creating a state of stability. Humans, Wu said, seek energy-efficient movement. The way you sit in a chair, or the speed at which you walk, is your body seeking a state of stability and energy efficiency. For Turner, his old swing, cultivated over decades, was a state of stability, even if it wasn't necessarily the best way to send a ball flying into the stratosphere. Dynamical systems theory would say that Justin Turner and J. D. Martinez changing their swings would be challenging, because it would require unlearning a preferred motion.

"What J.T. and J.D. did from a swing perspective is crazy, because they swung a preferred state, and their new swing, a nonpreferred swing, was energy-intensive," Wu said. "So it's phenomenal they were able to make the changes."

None of that mattered much to Turner, the one who actually had to make the changes. He wasn't concerned about preferred motions or generalized motor programs. He just knew that he hadn't hit all that well for his entire career, that he'd had a brilliant month, and that he wanted to understand how he had done it.

From the beginning, the skill was there. After one session with Turner, Latta remembers turning to Byrd and saying, "Does he know what an impact player he could be?" He didn't, yet. But he was ready to find out.

Turner trekked to the Ball Yard for three hours a day, five days a week, to hit with Latta and Byrd. He'd hit a round in the cage, then step out to review the video, just as Byrd had done the winter before. Latta would see a move that looked out of sync, Turner would fix it, and they'd evaluate the results. They worked on his leg kick, the position of his hands, how he moved his shoulders. This went on for months, with more bad days than good ones. Turner's body kept fighting back—his hands wanted to move backward, to "load up," to generate power. He had to force himself not to. When the swing was right, it was fluid and smooth. "It feels like you're not even swinging," Turner said. "It's effortless."

Some days Turner would hit live on the field at Cal State Fullerton, where he'd gone to college, then report back to Latta about how he did. Sometimes he'd hit with Latta in a group of five or six hitters. Other times they met one-on-one. It was a constant process, but Turner was committed to it, and as spring training drew near he felt like he could repeat the swing. He

Justin Turner's swing, before and after Doug Latta's intervention.

had found it, the way Byrd had found it before him. He believed in it. Unfortunately for Turner, some people didn't believe in him—and they were the ones who controlled his fate.

On December 2, 2013, Justin Turner was set to drive from his home in Los Angeles to San Diego to attend a union meeting. He was the Mets' player representative. Kourtney, his girlfriend at the time (and now his wife), was with him.

As Turner was packing up the car, his phone rang. He had not been expecting a call from the person on the other end of the line. It was Sandy Alderson, the Mets' general manager, and he wasn't the sort of person who called just to say hello. Turner was confused, but not alarmed. He wasn't a star by any stretch of the imagination, but he had carved out a place for himself as a productive role player for the Mets. The team's manager, Terry Collins, loved him for his versatility and professionalism. His scorching September hadn't hurt either. Unconcerned, Turner didn't answer, figuring he'd call Alderson back from the road.

When the two finally connected, the conversation was brief: Alderson informed Turner that the Mets had decided not to tender him a contract for 2014, making him a free agent. It wasn't that Turner was expensive—he had earned $504,547 in 2013 and would have received only a modest raise if the Mets had kept him. The Mets had simply determined that Turner no longer fit on their roster, and that was that. Turner never saw it coming.

"I didn't expect that at all," Turner said. "I thought I had a really good year, and I was excited about the adjustments I had made."

"I thought he was kidding," Latta said.

Why exactly the Mets nontendered Turner remains a bit of a mystery to this day. In the months that followed, reports surfaced that the Mets cut him loose because members of the front office had become frustrated with his perceived lack of effort and hustle. Alderson himself stoked those flames at the time when he told reporters, "Don't assume every nontender is a function of money." Turner resents those rumors to this day.

Since then, other theories have been circulated as well. In October 2017, writer Marc Carig authored a story for *Newsday* suggesting that the Mets were upset that Turner had declined their request to spend part of his winter training with Mike Barwis, the team's new strength and conditioning consultant. There was speculation that the Mets were dissatisfied with Turner's off-field behavior, though that, too, had never been raised as a problem in the past. The most likely answer is a lot less nefarious: the Mets didn't think Turner would ever be a more productive player than he currently was, and they felt they could find somebody even cheaper—and maybe better—to fill his role. Nothing more than that.

Whatever the case, Turner was now on the open market. He

had a brand-new swing, but no job where he could show it off. Almost as important, he had no equity with another organization. He knew the Mets. If he reported to spring training and told them he wanted to show them a new approach at the plate, they might listen and give him a chance to prove that he had fundamentally changed as a hitter. It was much harder to convince a new team of his transformation. Turner was going to have to do this the hard way: by clawing his way back from the bottom.

While his agents went to work trying to land Turner a job, Turner kept up his regimen with Latta and Byrd, honing his new swing. He figured that no matter where he landed, he would have to prove himself, and he was comfortable with that, even as the feeling of rejection still burned inside of him. His unemployment lasted all the way into the first week of February, when he signed a minor league contract with the Dodgers. It wasn't much, but it wasn't nothing either. At least it was a chance to show the world what he could do.

Right before Turner left for spring training, Latta and Byrd made a prediction: if he got a reasonable share of at-bats, they told him, he would hit 15 or 20 home runs. In his entire career to that point, he had hit eight.

Early in spring training in 2014, Doug Latta's phone rang. It was Justin Turner.

"Hey, Doug, I hit six home runs in a round of six today," Turner said.

"Great!" Latta responded, thrilled that Turner had made such a strong first impression.

Then Turner's tone changed.

"No," Turner continued. "They're telling me that's not what I do."

Turner's coaches still saw him as the light-hitting middle in-fielder he had been with the Mets. They immediately started giving him the same old instruction—instruction that Latta and Marlon Byrd had beaten out of him that winter. He was told to "stay back" and "load your back leg." He was criticized for hit-ting fastballs out in front of the plate rather than letting them get deep into the hitting zone. Essentially, they told him to do everything he had been taught his entire life except for his few months at the Ball Yard.

At first, Turner explained why he was swinging that way. He would try to give the coaches insight into what he was thinking, what he was trying to do, why he was doing it. This was generally met with skepticism. Turner had reached that moment of truth. The results were telling him that what he was doing was work-ing. His coaches disagreed.

"There are a lot of things that Doug's hitters have to go through," Byrd said. "Whenever you go somewhere else, people want to change you. You hit homers, they go, 'Uh-uh, no, that's not good.'"

In this case, there was no choice at all. Turner thought back to Byrd, who had arrived on the Mets the season before on a mi-nor league contract, the same kind of deal that had brought him to the Dodgers. Turner watched as Byrd never lost faith in his swing and was rewarded for it. Turner was determined to do the same. If he wasn't going to make it, he wasn't going to make it on his own terms.

So eventually Turner stopped trying to explain what he was doing. He simply held firm.

"Listen," he said, "I spent four months hitting every day doing this, getting where I want to be. And this is where I want to be."

Very quickly, it became clear that Turner was exactly where he was supposed to be. He tore up the Cactus League with his

Latta-approved swing, hitting .389 with five doubles in 36 at-bats for a whopping 1.005 OPS. The Dodgers started the regular season against the Diamondbacks in Sydney. On opening day, Justin Turner was no longer on a minor league contract. He was starting at second base for the Dodgers and batting second. He had earned it.

"When you have success, it makes it a little bit easier to have those conversations," Turner said. "If it wasn't working right away, then they probably would've been like, 'Yeah, see, what you're trying to do isn't working. We need to make some changes.'"

And in fact that nearly happened. Once the regular season started, Turner's bat cooled down. Despite his opening-day start, he wasn't a regular, and sporadic playing time made it more difficult for him to keep his updated swing sharp. After an 0-for-4 showing on May 21—coincidentally against the Mets—Turner's batting average sunk to .218. He had yet to hit a home run.

Something else happened on May 21, however. Juan Uribe, the Dodgers' regular third baseman, went on the disabled list with a strained hamstring. Suddenly, a spot had opened in the infield, and Turner was there to fill it. Almost immediately, he found his stroke. The very next night, he hit his first home run as a member of the Dodgers, a line drive to deep left field off Jon Niese of the Mets, the team that had just cut him loose. Three days after that, with the Dodgers now in Philadelphia, he hit another home run, this one a shot to straightaway center.

By the end of May, Turner's average was up to .250. He went 22-for-55 (.400) in June, bringing his average on the year up to .302. An injury of his own kept him sidelined for the first couple of weeks of July, but no matter. He hit .386 with six extra-base hits in August. In September, he hit a ridiculous .422, with five doubles, three homers, and 12 RBIs. It was a barrage of slug.

When the regular season ended, Turner had appeared in 109

games. His batting average was .340, the best in the National League among all players with at least 300 plate appearances. With runners in scoring position, he hit .419. And while he didn't quite make good on Byrd and Latta's prediction, he hit seven home runs in just 288 at-bats, a feat that had seemed impossible a year earlier.

"I was like, 'Holy crap,'" Turner said.

"He believed," Latta said. "He realized, 'Man, we're going somewhere.'"

J. D. Martinez was going somewhere too—to Santa Clarita to meet with Craig Wallenbrock for the first time. He arrived with a simple request: to be taught to swing like Jason Castro. It was the off-season before the 2014 campaign, the same winter Justin Turner was in the lab with Doug Latta. Martinez was ready to revamp his swing.

As he looked around the room, its walls lined with bats, Martinez couldn't help but notice a note hanging there. "Craig— Thanks for everything," it read. "I wouldn't be where I'm at today without your help." It was signed by Ryan Braun.

Not long after Martinez arrived, Craig Wallenbrock and Robert Van Scoyoc asked him to swing, to get a sense of what they were dealing with. "It was horrible," Van Scoyoc said. "It was disconnected. He drifted a lot. He hit in a very short zone. It was very flat and across the ball."

Wallenbrock had completely overhauled swings before. That was his job. But that sort of remake was usually reserved for younger players, impressionable amateurs whose bad habits were less ingrained and whose minds were more open to something new. The professionals Wallenbrock had helped in the past had never needed anything beyond a tune-up. And now

Craig Wallenbrock, at his cage in Santa Clarita, flipping balls to a hitter.

here standing before him was J. D. Martinez, an established major leaguer, who needed him to build a brand-new swing practically from scratch.

"I want you to understand something about Braun," Wallenbrock told Martinez. "Braun was not a remake. Braun was a polishing. He was a guy that I just had to polish. Castro I had to make some changes, but basically, he just took a little more polishing.

"J.D., I need to remake you, and you're going to have to spend more time. Because we're going to change a lot of stuff. Your whole foundation is bad. We've got to start over again, buddy."

Martinez didn't flinch. It had taken some time, but he had finally come to realize that his struggles with the Astros weren't because of bad luck, nor would they magically be corrected with more at-bats. His struggles were because of him.

"I'm all in," Martinez told Wallenbrock. "Whatever you guys want to do with me, I'm ready to go. I'll do it."

A few months earlier, Martinez would've scoffed at such a suggestion, especially one coming from somebody like Wallenbrock, a man who had accomplished far less in baseball than he had. What he had come to understand was that Wallenbrock and Van Scoyoc weren't trying to sell him on what was right. They were simply showing him what so many great hitters before him had done, and how to do it himself. It wasn't revolutionary—it was historical.

Martinez spent two weeks in California that first time, working every day with Wallenbrock and Van Scoyoc. Little by little they made changes. They worked out the hitch, teaching Martinez to keep his hands quiet, to stay balanced, to use his body more than his arms. They showed him how to keep his barrel in the zone longer and how to finish high. They instructed him not to chop down on the ball but to swing up on it.

The drills were different and foreign at first. There was the "towel bat," a Wallenbrock favorite. It was exactly what it sounds like: a towel attached to the top of the bat. The object was to snap the towel out in front of the plate. If it didn't snap, it meant the hitter went around the ball. If it snapped, he maintained the angle of his bat path. They gave Martinez exercises to swing just with his top hand and others to work on his bottom hand. Martinez just went with it, believing that if he put his head down and worked, it would pay off.

Later, I would ask Wallenbrock why he thought Martinez was so willing to listen to him, seemingly without any hesitation at all. Wallenbrock thought back to one of his first conversations with his new pupil, when Martinez admitted, "I'm going nowhere with what I'm doing right now."

Then Wallenbrock thought back to Paul Simon.

"He thought he was gliding down the highway," he said. "But in fact, he was slip-slidin' away."

After two intensive weeks embedded with Craig Wallenbrock in his Santa Clarita laboratory, J. D. Martinez needed a place to try out what he was learning against live pitching. He received the opportunity in the Venezuelan winter league—the kind of place where major leaguers go when they're on their last legs. In the winter before the 2014 season, that described Martinez.

Martinez didn't go outside much during the time he was in Venezuela. He was told it wasn't safe. So when he wasn't in the ballpark, he stayed holed up in his room and continued to obsessively pore over video. Martinez described this time as his "trial-and-error period." He was going to figure this out.

It didn't take long to prove to himself that the work he had done with Wallenbrock and Van Scoyoc was paying off. In his very first game, he hit two home runs. Both of them came on pitches that Martinez used to roll over and hit weakly on the ground. When he returned to the dugout after the second homer, he rushed over to Javier Bracamonte, the Astros bullpen catcher who had accompanied him to Venezuela and who had made an outlandish guarantee: Martinez was going to hit 30 home runs in the majors that next season.

In 24 games in Venezuela that winter, Martinez hit .312 with six doubles and six home runs. When he returned to the States, he quickly traveled back to California for another intensive week with Wallenbrock and Van Scoyoc before reporting to Kissimmee, Florida, for spring training. Martinez couldn't wait to show the Astros what he had done over the winter. He felt like a new man, and soon his bosses with the Astros would know it too. Martinez wasn't talking about Craig Wallenbrock yet. In an interview early that spring, Martinez discussed watching video and realizing that his swing had "a lot of weird mechanics and a lot of bad habits." He said his bat was now "in the zone longer" and that he was "using his legs" more than ever. The language had come from Wallenbrock, but the world wasn't ready yet to hear about the Oracle of Santa Clarita.

Unfortunately, the Astros weren't all that interested in J. D. Martinez anymore. They had new players coming through the system who didn't have three lackluster major league seasons on their résumés—including outfield prospect George Springer, a first-round draft pick who would go on to win World Series MVP in 2017. Martinez had become an afterthought.

Early in spring training, Martinez felt particularly strong at the plate. He was launching rockets all over the field in batting practice, sending balls soaring over the fence with ease. In between rounds, he approached the then-Astros' general manager, Jeff Luhnow, who was watching nearby, and asked to set up a meeting so they could talk about the adjustments Martinez had made. Luhnow agreed, though Martinez couldn't help but feel that he didn't sound all that jazzed about the idea. After a few more rounds in the cage, the Astros' manager, Bo Porter, shouted at Martinez to come join him in left field, where he was stationed. "J.D.," Porter said, "those were the most impressive rounds of BP I've ever seen you take."

At least somebody had noticed, Martinez thought, and he told Porter that he wanted to set up a meeting with him and Luhnow. It happened later that afternoon. "I know you guys have your team and have made your rosters," Martinez told them. "But I'm telling you I'm not the same hitter I was and I am begging you right now to give me an opportunity." It was an impassioned plea, and when the meeting broke up, Martinez was optimistic that he had been heard. But when the Grapefruit League schedule started, it quickly became clear that the Astros had no intention of making him part of their future.

The Astros gave Martinez just 20 plate appearances in spring training in 2014. Martinez picked up three hits, for a .167 batting average. Springer batted 46 times. Robbie Grossman, another prospect who had come up the year before, had 56 plate appearances. On March 22, 2014, the Astros released J. D. Martinez, the once-promising outfielder who no longer seemed destined for stardom.

After the Astros released Martinez, players like José Altuve, Matt Dominguez, and Chris Carter approached him, expressing their sympathy and telling him to stay positive. Martinez was defiant. "Don't feel bad for me. Don't feel sorry for me," he told them. "I guarantee you guys you will see me along the road."

Martinez had a reason to feel so confident. "I had this little freaking golden egg nobody knew I had, and that was my swing," he said. "I remember having this little trick, and nobody wanted to let me prove myself." Two days after the Astros let Martinez go, another team came along that was willing to give him that chance. The Tigers signed him to a minor league contract and brought him to spring training. It was far from a guarantee, but it was something. For Martinez, it was enough.

In a delightful twist of fate, Martinez's first spring game with the Tigers was a minor league contest back in Kissimmee against the Astros, the team that had just cut him loose. Martinez went 3-for-4 with a home run—and one audacious bat flip. Shortly after that the Astros' minor leaguers visited Lakeland for another game against the Tigers. Martinez hit three home runs, plus a fourth drive that banged off the top of the wall. That's when it dawned on Luhnow: perhaps he had made an enormous mistake.

Martinez opened the season with the Toledo Mud Hens, the Tigers' Triple A affiliate. In his first 17 games there, he hit 10 home runs and had 22 RBIs, showing very quickly that he didn't belong in the minor leagues. The Tigers promoted him to Detroit on April 21, and Martinez kept on hitting. He finished the year with a .315 batting average in 441 at-bats, hitting 23 home runs and posting a .912 OPS. It wasn't quite the 30 bombs he had promised Bracamonte, but it was close. If not for those first few weeks in Triple A, he might've gotten there.

As for the Astros, they survived losing J. D. Martinez, as evidenced by their championship in 2017 and return to the World Series in 2019. Luhnow, who was himself let go by the Astros in January 2020, doesn't regret the decision to cut Martinez, because he believes the process behind it was sound. Nothing they had seen told them that Martinez truly was different. Besides, players often say they made off-season changes and then do nothing to demonstrate the truth of that claim. But it's impossible not to wonder what might have been if they had given Martinez a few more at-bats in spring training in 2014.

"Our industry is littered with mistakes from the past," Luhnow said. "Cutting J.D. loose was a mistake."

Why didn't the Astros know that J. D. Martinez was on the verge of a breakout? Why couldn't they recognize that the J. D. Martinez who arrived in Kissimmee for spring training in 2014 was a fundamentally different hitter from the one who had left Houston for Santa Clarita just a few months before? The answer is fairly straightforward: they didn't have the tools to see it.

Until recent years, pitching has held a significant advantage over hitting across the major leagues, resulting in a record number of strikeouts and a lower collective batting average than at any point in decades. In part this advantage is due to advances in technology, which has long favored pitchers. For years, tech systems have been used to analyze the biomechanics of pitchers in an effort to help them throw faster, and it clearly has worked— pitchers now throw harder and put more spin on their breaking stuff than ever before.

For a long time, there was no comparable and widely accepted tech system to help hitters, which seems strange considering that perhaps the best hitter ever to live, Ted Williams, wrote a book called *The Science of Hitting.* Williams was about as scientific a hitter as there ever was, since he understood, even without the benefit of sophisticated technology, that hitting is science. But yet another great hitter, Tony Gwynn, wrote a book called *The Art of Hitting,* and that perception of hitting as "art" has persisted.

"Pitchers had a tech advantage if they were willing to use the technology and make changes as a result of it," Jeff Luhnow said. "Batters are now responding."

Technology sparked the fly-ball revolution. Luhnow believes that if today's technology had existed a decade ago, the Astros might never have cut J. D. Martinez.

At the beginning of the fly-ball revolution, there were people like Craig Wallenbrock who used video analysis to study swings decades before such a practice was considered mainstream in the baseball world. Later, Bobby Tewksbary and others would utilize the power of the internet to study components of the swing that few others were capable of seeing. These were the pioneers in a hidebound industry.

In 2015, Major League Baseball finally brought some of these technological advances to the masses, turning a small movement into a full-blown revolution. That's the year when the league debuted Statcast, a sophisticated player-tracking tool that uses radar and high-speed video to provide data that previously had been unmeasurable.

Statcast introduced to the lexicon the term "launch angle"—the vertical angle at which the ball leaves the bat after being struck. Every baseball that has ever been hit with a bat throughout human history has had a launch angle. It's a measurement, nothing more. But it wasn't until the advent of Statcast that analysts could track it. Once Statcast went live, an arms race broke out across the baseball landscape to understand this new treasure trove of information. Quickly it became clear that the ideal batted ball has a high exit velocity—another measurement made possible by Statcast—coupled with a launch angle of 25–30 degrees. Launch angles above 30 generally lead to routine pop flies, and very low launch angles result in (gasp) ground balls.

In the years that followed, launch angle exploded, emerging as a savior to some and the ultimate bogeyman to others. Launch angle data helped identify players who generally hit the ball hard but too frequently on the ground, suggesting that they might consider a swing change. Hitters like Christian Yelich, Jed Lowrie, and Yonder Alonso saw their production soar when they turned their sharply struck grounders into balls in the air, demonstrating the power of Statcast when utilized correctly in coaching.

Some critics saw launch angle as nothing more than a fad that was ruining baseball, and they blamed it for the rise of strike-outs across the game. Critics labeled players like J. D. Martinez and Justin Turner "launch angle guys," as if it were some sort of pejorative. In a June 2017 piece for ESPN, baseball writer Buster Olney quoted a host of anonymous baseball officials dismissing launch angle as a concept. One American League staffer said, "Changing every hitter's swing to produce a better launch angle is a mistake." A National League talent evaluator added, "I think too much is being made of fly balls and launch angle in general."

These people weren't necessarily wrong. Indeed, simply chasing "launch angle" without a full understanding of how to do it is a good way to ruin a swing. After stories about Turner's and Martinez's surges rocked the baseball landscape, plenty of hitters attempted to mimic their success by changing their swings to improve their launch angle—almost always without the assistance of an outside coach. Most saw their performance decline.

It's for that reason that most of the renowned "Swing Kings" avoid talking about launch angle at all, creating a lovely bit of irony: the people most often thought of as disciples of launch angle don't actually use the term "launch angle" to describe what they do. Craig Wallenbrock called launch angle "misunderstood and way overplayed." Martinez, a hitter who understands a thing or two about the swing, said, "People don't understand— they just say 'launch angle swings' without breaking down and understanding what they are and what they do." David Matranga put it best: "Launch angle is a by-product of swinging correctly."

Whatever the case, this much is certain: Launch angle, for better or worse, is now a part of the baseball vocabulary and will be for the foreseeable future. In spring training in 2018, Marc Topkin of the *Tampa Bay Times* saw the Rays conducting a most unusual drill. The team had positioned a wall of giant screens all around the infield, on the lip of the grass. Their presence sent a clear message: the goal is to hit the ball over the screens, not into them.

Here was a major league team actively preaching the gospel of the air-ball and taking a tangible step to encourage buy-in from its hitters. An idea once limited to the mad scientists on the outside had entered the mainstream. Now everyone knew about "launch angle screens."

"Even a guy that is your speed guy that looks to slap the ball the other way and let his legs run, he can still benefit from getting the ball off the ground, up in the air," Rays manager Kevin Cash told me. "We've done countless studies that say that trajectory more times than not benefits everybody."

With a seemingly endless array of software, wearable devices, and data collectors now flooding the marketplace, Statcast has become a small part of the technological wave being used to train hitters. In May 2018, I had a chance to experience some of the other innovations at Bobby Tewksbary's facility in Nashua, New Hampshire. It was a big day for Tewksbary—a Hall of Fame–caliber hitter was in town and planning (anonymously) to pop in for a session. I was the warm-up act for a slightly anxious Tewksbary.

I had told Tewksbary about my quest to refine my swing for the media baseball game, and he was all in, so into the cage we went. But first he brought me over to a monitor to enter my name into one of his technological teaching tools, HitTrax, a data capture and simulation system that transforms any batting cage into a superpowered analytics center. HitTrax, in real time, captures data like the exit velocity and launch angle of every batted ball and uses that data to show in gorgeous color animation exactly where the ball would go on a field. You can even overlay that trajectory onto any major league ballpark. We chose Yankee Stadium, the site of my game, so I could digitally take aim at the short porch in right field.

HitTrax doesn't teach swing mechanics. That job belongs to the coach. But it does give hitters instant feedback on the result of their swing. No longer do they have to wonder whether they truly hit a ball as solidly as they thought. With HitTrax, that information is right there on the screen.

Putting me in a batting cage connected to HitTrax was mostly a sad reminder of my limited ability. After one of my early swings off a tee, Tewksbary looked back toward the screen.

"Sixty point two on the exit velo," he said. "Not quite major league stuff."

Tewksbary went to work. He had me lower my hands and adjust the angle of my barrel when I swung. We worked on my bat path, fixing my tendency to swing around the ball instead of swinging through it. With every tweak, the exit velocity number on the HitTrax machine ticked higher . . . 62 . . . then 65. It was intoxicating. Every extra mile per hour off the bat felt like an accomplishment, and keeping that number climbing became my mission.

Eventually, I graduated from the tee to live pitching, with Tewksbary throwing me batting practice. After each round, we'd go to the video and Tewksbary would recommend changes. I was a bit of a challenge compared to his typical clients. Not only was I terrible, but I was also old—too old to easily train my body to move in a new way. I did have a solid understanding of what my hands should be doing to generate lift, but my lower body was a disaster. My hips weren't explosive, and my core was weak, making my hands and arms do all the work.

To help remedy that, Tewksbary made a recommendation: when he started to throw the ball, he wanted me to bring my front knee back toward the catcher, before launching into my swing. He said to lift my front knee so far back it felt wrong. As I finished my swing, he wanted my back facing the camera situated in the right-handed batter's box. Basically, he wanted to work on big, exaggerated moves, believing it would help my body break years of bad habits.

Will Wu, the motor learning expert, said that Tewksbary's approach makes scientific sense. What he was probably trying to do, Wu said, was to have my "perception match reality."

"A lot of the athletes I work with, the common exchange we have is they report that it 'feels weird' from their previous movement strategy, and I respond, 'But it looked good,'" Wu said. "I think Tewks is trying to resolve your perception of what you did previously with the reality of the altered movement strategy."

"What I'm trying to do here is get your body to move better, because if your body's not moving well, your hands have nothing to connect to," Tewksbary told me. "The way your brain is working, you have to go so far you think it's wrong, and then something different will happen."

Something different did happen. This new swing felt weird, but the results didn't lie. The ball started jumping off my bat, unlike anything I had felt up to that point with Tewksbary.

After one *crack!* we looked up to the monitor and the numbers flashed onto the screen: 75.7 miles per hour. Now, keep in mind that in the major leagues a hard-hit ball travels 100 miles per hour or more. I was still only three-quarters of the way there. But considering where I had started, it felt like a major accomplishment. The numbers showed that I could improve if I kept working. Maybe, with time, I'd actually look semi-athletic. Swinging in a cage with HitTrax certainly did wonders for my confidence, if nothing else. The technology wasn't a substitute for good coaching, but it was another tool at the coach's disposal.

HitTrax is far from the only piece of advanced technology that high-level coaches are using to analyze hitters. Many coaches have become enamored with a system called Rapsodo, which measures not only exit velocity and launch angle but also charts the spin rate and spin axis of batted balls, and creates 3-D models of their flight paths. Many professional organizations use Blast Motion, a motion sensor that attaches to a hitter's bat, and other new devices are entering the marketplace all the time. Driveline and others are into something called a K-Vest, a wearable piece of tech that measures the kinematic sequence of a hitter's swing, showing exactly how the body moves. Increasingly sophisticated sensors in bats have all but settled any debate about the ideal swing path, since these devices show, indisputably, what elite hitters do when they swing. Many of these technologies and similar ones have been used to better understand golf swings for years. Baseball is finally starting to catch up.

Not all private hitting coaches believe in the technology. Doug Latta doesn't use anything besides video analysis at his facility and believes the internet hitting community puts data ahead of teaching athletic swing mechanics. Richard Schenck is adamantly against most technology and will ferociously attack anybody online who advocates for it.

"It's the biggest gaffe in the game," Schenck said. "When college recruiters and professional scouts are recruiting or drafting players based on their exit velocity, they're making a huge mistake."

That's a minority opinion. But then again, Richard Schenck has never minded being in the minority.

David Matranga believed in Richard Schenck. He had for years. The difference was that now, in the off-season following the 2016 season, he had a platform, and he had test subjects. Matranga was working for PSI Sports Management, the agency that represented him as a player and was led by Page Odle, a minor leaguer in the 1980s who later moved into the agent world.

Matranga helped bring Schenck further into the fold. He would send Schenck videos of potential clients, players like Kole Calhoun, Kolten Wong, and Rob Refsnyder, whose swings Schenck would analyze from afar. One of the players Matranga sent Schenck video of was a young client named Aaron Judge.

Matranga had been "looking for the perfect opportunity" to introduce Schenck to his players. Finally, a guinea pig—a very large guinea pig—had emerged.

Matranga called Judge to broker a meeting with Schenck. "I said, 'Do me a favor: fly to Arizona and give me five days with one of my really good friends who I believe can drastically improve your swing and tap into your true potential,'" Matranga said. "'Give me five days, and if you think it's horseshit, you can go back to doing whatever you were doing.' I said, 'What can you lose?'"

Nothing, Judge reasoned. So in November 2016, he headed out to Peoria for a crash course: two sessions a day for five days at the D-BAT baseball training facility with Schenck and Matranga in an effort to overhaul his swing. Refsnyder and Odle were there. So was Jose Vargas, the independent league player Schenck had worked with a few months earlier. Coincidentally, Vargas himself had previously been represented by Odle and PSI. Schenck put Vargas up in a hotel on his dime, figuring that would boost Schenck's street cred with Judge and Refsnyder.

"I'm working with two major leaguers, and this is Rich from the Basement," Schenck said. "Why are they going to give me any respect? I'm going to bring this guy who can demonstrate what I teach."

That didn't help with Schenck's nerves. It's not that he wasn't confident. Clearly, Schenck never lacks for confidence when it comes to his theories on the swing. But this was different from working with kids on the internet, college players, or even a pro like Vargas. This was Aaron Judge, one of the top prospects in professional baseball, putting his swing—and his career, really—in the hands of Rich from the Basement.

Matranga warned Judge ahead of time that Schenck's drills would probably feel weird. Judge went along with it because he trusted Matranga. Even after all those warnings, it didn't go well at first. Vargas remembers speaking with Odle shortly after they arrived and spending the entire conversation defending Schenck, his methods, and his credentials.

"Page was a little skeptical," Vargas said. "He was like, I just met this guy off the internet and he's supposed to be some hitting guru? That's when he started asking me a whole bunch of questions. He had his worries."

Judge did too. On the first day, Schenck had Judge and Refsnyder warm up the way they always would. Right away, he saw Judge swinging in the traditional manner: down, led by his top hand, his barrel pushing forward. So the laptop came out, and Schenck feverishly showed Judge and Refsnyder video clips from his vast library of some of the best hitters throughout history to help them visualize what they should be doing.

Then came the drills. Weird drills that Judge and Refsnyder had never experienced.

"Some of his drills were pretty out there," Refsnyder said. "Pretty extreme."

Schenck had them swinging with pipes and broomsticks, like he had me doing in Tampa the first time we worked together. He asked them to swing with one leg elevated off the ground, another drill I had tried. He ran through all his terminology about the stretch and the swivel and the tilt and, of course, the *snap!*

It didn't go well.

"Judge said after the first session, 'This is really weird, what is this?'" Matranga said.

"I remember the second day they came back, and Rich was like, 'How are you guys feeling?'" Vargas said. "And Judge was like, 'Eh, I don't know about this.'"

The "this" Matranga and Vargas were talking about was the culmination of everything Schenck had spent the last decade working on—everything he had learned since his "eureka!" moment watching Barry Bonds. It was his dream realized: a chance to teach a real-life Major League Baseball player to tilt, stretch, and *snap it!* Schenck just had to figure out a way to keep Judge from leaving before he could make him a believer.

* * *

Richard Schenck has come up with a lot of strange teaching methods over the years. I personally had a chance to try a lot of them—swinging while keeping my front foot in the air the entire time was particularly memorable.

But if he has a favorite child among his motley assortment of invented exercises, it is the "command drill." Schenck puts the ball on a tee and tells his hitter to enter the load position, the moment right before the swing when all of his energy is stored up, just waiting to be unleashed on the ball. Then he calls out, "Swing!" and the batter attacks. The idea, Schenck says, is to teach "launch quickness," which he believes to be a principal tenet of swing mechanics.

"There should be zero time between hearing the command and launching the bat," Schenck said. "Most hitters still have a move they have to make between their decision to swing and the actual launch of their swing. And pitchers exploit that. Nobody in the world that I have encountered teaches launch quickness. I do."

Back in Arizona, Schenck hoped this would be the drill that would click with Judge. He set a ball on the tee in front of Judge and another in front of Refsnyder, then grabbed a bat himself and stood at a third tee next to them. He presented Judge and Refsnyder—major league hitters, mind you—with a simple challenge: beat me to the ball.

Vargas stood on the sidelines giving the commands. He shouted, "Load!" and then, "Swing!" The results were, let's say, unexpected.

"I destroyed Aaron," Schenck said. "I'm 62 years old at the time, and I can get my barrel to the ball before Aaron can get his barrel to the ball.

"I whooped Aaron, and I whooped Robert. And they both looked at me like, 'What are you doing, old man?' I got their attention. 'How can this guy, who is this old, get his barrel to the ball before I could?'"

That outcome wasn't unexpected to Vargas. Schenck had done the exact same routine with him a few months earlier, when they first started working together. It was no contest. This is one of Schenck's favorite party tricks, like the chess wizards who take on all comers for cash in Washington Square Park or the three-card monte hustlers on the street corner—it's a game that seems too easy to lose but in reality is impossible to win. When it ends with the mark inevitably shell-shocked and bamboozled, Schenck offers his sales pitch.

"I'm not more athletic than you," he says. "I've just done it more than you. I understand it better. I can snap that thing. And when you get the right feeling, you'll be able to snap it too."

Losing to Schenck in the command drill was a seminal moment in the transformation of Aaron Judge. He still wasn't exactly sold on Schenck, but clearly, Judge reasoned, this guy knew something about the swing. Maybe these bizarre drills had a point after all.

Judge's shift didn't happen right away. Vargas remembers watching bad swing after bad swing, failure after failure. Except every once in a while, something would click and the ball would explode off his bat. Schenck lives for those moments, when a hitter does something he has never done before. It's the moment when a hitter looks at Schenck and says, "I just felt something new. I kind of like it, I don't understand it, but I felt something new." Just describing such a moment, Schenck's face positively glows with pride.

It happened with Scott Kingery, a Phillies infielder and a Schenck disciple. It happened with Eric Hosmer and Ian Happ and Joc Pederson, a few other well-known players who have quietly worked on their swings under Schenck's guidance. And it happened with Aaron Judge—in the second session on the fourth day of the five-day boot camp. Judge started *snapping it!* Not every time, and not perfectly, but things were starting to click.

"I go home, and Aaron kind of bought in," Schenck said. "He had a lot of work to do, but it was, 'Okay, I kind of understand what you're doing here.' And somewhere along the way, Aaron really felt something."

Richard Schenck had a new believer. His name was Aaron Judge. Baseball was about to change.

SUCCESS

The best year of Bobby Tewksbary's professional life came in 2015, the year after J. D. Martinez and Justin Turner burst onto the scene after remaking their swings with outside hitting instructors. A few months before spring training, the Blue Jays swung a blockbuster trade that stunned the baseball world: they sent a package of four players to the A's for Josh Donaldson, who in 2014 had slugged 29 homers, driven in 98 runs, and made his first All-Star team. This was a bold move for the Blue Jays, who hadn't been in the playoffs since 1993. Adding Donaldson to a lineup that already featured José Bautista and Edwin Encarnación put them in position to compete with their division rivals, the Yankees and Red Sox. The night of the deal, Alex Anthopoulos, the Blue Jays general manager at the time, admitted, "We didn't expect him to be available."

Barely a week later, the Blue Jays made another move that didn't receive quite as much attention. Actually, it barely made the wires at all: they claimed Chris Colabello off waivers from the Twins, bringing him in to provide additional organizational depth. When the official Blue Jays Twitter account announced the news, the responses didn't exactly exude enthusiasm. "Can y'all buy superstars and not buy nobodies?" one user wrote. "Never heard of him," chimed in another.

The confusion in Toronto was understandable. Colabello still was a nobody. He had hit .229 in 59 games with the Twins in 2014, his age-30 season. He had made it, but he hadn't Made It, and it didn't seem likely that he ever would. But the Blue Jays saw *something*. Colabello had shown flashes in 2014. He finished April with a .295 batting average and 27 RBIs. If he could do it for a month, he could do it for longer.

For Bobby Tewksbary, this was a dream: Colabello and Donaldson, two players whose swings he had a hand in shaping, were on the same team. What more could he ask for?

As the season began, it quickly became clear that even if the mainstream baseball world still didn't know his name, Tewksbary knew quite a bit more about the swing than his modest background in baseball would suggest.

Donaldson started the party, immediately taking an enormous step forward from the progress he had shown the year before. In his first 27 games as a member of the Blue Jays, he went 33-for-105 (.314), with six home runs, 18 RBIs, and a .939 OPS. He was red-hot, and he was about to have company.

Colabello played his first game with the Blue Jays on May 5. He had earned it with a brilliant start in the minors, hitting .337 to that point. When he arrived in Toronto, nothing changed. In his first two games, against the Yankees, he went 6-for-8. In the next series, against the Red Sox, he went 4-for-10. When the calendar turned to June, Colabello was hitting .368 and had established himself as an everyday player, while Donaldson's 15 home runs had locked him into the prestigious number-two spot in the Blue Jays' lineup. Attendance at the Rogers Centre in downtown Toronto, which had lagged for the previous two decades, was starting to surge.

Inside the ballpark, the home clubhouse had quickly been transformed into some combination of a scientific laboratory and the Roman Forum—a place exclusively for the nerdiest of all hitting nerds. Donaldson and Colabello lockered near each other, and they spent every free moment discussing the ins and outs of the swing, new ideas, thoughts they had picked up from Tewksbary or anybody else in their orbit—whatever was on their minds. Their banter intrigued their teammates, who started to join in. A lot of it, Colabello said, was "shit they had never heard of." One night after a game, Colabello, Donaldson, and José Bautista stuck around until two in the morning talking about moves in their swings. It was like the internet message boards that Tewksbary had frequented for years, only the posters weren't random dads screaming at each other about their children, but sluggers at the pinnacle of the game.

Tewksbary will always remember Monday, July 6, 2015. The Blue Jays were in Chicago to begin a four-game series against the White Sox. Chris Sale was the opposing pitcher, and he dominated that night. He threw a complete game, allowing two runs on six hits in a 4–2 White Sox win. But it was how the Blue Jays scored their two runs that mattered to Tewksbary. In the third inning, Colabello hit a home run to left-center field. Three frames later, Donaldson took Sale deep into left for his 20th home run of the season. Tewksbary's two most famous success stories, coincidentally brought together as teammates, had both homered in the same game off one of the best pitchers on the planet. It was a dream.

After the game, Donaldson and Colabello received text messages from Tewksbary congratulating them on their homers. Colabello called him back.

What Tewksbary didn't know when he picked up Colabello's call that night was that Donaldson had recently accepted an invitation to participate in the Home Run Derby being held in Cincinnati the following week. Ever since Donaldson decided to participate, Colabello had been badgering him about who he planned to have pitch to him at the event. Part of the fun of the Derby is that players get to choose their batting practice pitcher, so that a family member, a close friend, or a beloved mentor gets the chance to throw on a major league field. Colabello thought Tewksbary deserved it.

In the moments before Colabello called Tewksbary, Donaldson was close to making a decision. He just had one question for Colabello about Tewksbary: "Can he handle it?" Colabello responded by handing Donaldson the phone, with Tewksbary on the line.

"I was going to ask you to throw in the Derby," Donaldson said. "But I don't know if you can handle it."

"Fuck you," Tewksbary shot back. "I can fucking handle it."

Just like that, it was done. Bobby Tewksbary, who had spent his entire life dreaming of the major leagues, was on his way there, at least for one day.

It was about 10:30 at night when Tewksbary hung up the phone. He had just pulled into his garage after a full day working at his hitting facility. Before heading inside, he paused for a moment in his car, took a deep breath, and basked in the surrealness of the moment. He almost couldn't process it. He went upstairs and woke his fiancée. "Ummm, I think this is happening," he said. "It's exciting if it is."

Too exhilarated to even think about sleeping, Tewksbary went back downstairs for a video session. He turned his television to ESPN's *Baseball Tonight,* which that night was featuring Curt Schilling and John Kruk as commentators. He couldn't believe what they were talking about. That year the Home Run Derby was set to introduce a new format. Previously, batters tried to slam as many home runs as possible around a set number of "outs"—any batted ball that didn't land over the fence. Because pitches they didn't swing at didn't count, they could take as many pitches as they wanted without penalty. Now, however, each batter would have a set amount of time in which to hit as many home runs as possible, so every bad pitch would seriously hurt his chances of winning. As Kruk and Schilling pointed out, all of the pressure was now firmly on the pitchers.

Shit, Tewksbary thought to himself. *That's me. That's me and seven other people in the world that this applies to right now.*

There was no time for nerves, because the next few days were a whirlwind. The traveling secretary from the Blue Jays contacted Tewksbary to arrange his flights from New Hampshire to Cincinnati. First-class, of course. This was the big leagues. ESPN sent him a form to fill out, asking Tewksbary questions about himself that the announcers could discuss on the TV broadcast. Equipment suppliers needed to know Tewksbary's jersey and hat size. Friends from throughout his life reached out. Many of them said that he should probably practice throwing batting practice before the big event, a suggestion Tewksbary found hilarious, since he had thrown batting practice pretty much every day for the past seven years.

"He's one of the first guys who sort of broke down swings with me before, I guess you could say, I became good," Donaldson told the Toronto media that week. "I think he's going to be in heaven being out there with these Major League Baseball guys because he's really worked hard the past few years spending time on the evolution of swings, guys who are good and putting it together. For him to be able to see guys he's studied on is pretty cool."

Tewksbary and his fiancée departed for Ohio on Sunday, July 12. His bride-to-be had to leave her own wedding shower a half-hour early to make the flight. Tewksbary was nervous. Of course he was. It was true that he had thrown batting practice every day—but never in front of the 7 million or so people who would be watching him during the Home Run Derby. When he went down to the hotel lobby to head to the park, a throng of fans were waiting outside, seeking autographs. On the bus ride over to the ballpark, J. D. Martinez—who naturally was familiar with Tewksbary's work from his own quest to revamp his swing—came over to Tewksbary, put his hand on his chest, and asked, "How's your heart rate?" Tewksbary mustered up enough confidence to say he was feeling just fine.

When Tewksbary walked into the visitors' clubhouse at Great American Ball Park for the first time, the nervousness immediately turned to awe. He found his locker, with Donaldson on one side and Blue Jays catcher Russell Martin on the other. In the nearest corner were Mike Trout and Albert Pujols. On the other side, he saw Manny Machado, Nelson Cruz, and José Altuve, some of the biggest stars in the game. In his locker was a uniform, black with red sleeves. The front said AMERICAN, for the American League. On the back was the number 28, sitting below the most incredible part: his name, TEWKSBARY. Tewksbary tried to blend in and act like he'd been there before, even though he hadn't. That became especially clear to him when he walked into the clubhouse bathroom and noticed who had stationed himself at the urinal next to his: Machado, then a star Orioles infielder.

"It was one of those, 'Everybody pees' moments," Tewksbary said.

A few hours before the Derby, Tewksbary went out to the field to soak in everything. Dallas Keuchel of the Astros and Darren O'Day of the Orioles had approached him to say hello, a gesture he appreciated. He spent some time chatting with Chris Berman, the famed ESPN sportscaster, and introduced himself to Frank Thomas, the Hall of Fame first baseman. Tewksbary went up close to the cage during batting practice and even whipped out his phone to take some video to add to his library since, he figured, he'd never get another chance to film all of these great hitters up close. Most of all, he tried not to seem like too much of a weirdo in front of some of his heroes.

Eventually, it was time to pitch. That was the easy part. Bobby Tewksbary might not have been a major leaguer, but he was a baseball player, and he possessed the superhuman tunnel vision that all elite athletes possess. He was able to block out the size of the stadium and the noise from the crowd and simply focus on the umpire giving him the okay to throw another pitch and on the catcher's glove. It was good enough for Donaldson to bash nine home runs in the first round, beating Cubs first baseman Anthony Rizzo to advance to the semifinals. One of his homers traveled 465 feet. Donaldson eventually bowed out despite hitting nine more homers in his semifinal matchup against Reds third baseman Todd Frazier, the hometown favorite. Tewksbary had handled himself admirably. Throwing strikes was never an issue. Later, Donaldson gave Tewksbary a signed bat. On it, he wrote, "Sick BP."

And that wasn't all Tewksbary took home with him. He brought a T-shirt that he wanted all four AL Home Run Derby participants to sign, and he quickly secured autographs from the first three: Donaldson, Machado, and Rangers first baseman Prince Fielder. He just needed Pujols. Once again, the nerves came roaring back. Albert Pujols was essentially a god to Tewksbary. A clip of Pujols's swing had sent Tewksbary on his quest of discovery in the first place. Everything he knew, everything he had learned, had all started with Pujols. Now, after a huge contingent of Spanish-speaking media had finally dissipated from Pujols's locker following the Derby, it was time for Tewksbary to approach him. So he gathered his courage, walked up to him—and promptly started geeking out.

"If I hadn't seen you swing," Tewksbary told Pujols, "I'd never be here."

"Aw, that's so cool, man," Pujols said, before pulling out a bat, signing it, and handing it to Tewksbary.

And then it was over. Tewksbary left the ballpark, went out for a fancy steak dinner with Donaldson and his representatives, sat in the stands for the All-Star Game the next night (Donaldson walked in both of his plate appearances), and on Wednesday returned home to his normal life in Nashua, working with kids at his hitting facility. In the days after the Derby, he got more than 700 emails from people wanting to hit with him.

Later that week, Tewksbary coached a 14-and-under game, a stark reminder that his stint in the major leagues was just a visit, not a permanent stay. Walking around town or at the mall over

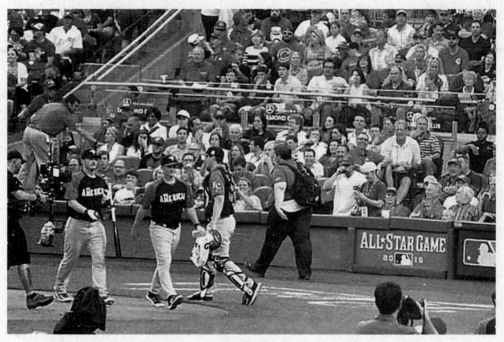

Bobby Tewksbary (holding towel) walking off the field at the 2015 Home Run Derby in Cincinnati.

the next few days, he'd bump into old friends from high school who excitedly told him they had seen him on TV. "Yep, I did that," Tewksbary would say in response. "That was me."

For his entire life, Bobby Tewksbary had wanted nothing more than to be in the major leagues. He never made it—except for one night, on the pitcher's mound in Cincinnati.

"It wasn't my dream to be a Home Run Derby pitcher," Tewksbary said, wistfully. "What I always say is, it was a cool experience. It was a really, really awesome experience. And it was a lot of validation for all the hours I have put into everything I have done."

For the trio of Bobby Tewksbary, Josh Donaldson, and Chris Colabello, the rest of 2015 was beyond their wildest imaginations.

Colabello never went back down to the minor leagues, because he never stopped hitting. He finished the season with a .321 batting average in 101 games, to go along with 15 home runs, 54 RBIs, and an .886 OPS. Donaldson never cooled down following his red-hot first half. He hit .297 with 41 homers and 123 RBIs, the most in the American League. He was named the AL MVP.

For the Blue Jays, too, the bets paid off: Donaldson and Colabello powered them to a 93–69 record and a postseason berth. Toronto advanced all the way to game 6 of the AL Championship Series before bowing out to the Royals. Colabello had two homers and three doubles in 10 playoff games, while Donaldson homered three times.

It was a remarkable accomplishment for Donaldson, not just because of where his swing had been just a couple years before, but also because of what he had overcome in his life to arrive at that moment. Born in Pensacola, Florida, Donaldson, an only child, was raised by a single mother, Lisa French. His father, Levon Donaldson, spent most of Josh's childhood in prison, serving more than a decade on charges of domestic violence, drug offenses, false imprisonment, and aggravated battery. He has distinct memories from early childhood of his father viciously attacking his mother in a fit of rage. Partway through high school, his mom landed him a spot at Faith Academy in Mobile, Alabama, where Donaldson managed to develop into a baseball star and, more important, started to conquer some of his emotional demons.

Donaldson rarely speaks publicly about his difficult road to becoming the MVP of the American League. But there is no question his rough upbringing had a significant effect on the rest of his life.

"I'm not going to get too colorful with it, but it wasn't pretty," Donaldson told Rosie DiManno of the *Toronto Star* in 2016. "The best way I can describe it is I can still remember things from when I was from three to five years old that are very vivid in my mind to this day. And it's not something I would want anybody else to go through."

Donaldson endured those difficulties and managed to flourish in spite of them. As he and Colabello and the Blue Jays were making their playoff run in 2015, Bobby Tewksbary accomplished something of his own: he got married, capping off an incredible year that had made him, at least in baseball circles, a household name. Colabello was now an indispensable member of a major league lineup after so many years in independent ball, while Donaldson had given Tewksbary's ideas about the swing legitimacy by bringing him to the Home Run Derby for the world to see. After years toiling away in obscurity at a batting cage in New Hampshire, everything, Tewksbary thought, was looking up.

* * *

When Justin Turner returned to the Dodgers for the 2015 season following his breakout performance from the year before, he had nothing left to prove to himself—but he had plenty to prove to virtually everybody else. His production in 2014 had been nothing short of remarkable, but many in the baseball community viewed his dream campaign as a fluke, a statistical quirk, and expected him to revert back to normal the next year. Baseball is a game of numbers, and that makes it hard to believe that a player at the stage of career where Turner was could suddenly improve so dramatically.

In fairness, there were some numbers that raised alarm bells. Most notable was Turner's 2014 batting average on balls in play (BABIP). This popular metric in the analytics community shows a hitter's batting average only on balls hit in the field of play and excludes strikeouts and home runs from the calculation.

It's extremely difficult to sustain a very high or very low BABIP over the course of multiple years. A BABIP well below average suggests that a hitter has been unlucky in finding holes and is due for a breakout. A high BABIP can indicate that a hitter making weak contact has simply gotten lucky as his grounders have disproportionately bounced into the outfield rather than finding an infielder's glove. Turner's BABIP in 2014 was an insane .404, the highest in the National League among players with at least 300 plate appearances.

The Dodgers weren't sure what to expect from Turner in 2015. They had crunched all the numbers and seen the warning signs, just like everybody else. But they had also spent a season with Turner and watched him hit. They had seen the changes in his swing in a way a statistical analyst never could. And they were excited to find out what Turner could do.

This year, at least, Turner didn't have to worry about finding a job. The Dodgers signed him to a $2.5 million contract in January, more than double what he'd made the year before. What Turner didn't have was a place in the starting lineup. Uribe was healthy and back at third base. The Dodgers had traded for a new shortstop, the former Phillies infielder Jimmy Rollins. They had also acquired a new second baseman, Howie Kendrick. These moves left no everyday job for Turner—a sign that, at the very least, the Dodgers were hedging their bets.

Turner was undeterred. He hadn't even had a major league contract heading into spring training in 2014, let alone a spot in a lineup. He'd just have to hit his way onto the field, as he'd done the year before.

That's exactly what happened. By the middle of May, Turner had secured the Dodgers' third-base job. He didn't hit .340 again. As the analysts had predicted, that above-.400 BABIP was unsustainable. It dropped to .321, and with it, so did his batting average, which settled in at a respectable .294 in 385 at-bats, to go along with his .861 OPS. His power continued to develop. Turner finished 2015 with 16 home runs, or one every 24 at-bats. Up until that point in his career, Turner had homered every 75 at-bats.

When the dust settled, Turner couldn't help but think back to what Latta and Byrd had told him. When they had predicted 15 homers in a major league season, Turner didn't believe them.

"They weren't lying," Turner said. "Never in my wildest dreams did I think I was going to do something like that in the major leagues."

But he had, because Justin Turner had fundamentally changed as a hitter. The swing he had crafted with the assistance of Doug Latta and Marlon Byrd had turned a player who was on the verge of being out of baseball altogether into an absolute monster at the plate. Creating that swing was an intense, difficult process, requiring countless hours of work and a willingness to reconsider everything he had ever thought about hitting. The result of the new swing, however, was shockingly simple: Before Turner joined the Dodgers, close to half of his batted balls were on the ground. In 2015, the year Turner hit 16 home runs, that number had plummeted to about 36 percent. That wasn't luck. It was a revolution.

"I knew nothing about hitting—nothing," Turner said. "I was completely backward in everything I thought."

Now he had awoken, and there was no going back. By the end of the 2015 season, Latta's name was out there. Sure, Byrd had talked a bit publicly about his work with Latta, but it wasn't the same. Turner was emerging as a star for the Dodgers, a big-market team with annual postseason aspirations. Turner acknowledging that he had changed his swing with the help of, in the eyes of the baseball establishment, a nobody meant something.

By that point, Turner no longer feared repercussions. He had proven himself. So on June 25, 2015, an article written by Phil Rogers appeared on MLB.com with the headline "The Secret behind Turner's Big Breakout." Rogers wrote that Latta "teaches hitting to the hardcore out of a batting cage in an industrial park in the San Fernando Valley." He also quoted Mark McGwire, then the Dodgers' hitting coach.

"Thank you, New York Mets, for letting him go."

If there were any lingering doubts about whether J. D. Martinez's breakout season in 2014 was a fluke, he quickly put them to rest the next year. In 2015, Martinez blasted 38 home runs and tallied 102 RBIs. In 899 at-bats for the Astros, he had hit a grand total of 24 homers. Now he had smacked 38 in one season.

He made the All-Star team and won a Silver Slugger. He even got some MVP votes.

The baseball world had taken notice. Before the 2016 season, he signed a two-year extension with the Tigers worth $18.5 million and then continued to produce at the plate. He hit .307 with 22 homers and a .908 OPS in an injury-shortened campaign that kept him limited to 460 at-bats. The 2017 season was even more impressive. A stint on the disabled list again cost him a month, but it didn't matter. He mashed a whopping 45 home runs, including 29 in 62 games following a July trade from the Tigers to the Diamondbacks, further establishing himself as one of baseball's premier sluggers.

His work ethic and commitment to refining his swing had become legendary around the game. Nothing short of perfection satisfied him. In an endeavor where immortality means failing 7 out of 10 times, Martinez didn't think that way. Wallenbrock laughed when he recalled a game when Martinez had three hits and two doubles. Wallenbrock texted Martinez to congratulate him. Martinez responded with an expletive, insisting that Wallenbrock knew those swings were far below his expectation. When Wallenbrock informed him that they were good swings for 99 percent of players, Martinez delivered what could best be described as his worldview: "I hold myself to a higher standard. So stop trying to placate me."

As the years passed, Martinez continued his work with Wallenbrock, honing and refining the swing that had made him such a force. But over time Martinez found himself gravitating even more toward somebody else: Robert Van Scoyoc, Wallenbrock's apprentice, who was slowly but surely proving himself capable of so much more. Martinez and Van Scoyoc's relationship developed in part out of necessity. Wallenbrock by then was approaching his seventies and had undergone hip replacement surgery. It was no longer easy for him to fly to Detroit for a few days to give Martinez a tune-up or to visit him in Florida over the winter. As Van Scoyoc began to make those trips instead, he taught Wallenbrock's basic curriculum but also imparted valuable wisdom of his own.

"J.D. is a lot to keep up with," Van Scoyoc said. "Being younger, having a little bit of a bigger engine at the time, I was able to fill that need for J.D."

It was more than just logistics, however, that drew Martinez to Van Scoyoc. In Van Scoyoc, Martinez saw not just a coach but a peer and a companion. They were about the same age, both trying to rise to the top of their chosen profession. Martinez and Van Scoyoc were a team, growing and learning together.

To Martinez, it helped that he and Van Scoyoc were of the same generation. Van Scoyoc spoke a language Martinez comprehended. When Martinez found himself confused sometimes in his early sessions with Wallenbrock, unable to follow the older man's tangents, Van Scoyoc, who typically wouldn't say much and generally let Wallenbrock do the talking, was there to clarify Wallenbrock's points in a way that Martinez understood. When they were apart, Martinez started sending film of his swings directly to Van Scoyoc, who was ahead of Wallenbrock from a technological standpoint. Wallenbrock might have been an early adopter of video in his youth, but he wasn't in any hurry to upgrade his flip phone. At first, Van Scoyoc would show the video to Wallenbrock and report back to Martinez. Over time Van Scoyoc felt more and more comfortable giving his own thoughts directly to Martinez. When Martinez first met Van Scoyoc, he had thought of him as little more than "Craig's sidekick." Now Van Scoyoc had become his main man.

"Robert has taken all of the things I've done," Wallenbrock said, "and in some cases he's taken them to a new level."

* * *

Aaron Judge worked with Richard Schenck one more time before reporting to spring training with the Yankees in 2017. It was
in January, about two months after the Arizona Summit, in Ventura, California, at a clinic put on by PSI Sports Management, the
agency that represents Judge. Twice a day for five days, Schenck
worked with about a dozen of PSI's players, including Judge,
Rob Refsnyder, and Phillies infield prospect Scott Kingery.

By the time Judge arrived in Tampa in February, there was no
doubt that his swing was ready. The bigger question was whether
the Yankees were ready to accept it.

"Aaron was doing a lot of drastic stuff, and it wasn't like he was
coming off a very successful season," Refsnyder said. "He was doing a lot of things that weren't considered normal, so there were
definitely a lot of raised eyebrows."

Indeed there were. The Yankees' hitting coaches didn't understand what Judge was doing. His swing looked weird, with
the knob snapping upward and the barrel zooming rearward.
Even worse, they had absolutely no idea where he had learned
those mechanics. They certainly didn't know Schenck. As spring
training went on, some in the organization encouraged him to
abandon whatever changes he had made.

The skepticism was challenging for Judge. Although his enormous physical stature might make him look tough, he is actually
quite gentle, and the idea of showing up his coaches was horri-
fying to him. He believed wholeheartedly in his new swing, and
in Schenck, but he also cared deeply about the people around
him on the Yankees, and he was too polite and respectful to ever
publicly indicate that he might not agree with their ideas about
swinging a baseball bat.

It left Judge in an uncomfortable position, trying to walk the
line between being gracious toward the Yankees coaches trying

to help him while also maintaining a commitment to the swing he had learned from Schenck, the swing he believed in. Finding that balance was the most challenging part of all for Judge, even more challenging than figuring out how to *snap it!*

"When I first started doing it, there was a lot of negative feedback from it, people saying, 'It won't work, you shouldn't do it,'" Judge told Marc Carig of *The Athletic* in May 2018. "But you've just got to have faith. It's my career. It's nobody else's career. If I'm going to fail, I'd rather fail my way."

There were some crises of faith at the beginning. After a bad game or two, he couldn't help but wonder if the critics were right: maybe his remade swing wasn't going to work and he should revert back to what he was doing before. That would have been the safe approach. But Judge stuck with it, and by the end of spring training he had hit .333 with three home runs in 63 at-bats, beating out Aaron Hicks for the everyday job in right field.

The regular season started a bit slow, with Judge going two for his first 15. His swing needed a tune-up, especially with outside pitches, which he felt were causing him to roll over and hit weak grounders. So he texted Schenck, who rushed to New York to work directly with Judge in person on an off-day at a batting cage in Manhattan. Together, they focused on keeping Judge's barrel under the ball so he could lift outside pitches to the opposite field instead of pulling them on the ground. The next day, facing Jumbo Díaz of the Rays, Judge hit a line-drive single up the middle that was measured at 116.5 miles per hour off the bat. The hit nearly killed Díaz, who moved his head out of the way at the last possible second. There were only 31 balls hit harder all season. Eleven of those came off Judge's bat. By the end of April, Judge's batting average was .303. The rest is history.

Judge and Schenck reconnected intermittently throughout

the 2017 season. In the second half, Judge sank into a dreadful slump, hitting just .185 in a 55-game stretch. A shoulder injury that would require off-season surgery was the main culprit. Even when he was able to play, the discomfort led to bad habits, and his swing mechanics deteriorated.

With Judge reeling, the Yankees sent Schenck videos of Judge swinging that were unavailable to the public, so that Schenck could diagnose any problems from a more conducive angle than what's shown on television. The two worked together in person a few more times. The Yankees hadn't necessarily come around on Schenck, but they knew that Judge, who had very much established himself as the best hitter on the team, was all in with him. If Judge thought Schenck made him better, it behooved the Yankees to be quiet and get out of the way. Judge eventually snapped out of his funk, of course, even hitting four home runs in the playoffs, which ended in a seven-game loss to the Astros in the American League Championship Series. Shortly thereafter, Judge was the unanimous choice for Rookie of the Year. He had arrived.

The next time I got in the batting cage with Richard Schenck was in July 2018. The Teacherman was spending a week in New Jersey running a clinic at the Gamers Baseball Academy in Kenilworth. Two days later, he was planning to fly to Cleveland at Aaron Judge's request. Judge needed a tune-up.

These sorts of calls were becoming more frequent. I had spent some time with Schenck in New York about three weeks earlier under similar circumstances. "Emergency call yesterday," Schenck texted me one day. "On a plane now." Schenck had been on vacation with his family in Colorado when he heard from Judge. His vacation ended early.

These "emergency calls" were actually a little more complicated than they might seem. Schenck isn't a team employee, so he can't work with Judge at Yankee Stadium. The grind of a Major League Baseball season doesn't exactly leave a lot of free time either. So Judge and Schenck devised a solution: they would meet at midnight, after games, to fix Judge's swing in secret, in a private setting where nobody would bother them. To make this happen, Schenck would convince the owner of a baseball facility to open the doors for him and Judge late at night. Considering the star power of the unexpected guest, it wasn't too difficult to find somebody willing to oblige.

On this night, the Yankees had played a particularly long game—3 hours, 28 minutes—and had a 1:00 p.m. first pitch scheduled for the next afternoon. But that didn't stop Judge from trekking to the Upper West Side to meet Schenck, who quickly pointed out some issues with Judge's swing mechanics. He wasn't coiling one of his legs enough. The result was a swing driven by his arms rather than his lower body, where power is generated. Afterward, Judge seemed pleased. About 12 hours later, he homered off Mariners ace James Paxton.

"It was the quickest session we've had," Schenck told me later. "I traveled 10 hours for a 20-minute session."

Aaron Judge—Aaron freaking Judge—not only credited Schenck with repairing his swing, but *flew him around the country whenever he thought he needed help*. Many hitters FaceTime with their coach for a fix during the season. Lots of players would meet up with Craig Wallenbrock or Doug Latta when their teams visited Los Angeles or Anaheim. But it is, to say the least, unusual to fly in a guru for a midnight hitting rendezvous.

I still didn't feel that I had personally figured out the gospel according to Schenck, which is why I found myself in a batting cage in Kenilworth with the man himself that afternoon in July.

I brought batting gloves this time—Mike Trout's model, figuring that maybe if I wore gloves bearing his name a smidgeon of his otherworldly hitting ability might rub off on me. But of course, Schenck didn't want me to hit baseballs with a bat. That would be too normal. Instead, he pulled out one of his favorite tools: a PVC pipe.

Schenck set a ball on a tee in front of me. Not a baseball, mind you. A Wiffle ball. The object of this first drill, I was told, was to hold the pipe in the middle and then aggressively twist it counterclockwise so that the bottom—the equivalent of the knob on the bat—hit the ball. This was *snapping it!* Apparently. At least, that's what Schenck was telling me. If I could hit the Wiffle ball by snapping the bottom of a PVC pipe upward, I could be a great hitter or something.

Well, guess what: I couldn't. Most of the time, I flat-out missed the ball. Occasionally, by the grace of God, I'd graze the ball with the pipe every few swings—could I even call what I was doing "swinging?"—and it would trickle away, pitifully. This happened, Schenck said, because I didn't trust in the snap. Instead of *snapping it*, I was dropping my hands and trying to push them at the ball. He talked a lot about trusting the snap. I told him I did trust it. In reality, I wasn't really sure what he was talking about.

After a few minutes of embarrassing myself, Schenck decided that perhaps we should start with something else, since his lesson in snapping wasn't going too well. So instead, we decided to work on what he calls the "stretch," or "tilt." It involves leaning back toward the catcher and stretching against and around the rear leg. This was another central tenet of the Teacherman swing: first the tilt and then the *snap!* On these swings—again, was I actually swinging?—Schenck told me to imagine there was a laser on the knob of the pipe. I should think about slicing the ball in half with the laser. (Not long after we met, Schenck created a bat with a red light in the knob so that his hitters could actually see it while training.)

The tilting drill went a little better than the snapping drill. That doesn't mean it went well, because it surely didn't, but it was a little less pathetic, which meant it was time for the main event: me swinging a baseball bat and hitting actual baseballs. The way Schenck described it, the ideal swing involved tilting back first with the body and then *snapping* with the hands. If done correctly, the knob of the bat goes up and the barrel of the bat automatically follows right through the zone, resulting in solid contact. And here's the thing: as I hit—first off the tee, then with Schenck flipping balls underhand from a few feet away—I sort of, kind of understood it. If I snapped the knob with enough force, the barrel did in fact end up in the right place. In some ways, it wasn't that different from what the other Swing Kings talked about. Wallenbrock called it the "lag position." Tewksbary referred to it as a rearward motion. The common idea among all of these coaches was that the ideal swing doesn't involve pushing the barrel down and forward to strike the ball, but moving the barrel backward first to generate momentum behind the ball and connect with it on an upward plane. Schenck simply took it the furthest, essentially instructing his pupils to swing backward in order to hit the ball forward. It felt strange. It felt unnatural. I understood why some people didn't buy in.

Afterward, I started to wonder about Schenck's ideas about the swing. I saw how, theoretically, *snapping it* could create immense power. But it seemed to require immense strength to snap fast enough for the barrel to wind up in the hitting zone— strength that somebody like, say, Aaron Judge possesses but not many others.

As I dejectedly packed up my stuff and prepared to depart, I saw a couple of high school kids take my place in the cage with Schenck. They were doing the exact same drills I had been doing. Except when they did it, their bats whipped through the zone at lightning speed and the ball exploded into the top of the cage. Maybe Schenck wasn't the problem. Maybe I was.

THE YEAR THE REVOLUTION NEARLY DIED

If 2015 was a rocket ship for Bobby Tewksbary's professional life, shooting him to the stratosphere in the realm of hitting, 2016 was the equivalent of falling back to earth without a parachute.

In the winter before the 2016 season, Tewksbary was in high demand. Many Blue Jays players naturally sought him out after seeing Donaldson's and Colabello's success. The team even gave Tewksbary permission to hit with players at the team's facilities in Florida, though he didn't technically work for them. Maybe he should, they thought: the Jays were one of multiple teams to speak with Tewksbary that winter about coming on board in some sort of hitting consultant role.

"I wanted to win a World Series as a player. Can't do it as a player? Let's win it as a coach," Tewksbary said. "And I'm working with guys, I feel like I'm contributing and helping at that level of the game, which is incredibly exciting."

That was the pinnacle—followed by the plunge: by the start of the 2016 season, less than a year after Donaldson invited Tewksbary to pitch to him in the Home Run Derby, the two were no longer speaking.

What happened really isn't all that juicy. Tewksbary alienated some in the Blue Jays organization by making an absurdly high salary request, far more than the typical big league hitting coach earns, which is usually in the low-six-figure range. His negotiations with their executives wound up falling apart.

Tewksbary said he asked for so much money to compensate for having to close his business, uproot his life (and new bride), and take a job that would force him to travel six months a year. He also feared that a team would hire him, obtain his information and coaching philosophy, and then cut him loose. He never expected the Blue Jays to accept his demand, Tewksbary said, though naïveté and bravado likely played into how he handled the situation.

Whatever the case, the entire ordeal didn't sit well with Donaldson, who felt that Tewksbary was inappropriately leveraging their association, taking too much credit for his success at the plate, and being a little too eager, after the Home Run Derby, to play into the public perception that he was Donaldson's savior, the reason Donaldson had turned into a great hitter, when in reality he was only a part of it.

Tewksbary denies that he ever portrayed himself as the primary reason for Donaldson's transformation, but even if it was a misunderstanding, it led, at least in part, to their falling-out. Tewksbary removed Donaldson's testimonial from his website. The two haven't spoken in years.

Tewksbary and Donaldson might not have had a future together, but nothing could erase their past, which continued to intrigue. On April 13, 2016, baseball writer Gabe Lacques of *USA Today* published "From Gurus to Grainy Video, New Information Age Dawns for MLB Sluggers," an article describing Tewksbary's ascension and his work with Colabello and Donaldson. The story said that Tewksbary's "fingerprints were all over the major leagues' most prolific offense in 2015."

Donaldson wasn't quoted in the piece. Tewksbary was, and read now, knowing that he and Donaldson weren't speaking at the time, it's obvious that he was trying to avoid saying something that could be perceived as taking any sort of credit for Donaldson's success. The one thing he said about Donaldson was in regard to the Home Run Derby: "It was a very unique and special opportunity," he told Lacques. "And I'll be forever grateful to Josh."

Nonetheless, the whole thing was difficult for Tewksbary. He spoke with Lacques from Tropicana Field in St. Petersburg, Florida, where he was visiting Colabello for the Jays' opening series against the Rays. The interview was conducted by phone, but the paper also wanted a picture for the piece, so the photographer had Tewksbary stand in the dugout to pose for it. Tewksbary agreed, reluctantly. The entire time he kept looking over his shoulder, praying that Donaldson wouldn't come out of the clubhouse and see him there. Mercifully, he didn't.

That wasn't the end of Tewksbary's press tour either. On May 10, 2016, MLB Network invited him to appear as a guest on *MLB Now,* a program devoted to discussing the day's baseball issues from an analytical perspective. Tewksbary appeared for about six minutes, conducting an interview with host Brian Kenny and former first baseman Sean Casey. Naturally, the first 30 seconds of the segment featured—what else?—a highlight reel of Josh Donaldson. Kenny introduced Tewksbary as a "hitting guru to the stars." During the interview, however, Tewksbary avoided almost all mention of Donaldson. Instead, he focused on the swing itself.

"The bat's going to be working back, getting on plane as deep as possible so that it's going to enter the zone as deep as possible," Tewksbary said, attempting to distill what he had learned about the swing into one sentence for a national television audience.

This was—and in many ways still is—life for Bobby Tewks-bary: Publicly, he is known as Josh Donaldson's hitting guy, and he probably always will be. Privately, he most certainly is not that.

Bobby Tewksbary considers 2016 the worst year of his professional life. Chris Colabello considers it perhaps the worst of his life period—especially considering, for him as for Tewksbary, the incredible high of the year before.

The season started great. Colabello, now set as the Blue Jays' everyday first baseman following his brilliant 2015 campaign, jumped out to a hot start in spring training. He was approaching salary arbitration for the first time, which was likely to lead to life-changing money. To date, Colabello had earned roughly $1 million in the majors—nothing to snark at, but still a relative pittance by big league standards. Now Colabello had his sights set on a major contract extension that would keep him in Toronto for the rest of his career. Brian Charles, Colabello's agent, had flown down to Florida to broach the subject with the Blue Jays' management.

On March 13, after a short day at the team facility in Florida, Colabello and Charles went to lunch at a nearby Applebee's. Colabello's phone rang with a number he didn't recognize. Typically he ignored such calls and waited to see if the person on the other end of the line would leave a voice mail, but this day he was in a good mood. He decided he would answer it and use a funny voice to mess around with what he assumed was a telemarketer.

Instead, it was Bob Lenaghan, an attorney for the Major League Baseball Players' Association.

"Chris," Lenaghan said, "I'm afraid I have some bad news."

Colabello's mind immediately jumped to tragedy. Colabello was the Blue Jays' player representative to the union; he wondered if something had happened to Tony Clark, the union's executive director. Suffice it to say, Clark was fine.

"Sorry to tell you," Lenaghan said, "but you failed your spring training drug test."

At first, Colabello says he assumed it had to be some sort of prank. "Seriously, what's up?" he asked. "Seriously," Lenaghan responded. "I'm not joking."

Colabello froze. For the first time since he learned to speak, he couldn't find any words. Then suddenly, all of the words in his brain came spewing out at the same time, to the point that to Lenaghan it sounded mostly like gobbledygook.

"I don't know what somebody's reaction would be if they got caught with their hand in the cookie jar," Colabello told me. "But it couldn't have been this one. It couldn't have been, because it was raw. It was real."

Charles, Colabello's agent, eventually took the phone to try to figure out what was happening, because Colabello was in no state to continue the conversation at that point. Whatever the case, no amount of negotiation, protest, or genuine shock could change the truth: Colabello's urine tested positive for dehydrochloromethyltestosterone, an anabolic steroid also known as Turinabol that was famously used by East German Olympians. Trace amounts of the M4 metabolite found in his system had triggered the positive test.

Officially, the penalty would be an 80-game unpaid suspension, but in reality the punishment would be even worse: news of the failed drug test would undermine Colabello's entire journey up to that point in the eyes of the baseball world. The changes he had made to his swing with Bobby Tewksbary would be ignored. He was a lifetime independent league player who had just made it big in the majors. Of course he had done it by cheating. It made too much sense—way more sense than the idea that remaking his swing from scratch with a random guy in New Hampshire had turned him into a major league masher.

There had to have been some kind of mistake, Colabello thought. He was the guy who would have smoothie shops double-rinse the blender before serving him. He was the guy who would cross to the other side of the corridor whenever he passed a GNC at the mall so he "wouldn't breathe the damn air," he said. And yet he had tested positive, and his life was now careening in a way he never could have imagined.

The first step was to meet with representatives from the players' union to review any supplements he had taken. He said that all he ever took was a whey protein supplement, a multivitamin, and the occasional probiotic, all manufactured by the company Klean Athlete. The meeting lasted about three hours. Colabello says he cried for two and a half of them. When he did speak, he told them that he had voluntarily gone in for his spring training drug test five days early, praying that somehow this information would absolve him.

"It's the one drug test you know you're going to have," Colabello said. "Who the fuck fails the drug test that you know you're going to have? You have to be stupid."

But Colabello had failed it. Prepared to fight for his good name, he immediately filed an appeal, which allowed him to keep playing until the time came to present himself to an independent arbiter. In the interim, he did his research. It didn't take long for Colabello to discover that Turinabol was an old-fashioned steroid that was relatively easy for modern technology to catch, not some fancy designer drug created to evade testing.

"To find this stuff in today's day and age, you need to know the guy that knows the guy that knows the guy, and I don't even know the first guy," Colabello said. "So how the hell could I have gotten it?"

Over the next few weeks, Colabello had every substance and vitamin he was taking independently tested, in case a batch was tainted. He and Tewksbary pored over his credit card statement so they could check in with every restaurant he had eaten at. He tested medication that his mother and his dog were taking. He had his puppy's blood and urine tested. He spoke with somebody from Aegis Sciences Corporation in Nashville, Tennessee, to see if anybody there had insight into whether false positives with the M4 metabolite were possible.

Through it all, Colabello was still playing baseball, and it wasn't going well. He shut himself off from the world, instructed by the MLBPA to keep his positive test confidential during the appeal process. There was one time when his mom emailed him from the next room, offering support if he wanted to talk about what was bothering him, not knowing what was weighing on Colabello's mind. There was another time when one of his teammates, shortstop Troy Tulowitzki, came up to him and said, "CC, get your fucking head out of your ass. What the fuck is wrong with you?"

A lot was wrong, it turns out, and it showed on the field. With the specter of a suspension looming, Colabello went 2-for-29 to start the 2016 season. On April 22, with Colabello's appeal denied, MLB announced his suspension. Colabello's agent had called the Blue Jays' front office to warn them of what was coming, but Colabello took the step of personally speaking with general manager Ross Atkins, manager John Gibbons, and bench coach DeMarlo Hale. He called his teammates together and "cried my face off in front of those guys, which was the most embarrassing thing I had to do in my career," he said. He released a public statement that said, in part, "I have spent every waking moment since that day trying to find an answer as to why or how. The only thing I know is that I would never compromise the integrity of the game of baseball. I love this game too much!" By the end of the day, he had more than 300 text messages on his phone from family, friends, and acquaintances saying they supported him.

Chris Colabello hasn't played an inning in the major leagues since his suspension. As of 2019, he was back in indie ball, playing for the Kansas City T-Bones of the American Association. What was once the ultimate feel-good story has fizzled out.

But for Colabello himself, the story was just beginning. Since his suspension, Colabello has spent his life working not just to clear his name, but to help others avoid ending up in the same position. It turns out that, as Colabello was going through his troubles, he wasn't alone. Over the past few years, other players have tested positive for DHMCT and then insisted they had done nothing wrong, including Cody Stanley, Daniel Stumpf, Alec Asher, Boog Powell, and Thomas Pannone. To counter the belief that all of them cheated, they have banded together, hoping to prove their innocence.

Chris Colabello will go to his grave swearing he never used PEDs, and he insists that he won't rest until he is completely exonerated. Along with many of the other players who tested positive, he continues to search for the scientific proof that will vindicate him. It won't be enough to save Colabello's playing career, but he hopes that finding that proof will help future players.

Is Colabello telling the truth when he says he never took PEDs? It's impossible to know for sure. But when he makes his case, he's certainly convincing.

Here's what I do know with complete certainty: with the help of Bobby Tewksbary, Colabello reshaped his swing and his production improved. The changes were real, and they were meaningful. Chances are that baseball will always view him, fairly or unfairly, as a cheater. That doesn't change the fact that he was and always will be one of the most important people in the fly-ball revolution. But sometimes these stories don't have happy endings.

"Am I an idiot for wanting to climb the mountain my whole life?" Colabello said. "I get there, and it's, 'Fuck you, game. Here I am! I am here to stay.' And then that happens. It's a kick in the nuts."

Chris Colabello wasn't the only swing-changer whose career was upended in 2016.

While Justin Turner was ascending with the help of Doug Latta, the man who introduced them, Marlon Byrd was just trying to hang on. His stunning turnaround in 2013 was enough to earn him a two-year contract with the Phillies worth $16 million, a remarkable development considering his age and where he was just two years earlier.

When he arrived in Philadelphia, his confidence was soaring. It may have been soaring a little too high.

"I was thinking, 'Oh, I'm going to hit 100 homers,'" Byrd said. "It was the wrong mind-set. Then the cockiness came in."

The result was a notable decline in production. His batting average fell to .264, down from .291 the year before with the Mets and Pirates. His OPS dropped from .847 to .757. But one aspect of his game remained: the power he had never experienced before meeting Latta and reshaping his swing. He blasted 25 home runs in 2014, a career high, proving that he still had something to offer and that the Latta-approved swing he had debuted in 2013 was no fluke. Byrd spent 2015 with the Reds and Giants after being traded from the Phillies, and while his average sank even more, to .247, he still managed to hit 23 homers as a 37-year-old.

Nonetheless, Byrd knew he was reaching the end. The market for his services as a free agent in the winter before the 2016 season demonstrated as much. He was unemployed until March 18, just a couple of weeks before opening day, when the Indians brought him to spring training on a minor league contract. Byrd had been here before. He'd had his big breakout with the Mets in 2013 after coming to camp on a minor league deal. He didn't have much time to show the Indians that he could still play, but he took advantage of the opportunities he did receive, going 9-for-31 with six doubles, enough to earn a spot as a backup outfielder on the opening-day roster.

That's when everything came crashing down for Marlon Byrd.

Byrd played well enough in his first two months in Cleveland, hitting .270 with five home runs in 115 at-bats. But news broke on June 1 that, in the eyes of many in the baseball community, immediately undid everything he had accomplished over the past few seasons: he tested positive for Ipamorelin, a growth hormone–releasing peptide. Because Byrd was now a second-time offender, the punishment was a 162-game suspension.

When the penalty came out, Byrd released a statement saying that ever since his suspension for tamoxifen—which he never denied taking—he had been careful about what he put in his body and that he "had no intention of taking any banned substances." He retained legal counsel and hired a biochemist in an effort to uncover the source of the positive test, insisting, "I never knowingly ingested Ipamorelin." One of his attorneys released a statement attributing the positive test to a tainted supplement. But because Byrd did acknowledge taking supplements that weren't on the "NSF Certified for Sport" list, he did not appeal the suspension.

In my extended interview with Byrd for this book in the summer of 2018, he offered the same explanation.

"I would be a dumb-ass to take Ipamorelin," Byrd told me. "I did everything I could. I went and hired my own biochemist and tested all of my stuff. Everything came up clean. But it doesn't mean anything. You have to figure out why you tested positive, and that's what I couldn't do."

For Byrd, getting popped for PEDs again was a baseball death sentence. There was no chance of him ever playing again. To many, his explanation rang hollow, given his past. In spring training with the Mets, as he was coming back from his first PED suspension, Byrd famously said, "I think you have to be an idiot to test positive, and I was one of those idiots." Now he had tested positive again, which meant that, even if he wasn't consciously cheating, he was at the very least an idiot two separate times.

The pitchers Byrd had tormented since his post-Latta resurgence weren't particularly thrilled either. Justin Verlander, an outspoken critic of players caught using PEDs, tweeted out an angry emoji. Dan Haren asked if he could get back all the home runs Byrd had hit off him, and he wasn't exactly kidding. Jeremy Guthrie, in a tweet, called Byrd "a joke." That's what Byrd will have to live with—the knowledge that, despite his protestations, he will be forever known as the player who was suspended for PEDs twice.

"The second one was BS," Byrd said. "It was a huge shock to me *because* it was BS."

In many ways, it doesn't matter whether Byrd meant to use PEDs or not—to anybody besides Byrd himself at least. What matters is that his suspension put a major dent in the momentum of the fly-ball revolution. In the span of about six weeks, two of the key faces in the swing-change movement, Colabello and Byrd, had been suspended.

Given that, it was natural to start considering a disquieting possibility: maybe the work they had done with their outside swing gurus wasn't the reason for their offensive renaissances at all. Maybe the reason they hit so well all of a sudden was more artificial, more sinister. Maybe it wasn't that people like Doug Latta and Bobby Tewksbary knew a lot about the swing, but that they knew a good chemist. This was, admittedly, a cynical viewpoint, but also a giant plate of juicy red meat for those who doubted the revolution. Not long afterwards, one MLB general manager told me that he discouraged his team's players from going to outside hitting gurus because of the perception that their success stories were driven by drugs, not mechanics.

"The hardest part for me was how it compromised people I'm close with," Colabello said. "That's what shattered me. Bobby stands within that category."

For Byrd, it was particularly difficult. He said he tried to distance himself from Latta in order to protect the coach whom he credits with changing his career. Latta said Byrd's suspension left him shocked. But Latta wasn't the only one Byrd was associated with: he was also associated with Justin Turner, who had made no secret of working closely with Byrd and who attributed his turnaround with the Dodgers to Byrd's guidance.

"There's some ugliness that I've put on him," Byrd said.

Ultimately, nobody knows whether Marlon Byrd intentionally used Ipamorelin besides Marlon Byrd. There will never be any irrefutable evidence that either absolves him or proves his guilt. You can choose to believe him, or not.

Regardless, Marlon Byrd's swing changed in 2013 after he worked with Doug Latta. Anybody can see it, plain as day, immortalized right there on the videotape. That much is evident with the naked eye. To say that the swing changes aren't real would be willfully ignorant.

"That's what the naysayers are going to do," Latta said. "But there's enough proof to show that the actual physical changes that were made are real."

There's no question that Byrd getting suspended was a bad moment for the revolution. But it didn't kill it. Nothing could.

STARDOM

As Marlon Byrd shrank from the public spotlight in the wake of his second PED suspension, Justin Turner was struggling. He hit just .220 in his first 57 games of 2016. The swing he had perfected with Doug Latta was out of whack.

In the past, during a slump like this, Turner would run back to Latta for help. In the sanctuary of the Ball Yard, the two of them would diagnose and resolve the problem. But over the past couple of years something incredible had happened: Turner didn't need Latta anymore to figure out the flaws in his swing. He could do it himself, because he now possessed a better understanding of what made his swing work than any coach could ever have.

That's not to say that Turner had moved on from Latta. The two continued to talk and text, sharing thoughts and ideas. Turner would ask Latta what he was seeing in his swing, seeking feedback from another pair of eyes he trusted in case he was missing something when he watched video of himself. The difference, Latta said, was that early on in their relationship Turner relied on him and looked to him for help when things were going badly. By 2016, Turner was largely self-sufficient. "That," Latta said, "is every coach's dream."

After the slow start, Turner found his stroke that season.

Doug Latta smiling at the Ball Yard, with his star pupil on the monitor behind him.

He finished the regular season with a .275 average and 27 homers, the third straight year he had set a new career high.

Turner figured things out at the perfect time. When the 2016 season ended—in a loss to the Cubs in the NL Championship Series—Turner was officially a free agent. His last time on the open market came because the Mets released him. Nobody wanted him. Now he was coveted, with teams across baseball bidding for his services.

The result was a contract ensuring him generational wealth. On December 23, 2016, he signed a four-year contract with the Dodgers worth $64 million, money that not only all but guaranteed his financial future but validated everything he had done over the past few years.

When the Mets had cut Turner, he was approaching his 30th birthday and his career was foundering. The idea that he would one day sign a contract like this was more than improbable—it was laughable. Turner had said himself that he knew nothing about hitting. Nothing. Now he was a poster child of a revolution, and he wasn't slowing down.

In 2017, his first season after signing his big contract, Turner had perhaps his best year yet. Despite a hamstring injury that kept him out about a month, he finished the regular season with a .322 batting average, 21 homers, and a career-best .945 OPS. That postseason, he delivered what is to this day his signature moment: a walk-off home run in game 2 of the NLCS against the Cubs, coming 29 years to the day after Kirk Gibson's famous homer off Dennis Eckersley in game 1 of the 1988 World Series. A year later, Turner again hit a game-winning homer in game 2 of the NLCS, this time against the Brewers, helping power the Dodgers to their second consecutive pennant.

This will be Turner's legacy: his .310 batting average and .931 OPS in 54 postseason games through 2019 established him as one of the great October performers. He accomplished that by trusting his swing to an outsider on the fringes of baseball.

"Where would J.T. be if there was no Doug Latta?" Marlon Byrd said.

I asked Turner that very question one day as we sat at a table in the middle of the Dodgers' clubhouse at their spring training facility in Arizona. He considered it for a bit, then delivered an answer that was more thoughtful than I had expected. I figured Turner would lament the fact that he hadn't met Latta earlier. If he had, he'd probably be a lot richer. He certainly wouldn't have had to claw his way up from the bottom. He'd have played on more All-Star teams and won more awards.

Turner saw it a little differently. He reflected on the entirety of his journey, including the fact that he had made it all the way to the major leagues with a broken swing. He had taught himself to hit that way. He learned how to control the strike zone and how to handle the bat. He developed the grind-it-out mentality that he still brings with him to the plate every single time he steps into the box.

"Honestly, I think it was good to be able to not have the best swing and figure out a way to have success," he said. "I don't know, because I don't want to say that high school kids shouldn't start learning to hit, so it's a fine line."

Justin Turner had walked it. He had become a star.

Aaron Judge followed up his unbelievable 2017 season with another All-Star campaign in 2018. Though a broken wrist limited him to 498 plate appearances, he still managed to blast 27 home runs and post a .919 OPS. In 2019, he homered 27 times in 378 at-bats. He has further cemented himself as one of the premier sluggers in baseball, and there is almost certainly a nine-figure contract coming to him at some point before too long. Judge's future looks all but certain.

The bigger question is what the future looks like for Richard Schenck. Despite Judge's overwhelming success, Schenck remains controversial in the hitting community, both inside professional baseball and on the internet. That might come as a bit of a surprise, considering that Schenck had extremely positive results working with a player who has become one of the game's best hitters. There are lots of self-proclaimed swing gurus. Only Richard Schenck helped fix Aaron Judge.

Several teams have spoken with Schenck over the past couple of years about the possibility of bringing him aboard. During my reporting for this book, in fact, one major league general manager asked me for his phone number so the team could reach out to him and see if he could be an asset.

The problem with Schenck has never been about his knowledge. There is no doubt that he has progressive, high-level ideas about the swing and that, when he finds the right fit with a willing pupil, the results can be transcendent. Judge is proof of that. He called Schenck a "career-changer," and he isn't the only player who believes that. Nobody can ever take that away from Schenck.

Unfortunately, visiting the Teacherman hasn't worked for everybody. This in itself isn't necessarily alarming. Every hitting coach, even Craig Wallenbrock, has had experience with players whom they simply couldn't reach. Some hitters lack the athleticism or natural hand-eye coordination to become elite. Some have problems with their vision or with pitch recognition. Some have poor command of the strike zone. Some lack the mental fortitude to produce in the pressure cooker of the major leagues. And some fail for no discernible reason at all. Hitting, especially at the highest level of baseball on earth, is more than just mechanics. (I had been learning that myself!)

Lars Anderson, who played 30 games for the Red Sox from 2010 through 2012, explained this phenomenon perfectly. In a piece he wrote for *The Athletic* in August 2018, he described his own experience visiting Wallenbrock and Robert Van Scoyoc in the hopes of remaking his swing for the 2013 season.

"My rational brain agreed with everything they had said, as it should: They were making inarguable points," he wrote. "But what was my ego saying? How did I 'feel' about Craig and Robert's observations? My ego fucking hated it and I felt terrible. Even though I knew I needed help with my swing (or why else would I be there?), a large part of me was rejecting their insight despite it being 100% on point."

After working with Wallenbrock and Van Scoyoc, Anderson hit worse than he ever had before and was released.

In Schenck's case, the disappointments were a bit more high-profile and notable. Take Kole Calhoun, who worked with Schenck before his 2018 season with the Angels in the hopes of changing his swing and improving his consistency at the plate. Instead, Calhoun completely fell apart, hitting just .145 in 173 at-bats before an oblique injury landed him on the disabled list. The effect of his work with Schenck was the opposite of what he intended, with 56 percent of his batted balls through May going onto the ground, far above his career rate of 42 percent. That August he told Ben Lindbergh of *The Ringer* that despite his efforts to hit more balls in the air, "the way I was trying to do it wasn't the correct way." Calhoun never mentioned Schenck by name, but his production improved after he spent time, while injured, re-remaking his swing with the Angels' hitting coaches.

Asked about Calhoun's dismal start and apparent resurgence after abandoning Schenck's teachings, Schenck pointed to Calhoun's spring training, when he went 18-for-51 (.353) with five extra-base hits. He was doing it right then, Schenck insisted, and then he lost the feel and never got it back. Perhaps. But in an article by Jeff Fletcher of the *Orange County Register,* Calhoun said he "kind of got lucky" during the Cactus League slate. Calhoun told me that he had no hard feelings toward Schenck, but the two didn't connect and he had to look elsewhere for help.

There are others who failed to explode after working with Schenck. Ian Happ of the Cubs, who connected with Schenck in the middle of the 2016 season, saw his OPS plunge from .842 in 2017 to .761 in 2018. Because the Cubs believed he needed a demotion to work out his swing, he began the 2019 season in Triple A, and didn't return to Chicago until late July. "You can get really carried away with some of that stuff," Happ said. "I got to a point where I was trying to get the bat moving backwards so suddenly that I was really late. I was doing it to such an extreme that I created holes that I didn't previously have."

Granted, none of this is to say that these players' struggles were necessarily because of Schenck. There are lots of success stories out there as well, Judge chief among them. Schenck pointed out that he has worked more than 100 hours in person with Judge and more than 50 hours with Scott Kingery. With Happ, less than 15, as of late 2019. Regardless, multiple players who worked with Schenck said that his commitment to his beliefs about the swing sometimes hurts players, because he doesn't adapt what he teaches to the individual. Either you fit in his box or you're wrong.

"It doesn't work for everyone," Rob Refsnyder said. "I think there's universal truths in the swing, and I think Rich understands a lot of those. And I think he is good for a lot of people, and unfortunately, sometimes, some guys might take a lot of the stuff and maybe go in a negative direction."

"It's sink or swim," said Lane Adams, an outfielder who first discovered Schenck in 2016. "You have to use his terminology. That was the thing for me. Everybody perceives things differently, and not every one thing connects for everybody the same. But you have to use his terminology, or he'll freak out."

All that said, it's possible that none of that would matter if Schenck hadn't alienated so many people on Twitter.

After receiving a formal endorsement from Judge, Schenck's life changed forever. He was no longer "Rich from the Basement," a dude behind a computer without a real identity, a father searching for answers. He was Richard Schenck, swing guru for the stars. Yet even with his newfound status, his combative, abrasive, inappropriate, and at times straight-up offensive online personality persisted. He'd call other people "losers" and "idiots." He attacked their ideas. He would pick fights with anybody and everybody, most of whom had never worked with a single major leaguer, let alone one as successful as Judge.

Schenck had a particularly bitter feud with Driveline, the data-driven performance center outside of Seattle. He tweeted constantly at Jason Ochart, Driveline's hitting chief, badgering him to the point of harassment. The feud came to a fever pitch in August 2018, when Schenck tweeted that he would pay for any Driveline hitter to visit him in St. Louis, plus an additional $1,000, so he could prove that he knew more than what Ochart taught. (Ochart responded that if Schenck had an extra $1,000 lying around, he should give it back to Calhoun for ruining his season.)

"He is hated on the internet. Like, there are people out there who want him to be harmed," Ochart said. "He has what every private hitting coach dreams about, and he's going to go shit it away."

For the players who have worked with Schenck, his internet behavior is especially frustrating because it doesn't reflect the Richard Schenck they know. After a few Skype sessions with Schenck, including one with Happ, Adams decided to meet Schenck in person in St. Louis after being promoted from Double A Tennessee to Triple A Iowa in 2016. He said Schenck was kind and gentle, which is exactly how everybody who has met him in real life describes him. And while Adams prefers working with Craig Wallenbrock and Robert Van Scoyoc, he said Schenck was helpful and has smart ideas about the swing. The problem, Adams said, is that being associated with Schenck isn't worth the trouble.

"He's such an asshole online you don't want to give him the time," Adams said. "I want to tell him, 'You don't have to be a dick. Your stuff is good. You're good.'"

Indeed, plenty of players still think so, as evidenced by how many still reach out to Schenck, both for work on Skype and in person. Scott Kingery is one of them. He thinks Schenck has played a key role in his career and he continues to believe in him. After struggling in his rookie season with the Phillies in 2018, Kingery broke out in 2019, hitting 19 home runs in 458 at-bats. Schenck is a big part of the reason why.

But Kingery knows that not everybody in the baseball community agrees with Schenck. He just wishes that sometimes Schenck would tone things down on Twitter and focus on what he can control instead of what people on the outside are saying.

Many players get around Schenck's controversial online persona by contacting him privately. In many ways, that includes Judge, who has hardly talked publicly about Schenck at all over the past few years. There was the famous tweet from January 2018, when Judge introduced Schenck to the world and called him a "career-changer." There was a segment a few months later on the YES Network, the Yankees' channel, where Judge mentioned briefly that his agents had brought him to work with a hitting guy named Richard Schenck. And . . . that's been pretty much it. He declined to speak to me for this book.

In the winter before the 2019 season, PSI, the agency that had a relationship with Schenck, reached a crossroad. As much as David Matranga and his colleagues liked Schenck's stuff and believed he helped their clients, the connection was simply becoming bad for business. They were especially concerned about Judge, who had become a phenomenon with many corporate sponsors. They worried that being linked to Schenck ran the risk of damaging his brand.

"If Pepsi would call Judge and say, 'Are you still associated with Rich?' he'd have to say no," Schenck said. "At that point, it affects Aaron. So let's part ways if that's the issue."

Eventually, PSI issued what amounts to an ultimatum, a conversation Matranga described as "real talk." Schenck could continue working with its players as they saw fit, including Judge, under one condition: he had to clean up his act on Twitter. Matranga and his cohorts had told Schenck this before, imploring him, at the very least, to stop attacking people online, even those who instigated the conflict.

"We have to protect the best interest of our clients," Matranga said. "Whoever we associate with, we have to be careful that their values and what they're saying matches with our values."

Matranga had known Schenck for more than a decade at that point, and he knew what he considered to be the real Schenck—not the Schenck from behind a computer screen. He also understood why changing his online behavior wouldn't be as easy a decision for Schenck as it might sound. Schenck had spent years fending off critics and fighting battles on internet forums and social media platforms. He had been attacked and criticized, and he wasn't afraid to fight back. The problem was that sometimes, Schenck fought too hard and crossed a line.

Schenck thought of his Twitter persona as his "filter": it eliminated people who weren't truly serious about working with him. He said that his presence online nets him more clients, keeping his schedule filled with clinics and seminars and lessons with hitters of all ages. He also believes he needs to be able to defend himself from critics. "I am opinionated," he said. "But I don't think I do anything really, really bad." Matranga describes Schenck as "passionate."

Ultimately, Schenck realized that it would be a mistake to burn his bridge with PSI's players. He has no formal business relationship with the agency, but he still works with some of their clients, like Judge and Kingery, as an independent contractor. He and Matranga remain close.

Schenck has not stopped tweeting. His account is still filled with his musings about the swing. He doesn't respond to others as much as he used to, no longer picking fights or taking the bait when fights come to him—most of the time. In late 2019, he signed a lease to open Teacherman's Hitting in St. Peters, Missouri, a membership-based training facility for those interested in learning Schenck's swing.

The hitting coach who may have saved Aaron Judge insists that he is finally at peace.

"I didn't set out to be a guru," he said. "I set out to help my sons. I'm happy. I took serious criticism. Massive. Battled the war of words. Then I was vindicated by Aaron's success. Mission complete. I can go back to being Rich from the Basement."

The last time I visited the Ball Yard was in October 2018, while I was covering the Dodgers' run to the World Series for the *Wall Street Journal*. The setting had changed. In March 2016, Latta had closed the Ball Yard in Chatsworth and reopened it in a facility in Northridge, a few miles to the east. Like the old Ball Yard, it wasn't much, located in a nondescript office park near a Costco, a Best Buy, and an In-N-Out Burger. Inside were two batting cages, a small bathroom, a few old couches, and a workstation where Latta reviewed video. It didn't look like an elite hitting laboratory, but Latta liked it that way.

That summer I'd spent two days at the Ball Yard working with Latta. On one of those days, Marlon Byrd joined us. We'd take a round of batting practice, then go to the monitor to review the tape. Latta would offer a few pointers, and we'd head back to the cage to try to implement them. At one point, he and Byrd suggested I start with my hands lower and closer to my body. For the next 20 minutes, baseballs exploded off my bat. That one piece of advice made an enormous difference, and I haven't deviated from it since.

When I walked in that October, I found Doug Latta inside the batting cage, flipping baseballs to a hitter at the plate. This wasn't a surprise. Latta spends most of his time either in the cage or at the video screen just outside it, reviewing video of swings.

What was surprising was the person he was tossing pitches to. It was Hunter Pence, who had been a successful major league outfielder for 12 seasons, compiling a lifetime .280 batting average and making three All-Star teams during that span. He had spent the last six-plus years with the Giants, and in his final regular-season game in San Francisco he made an emotional farewell speech to the hometown fans—the kind of speech a player makes when he's preparing to ride off into the sunset.

Except Pence wasn't retiring, even with his 36th birthday coming in the first month of the 2019 season. He was trying to re-invent himself. Like Justin Turner and Marlon Byrd before him, Pence decided to hand his swing over to Latta and see where it led him. He had worked with Latta a few times before, hitting with him during the 2018 season as he was recovering from an injury. Pence's interest was only piqued further when his Giants teammate Mac Williamson saw results with Latta.

Pence was always a strange hitter. He seemed to succeed in spite of doing *everything* wrong at the plate. His stance was weird. His swing was weird. He stood at the plate like he had ants crawling up his pants, his limbs all twitchy and jittery and spastic, followed by a choppy, awkward cut. In 2013, *Sports Illustrated* convinced Pence to star in a fake commercial for a pretend youth baseball camp called "Hunter's Hitters." In it, he compared all the extra movement in his swing to "a hungry man chasing a taco."

That made Pence a fascinating challenge for Latta. The goal was to help Pence add lift to his swing without neutering the idiosyncrasies that defined him. Pence's swing would never be conventionally pretty. But it could be more efficient. That was Latta's job. For his part, Pence was all in: he visited the Ball Yard six or seven days a week for two months to remake a swing that had served him well for a long time but could no longer compete against the best pitching in the world.

"It's a massive overhaul with a whole new move," Pence told me. "Doug faces a lot of resistance because there are a lot of people in the game that won't allow players to make that move. I really love the move, and I believe in it."

Pence was just one of many major league hitters who had shown up at Latta's doorstep since his fortuitous encounter with Marlon Byrd in the parking lot six years earlier. Even Mookie Betts, the 2018 AL MVP, had worked with Latta. This was his new reality: players reaching out, asking for time at the Ball Yard, all day, every day, from the moment the season ended until the next spring training began. Latta calls the Ball Yard "a sanctuary." He will not publicly identify his clients unless the player outs him first. But the list is as extensive as it is impressive, and the batting cage is always full. All told, Latta has about 20 big leaguers coming in for regular work, not to mention the many others who stop by for a tune-up.

Latta long dreamed of a day when his and Wallenbrock's ideas would enter the baseball mainstream. Now that day has come.

Latta remains at the forefront, to this point choosing to remain independent and work personally with players rather than join some of his peers in employment on the inside. "I thoroughly enjoy my relationship with my clients," Latta said. "I don't want to jeopardize that with anything like exclusivity or questionable loyalties."

After fighting for acceptance for so long, this much now seems undeniable: Latta's stuff works. He has proven it, with Marlon Byrd, with Justin Turner, and with all of the new students showing up ready to learn. And sometimes he can even teach an old dog some new tricks: after an entire off-season working with Latta and a stint auditioning his new swing in the Dominican Republic, Pence landed a contract with the Rangers. Then something amazing happened: Pence turned back the clock in a way that seemed impossible and reemerged as one of the top hitters in the league. In July of 2019, at age 36, he was named an All-Star starter for the first time in his career, elected as the American League designated hitter. Though a groin strain prevented him from playing, the honor of being chosen was enough. It was his first All-Star selection since 2014. He finished the season with a .297 batting average and a .910 OPS in 83 games. Less than a year earlier, he wasn't even sure if he'd find a job. Then he walked into the Ball Yard to work with Doug Latta.

"What Latta is teaching is the most consistent I've ever felt," Pence said. "It's a really phenomenal movement."

Less than 20 miles up the 5 , Craig Wallenbrock, Doug Latta's old business partner, was watching his own success story with pride.

Not too long before, J. D. Martinez was a baseball afterthought. He had been cut, relegated to the scrap heap of the industry. His career had fizzled out, short-stopping before it had really gone anywhere at all. But by the winter following the 2017 season, all of that felt like a distant memory. He was a bona fide star, having put together four consecutive extraordinary seasons at the plate, and he seemed to be getting better still, even as he crossed his 30th birthday, the age at which players tend to see their production start to decline.

That off-season, Martinez was a free agent again, as he'd been after the Astros cut him in spring training in 2014. Only this time, he wasn't desperate. He was coveted. Even though the market crashed that winter as organizations across baseball retreated from long, expensive contracts for veterans, Martinez came away with a five-year deal with the Red Sox worth $110 million guaranteed. It was a sum of money that a few years earlier would have seemed inconceivable. He had earned every penny of it.

Martinez's debut with Boston was quite possibly his best season yet. He dominated, compiling monster numbers that kept him in the MVP conversation all through the summer and even put him in the running for the Triple Crown in the American League. When the regular season ended, Martinez had compiled a .330 batting average with 43 home runs and 130 RBIs, the most in the major leagues. He helped power the Red Sox to a season for the ages in 2018. They went 108–54, the best regular-season record for any team since the 116-win Mariners of 2001. They powered through the playoffs, knocking off the 100-win Yankees in the division series and the 103-win Astros in the championship series. In the World Series, they quickly dispatched Turner and the Dodgers in five games. Martinez hit .300 with three home runs and 14 RBIs in the playoffs. In the end, the Red Sox won 119 total games, the third-most of any team in history. The 2018 Red Sox were, unequivocally, one of the best teams ever. J. D. Martinez was a big part of the reason why. And therefore so was Craig Wallenbrock.

Wallenbrock spent his entire adult life trying to show the world that there was a better way to swing a baseball bat, that the way it had been taught for decades was wrong. This was a lonely pursuit. For decades, almost nobody listened— but his prize pupil changed all that. As J. D. Martinez's story spread, so too did the gospel of Wallenbrock.

Raúl Ibañez played 19 major league seasons and hit 305 home runs. In 2006, he was briefly a teammate of Joe Borchard's with the Mariners. Ibañez remembers Borchard talking about things like "bat lag" and "staying on plane," terminology he had learned from Wallenbrock. As he heard

J. D. Martinez with the Red Sox, after his Wallenbrock makeover.

Borchard talk, Ibañez suddenly flashed back to conversations he had had years earlier with one of his idols, Mariners slugger Edgar Martínez.

As a young player coming up to the majors, Ibañez asked Martínez how he got on top of the ball, a common baseball phrase that doesn't really mean anything, other than conventional wisdom says you want to do it. Martínez responded, "You don't get on top. You don't swing down. You swing up. The ball is coming downhill, so you swing uphill."

"So I thought what most people would think: my idol, Edgar Martínez, is crazy," Ibañez said.

Now here was Borchard saying essentially the same thing. For a while, Ibañez put it aside. He still was unsure—until three years later, when he was teammates on the Phillies with outfielder Ben Francisco. Like Borchard, Francisco was talking about bat lag and staying on plane, ideas he had learned from Craig Wallenbrock. Ibañez decided he had to meet this mysterious coach and his protégé, Robert Van Scoyoc. They started working together in 2010. One day Ibañez spent six or seven hours around the cage, seeing the duo work with hitter after hitter, ranging from high school players all the way to major league sluggers. He said that for every hitter, no matter their skill level, athletic ability, or experience, you could see a positive change within 10 swings. Ibañez was sold. "I had never seen anything like that before," he said.

In the winter before the 2016 season, the Dodgers hired Ibañez as a special assistant to team president Andrew Friedman. Not long after, Ibañez learned that an American League organization was in discussions to hire Van Scoyoc on an exclusive retainer. Ibañez sprang into action. "I said, 'Don't sign anything. Don't sign anything, don't do anything,'" he said. "If you're going to work somewhere, it has to be here."

Ibañez called Friedman and told him about Van Scoyoc and his mentor. He described them as superstars. Friedman called up Gabe Kapler, then the Dodgers' director of player development. Suddenly, Wallenbrock and Van Scoyoc were working for the Dodgers as consultants. And this time, unlike when Wallenbrock went to work for the White Sox as a hitting consultant more than a decade earlier, management wanted him there. It took until he was about 70 years old, but Craig Wallenbrock, the Oracle of Santa Clarita, was a hitting consultant for a major league organization.

A lot had changed across baseball in the 11 years between Wallenbrock's failed bid at consulting for the White Sox in 2005 and his hiring by the Dodgers in 2016. The biggest difference was the people calling the shots. Ken Williams, the White Sox general manager in 2005, was from the previous paradigm: he had played six seasons in the majors in the 1980s and early '90s before ascending through the front-office ranks.

Then *Moneyball* happened. Billy Beane became a household name. Teams across the industry started looking not for ex-players, but for nerds looking to use their powerful minds to construct the perfect baseball roster. One of them was Friedman: when he became the general manager of the Rays at age 28, he was coming to baseball from the world of high finance and private equity. Before Friedman's promotion for the 2006 season, the Rays had never won more than 70 games in a given year. By 2008, they were in the World Series, and they made the playoffs three more times through 2013, despite having one of the game's lowest payrolls. Friedman went to the Dodgers ahead of the 2015 season to work his magic again, but this time with an astronomical amount of money at his disposal. It has gone well.

The point is that Friedman had recently been an outsider before he crashed into a sport that didn't exactly respond well to people like him. He didn't have the traditional baseball background, but then he showed he could do the job better than virtually anybody else on the planet. Remind you of anyone?

When it came to hiring Wallenbrock, Friedman couldn't have cared less about his previous employment history or the fact that he didn't play professional baseball. History had proven that for generations, baseball teams weren't hiring the best possible people to run their front offices. To Friedman, it made perfect sense that those teams probably weren't hiring the best coaches either. He had even seen it himself: in 2009, one of his players on the

Rays, Ben Zobrist, had a breakout season because, Friedman would eventually discover, he had made a swing change under the eye of somebody outside the organization.

"That was the first time a hitting guy outside of the close-knit infrastructure of major league teams was that instrumental and influential, to my knowledge," Friedman said. "That's when it started piquing my interest, and I started learning more."

So it was settled. Craig Wallenbrock and Robert Van Scoyoc would be Dodgers. Bringing people like them into the fold was a natural evolution from the progress that stemmed from *Moneyball*. And it turns out that Friedman wasn't the only onetime outsider who felt that way.

SWING KINGS

In the winter following the 2018 season, a dam burst. By the end of April in 2019, 17 teams—more than half of Major League Baseball—had a different hitting coach than the one they'd employed the season before. The reason was simple: organizations realized they hadn't been tapping the most qualified people for the job. The rise of technology, the use of data, and improved knowledge of the swing had changed the role, forcing traditional coaches to adapt or die. Seemingly all at once, hitting coaches became younger and more tech-savvy. The idea that the swing should be tailored to drive the ball in the air wasn't a foreign concept to this new batch of hitting coaches—it was simply the truth.

That's why, by 2019, there were 13 major league hitting coaches who hadn't played in the majors themselves. Four of the coaches brought in that off-season were the ultimate interlopers in the baseball brotherhood—they hadn't even played in the minors.

For generations, hitting was taught more or less the same way: hitting coaches, almost exclusively former professional players, passed on the lessons they had learned from their hitting coaches. This cycle of teaching had been in place, uninterrupted and unchanged, for decades. These coaches' ideas weren't based on empirical truths, but simply on what they *believed* had made them talented hitters themselves. Only with improved video review and data analytics did it become abundantly clear that players often have no idea what they actually do at the plate. Alex Rodriguez, for instance, has said in many interviews through the years that he tries to bring the knob of the bat to the ball—to, essentially, "swing down." Albert Pujols says the same thing. In reality, neither player does anything close to that. They get their barrel behind the ball, matching the plane of the pitch, and they swing up through it.

That doesn't mean that what players think isn't valid. Whatever Alex Rodriguez tells himself at the plate is correct for him. The mental cue he gives himself results in a near-perfect swing, and no good coach would ever tell him otherwise. But the fact remains that there is a difference between what many great players tell themselves to do and what they actually do. The new crop of hitting coaches understand that, and they have the technological tools to back it up.

"Hitting was so far behind pitching and so far behind golf as far as the technology and science," said Andy Haines, whom the Brewers hired as their hitting coach before the 2019 season. "We've been able to move to evidence-based teaching from theory-based teaching, people teaching off their opinions. Slowly, we are guessing less than we have ever guessed."

Haines would know. He embodies the new breed of hitting coach sweeping across the league. As a player, he wasn't much, reaching the end of his road after his collegiate career at Eastern Illinois. He was taught what so many people were taught when he was growing up in the 1980s—use your hands, be short to the ball, swing down. And being the ever-coachable kid he was, he worked and worked and worked until he perfected those mechanics. He wouldn't learn until much later that he had spent the first couple of decades of his life practicing something that was incorrect.

The desire to figure out what he had done wrong was what drew him into coaching. Right after graduating, he got a job as an assistant at Olney Central College. From there he moved on to Middle Tennessee State, where he coached and earned a master's degree. Of course he dreamed about one day moving up to professional baseball. It just didn't seem like a realistic goal. "I didn't think people would take me seriously," Haines said. "I saw the people coaching at the professional level, and they weren't guys like me."

But the people in charge were changing. So when Haines had an opportunity to interview for a job in the Marlins organization, the executives there didn't care about where Haines had played. They just wanted to know if he could teach.

Haines worked his way up, managing Marlins farm teams in Jamestown, New York; Greensboro, North Carolina; Jupiter, Florida; and New Orleans before becoming the Cubs' hitting coordinator in 2016. That is the story of a Swing King. "Today's players don't care about your background—they won't even ask you," Haines said. "They just want to know if you can help them or not."

The ascension of Jeff Albert, who was hired as the Cardinals' hitting coach before the 2019 season, was just as improbable. He was, quite possibly, the first coach to be hired into professional baseball in large part because of his work on the internet.

In the winter before the 2008 season, the Cardinals had an opening for a hitting coach for their short-season farm club in Batavia, New York. Jeff Luhnow, the man who as the Astros general manager a few years later would make the grave mistake of cutting J. D. Martinez, was responsible for the hire in his role directing the Cardinals' scouting and player development efforts. Luhnow wasn't sure who to hire, but he did know one thing: "I wanted to see what would happen if we shook it up a little bit and brought in a fresh perspective from the outside," he said.

Luhnow himself was a baseball outsider then and is again now: He was suspended by MLB for the entire 2020 season, and then fired by the Astros, as punishment for the team's sign-stealing scandal that rocked the sport that winter. A US citizen born and raised in Mexico City, Luhnow has a dual bachelor's degree from Penn in economics and engineering, as well as an MBA from the Kellogg school at Northwestern. Before joining the Cardinals in 2003, he spent five years at the consulting firm McKinsey, served as a vice president of PetStore.com, and founded Archetype Solutions.

When he started considering candidates for the minor league hitting coach job, Luhnow quickly became interested in Jeff Albert. Luhnow knew Albert from his regular column about hitting on the BaseballAnalysts.com website called "The Batter's Eye," which he wrote while pursuing a master's degree in exercise science at Louisiana Tech. Albert also owned and operated his own website, SwingTraining.net. Albert's writings showcased his mind in ways that made it irrelevant that he had never played beyond college and a handful of at-bats in the independent leagues. For instance, he authored a two-part series on swing changes made by Alex Rodriguez and Andruw Jones, using video analysis to break down mechanics in a way unheard of by an amateur. He also wrote about Derek Jeter and Todd Helton and Justin Upton, with the same level of sophistication.

Albert had begun writing around 2005 as he started seeing videos of swings on the internet. He had dreamed about playing professional baseball himself but wasn't good enough, even though he managed to will himself into a college career that ended with two seasons at Butler. Albert essentially taught himself a high-level swing. He would record ESPN highlights of swings on VHS tapes and then try to match them with his own swings taken in the batting cage he rigged up in the dining room of the apartment he shared with his girlfriend (now his wife). "I don't think our neighbors liked it," he said.

His pursuit of video led him to the internet, specifically SetPro .com, an early online entrant in the world of renegade baseball discussion. The site's founder, Paul Nyman, was using scientific research into biomechanics and kinesiology to understand the swing, largely focusing on how to improve bat speed. Intrigued, Albert bought some of Nyman's products. Within a few weeks, he said, his bat speed had improved by 17 miles per hour. That season, his first at Butler after transferring from the Rochester Institute of Technology, he hit .331 and worked his way up from the third-string third baseman into the starting lineup.

Albert's success learning from unconventional sources made him want to be a coach. Before the 2008 season, he came close to accepting a strength and conditioning internship with an MLB team, thinking that was his best chance of entering the pro game. Then Luhnow called, offering him the short-season hitting coach job. "I didn't know if he could do it," Luhnow said. "But I wanted to take a chance on him because of the way his mind worked and his insatiable appetite to learn more and more and figure out how to transfer that knowledge."

Luhnow particularly worried about how some of the longtime Cardinals staffers would react to Albert. The organization's culture was imprinted on Batavia's manager, Mark DeJohn, who had been with the Cardinals since the mid-1980s. But halfway through the season, when Luhnow visited the team, DeJohn approached him and praised Albert and the decision to hire him, saying that Albert had a chance to move up. "No question experience plays a role to be a good teacher," Luhnow said. "But it doesn't have to be experience as a hitter yourself."

Albert did advance through the Cardinals organization. Eventually he followed Luhnow to Houston, where he became the major league second hitting coach in 2018. In the winter before 2019, the Cardinals brought him back—as their primary major league hitting coach.

"I was a no-name, a nobody," Albert said. "Big credit to Jeff's foresight and willingness to do something unconventional—he was at the beginning of the curve."

The hitting coach hiring spree was most notable at the minor league level. The White Sox, the organization that once let Craig Wallenbrock go, hired Matt Lisle to the newly created role of "hitting analytics instructor." Lisle had coached baseball and softball at the college level, at places like South Carolina and Missouri, but he was perhaps better known for proclaiming himself "the internet's most followed hitting coach," boasting a Twitter audience of more than 130,000. Lisle never played pro ball, but after the instructional videos he posted on his website, TheHittingVault.com, gained a large following, major league players began to seek him out for guidance on their swings. One of his main success stories, Daniel Descalso, hit a combined 23 home runs in 2017 and 2018, after hitting that many from 2010 through 2016. That was enough for the White Sox to give Lisle a chance. (He will coach softball at Fresno State in 2020.)

The Angels brought in a crop of private hitting coaches, including Ryan Parker, Tyler Jeske, and Derek Florko. Parker, once just a Twitter personality and *Baseball Prospectus* author writing about the swing, was hired as the team's "coordinator of hitting analysis." Jeske had done some video and scouting work for the Indians and Rangers before becoming the director of baseball operations at Missouri State—not exactly your traditional path to the big leagues. Florko had previously worked for Axe

Bat, a company that manufactures bats with biomechanically optimized handles.

The Phillies, as so many other teams had done in search of underground pitching coaches, tapped into the growing resources at Driveline by hiring Jason Ochart, its director of hitting, as their minor league hitting coordinator.

These are the people who are now responsible for helping the world's best hitters figure out how to combat a constant array of blistering fastballs and cartoonish sliders unlike anything ever before seen in baseball history. This guidance is coming from people who couldn't do it themselves—but might just understand the mechanics of swinging a baseball bat better than anyone.

More than anything, the winter before the 2019 season was the ultimate acknowledgment of Craig Wallenbrock's contributions to baseball. Three of the major league hitting coaches came directly from his tutelage. Very quietly, with little public acknowledgment or recognition, Wallenbrock had begat baseball's fastest-growing—and perhaps least likely—coaching fraternity.

It was this influence that made Wallenbrock the Oracle. He is the tree from which all of these branches have grown. Ted Williams might have been the first to talk about putting the ball in the air, and people like Mike Bryant helped bring that idea further into the forefront. But it was Craig Wallenbrock who truly sparked the revolution and changed baseball forever.

"Craig," Greg Brown told me, "is the source of all of our success."

Before the 2019 season, the Mariners hired Tim Laker, a former catcher who played for five major league teams over parts of 11 seasons between 1992 and 2006. Laker was a Wallenbrock original, having hit with him since the mid-'90s. He became one of Wallenbrock's most fervent disciples, and he continued to spend parts of his winters with Wallenbrock and Van Scoyoc. Laker was around when Martinez first started making the changes that saved his career. Laker's work paid off: in 2017, he joined the Diamondbacks as an assistant hitting coach—perfect timing, since for part of the season Martinez was one of his charges. Then Laker joined the Mariners. Without Wallenbrock, that wouldn't have happened.

"He's an innovator, that's the first thing that comes to mind," Seattle general manager Jerry Dipoto said of Wallenbrock. "His ability to teach it, not just to the players but to a series of coaches that have branched off to become something greater, is pretty awesome. It has changed the game."

In 2013, Laker brought somebody else into the fold. Johnny Washington, a former minor leaguer just starting out in coaching, had also become a regular with Wallenbrock. That was enough to eventually land him the hitting coach position with the Padres.

"The information he gives, it's fact," Washington said. "It's not opinion-based. It's fact. It's, 'Here's what you do and here's what great hitters do.'"

Laker and Washington are two of the three hitting coaches from the Wallenbrock fraternity who were hired before the 2019 season. The third one was the most interesting one of all.

When Raúl Ibañez helped bring Craig Wallenbrock and Robert Van Scoyoc into the Dodgers' organization as consultants for the 2016 season, it didn't take long to see meaningful results. That June, the Dodgers completed a trade, sending little-known pitcher Zach Lee to the Mariners in exchange for an even more anonymous name: Chris Taylor.

Taylor had already done a few stints with the Mariners before joining the Dodgers. He wasn't much of a hitter. In 233 at-bats with Seattle, he had a .240 batting average with exactly zero home runs. Then again, his lack of power shouldn't have been a surprise. All through high school, he hit a grand total of one homer—an inside-the-parker.

"I always thought, being a smaller guy, that was the best way for me to hit," Taylor said. "Fly balls to me then were outs."

When the playoffs came around that fall, the Dodgers left Taylor off their active roster. Instead, they sent him to their facility in Arizona for "Stay Hot," a program designed to keep players prepared in case the Dodgers decided to summon them back to the team. By that point, Taylor was already toying with the idea of making a change. He was 26. His chances of developing into a star player were diminishing. But he had followed Josh Donaldson's tremendous turnaround and heard him talk about the value of swinging to hit the ball in the air. And he had seen other players around his size put up power numbers he couldn't even fathom. Mookie Betts could do it. Trea Turner could do it. So could his new teammate, Justin Turner. Why could they drive the ball and he couldn't?

Fortunately for Taylor, he wasn't alone in the desert. Van Scoyoc was there too, working with Dodgers prospects at the instructional league. Van Scoyoc had seen Taylor hit before, as a rookie, when he was in Detroit for a tune-up with J. D. Martinez. He liked Taylor's tools, but not his swing.

So when Van Scoyoc noticed Taylor hitting in the batting cage, experimenting with some tweaks, he stopped by. The two would spend the rest of the week together, working to revamp Taylor's swing. When the off-season arrived, the lessons continued. Taylor would send Van Scoyoc video and then make adjustments based on his feedback, which focused mostly on bat path. Eventually he made the pilgrimage out to Santa Clarita, as

J. D. Martinez had done before him, to hit in person with Van Scoyoc and Wallenbrock. That's when the lessons became more sophisticated: Van Scoyoc and Wallenbrock talked about Taylor's rhythm to help create a natural move with his hands, rather than the push that had been defining his swing. Van Scoyoc had Taylor start with his barrel tilted, rather than holding it straight up and down, as a way to promote the new path they had built together.

When 2017 came around, it quickly became evident that Taylor was a different player. Van Scoyoc realized it on the day of the Dodgers' first full-squad workout, when he saw the ball popping off Taylor's bat when he was hitting on the back fields. The rest of the Dodgers realized it a couple of weeks into the regular season when, after being promoted from Triple A Oklahoma City, Taylor pounded two doubles and a home run in his first four at-bats. Taylor emerged as one of the key players for the Dodgers in 2017, a season that ended for Los Angeles in game 7 of the World Series. He hit .288 with 21 homers, 72 RBIs, and an .850 OPS. In 2018, he hit 17 homers and remained a vital part of a Dodgers team that reached its second consecutive World Series. Last season, he homered 12 more times. For all of that, he could thank Van Scoyoc.

"A lot of the best hitting coaches are guys that have grinded it out and weren't just naturally really good at hitting," Taylor said. "They had to work through it."

The rest of the league took notice of Taylor's success—and the man behind it. That attention made Van Scoyoc a commodity, more valuable perhaps than his consultant title. Before spring training in 2018, the Diamondbacks made him an offer too good to pass up: to become the organization's "hitting strategist."

The Diamondbacks had good reason to feel that way about Van Scoyoc. They knew the role he had in helping Martinez continue honing his swing, and they saw firsthand what Martinez could do as he led them to the playoffs down the stretch in 2017. Martinez left Arizona for Boston that winter because the Diamondbacks weren't quite willing to meet his contract demands. But if they couldn't stay in the J. D. Martinez business, they hoped that Robert Van Scoyoc would be the next best thing.

Van Scoyoc spent a year with the Diamondbacks, taking the reins in a broad role that exposed him to the organization's efforts in amateur scouting, pro scouting, player development, and major league coaching. But the Dodgers wouldn't let him leave Southern California forever. In late 2018, the revolution took an enormous step forward. Plenty of once-independent hitting coaches were hired by major league organizations in the winter before the 2019 season. Nearly all of them were assigned to mostly behind-the-scenes roles in the minor leagues. The Dodgers had other plans for Van Scoyoc: they shocked the baseball world by naming him their major league hitting coach. Other teams had started hiring outsiders in smaller roles. Some had even hired hitting coaches with nontraditional backgrounds. But nobody with a background as obscure as Van Scoyoc's had ever been hired to such a prestigious position. No coach could ever again be dismissed on the basis of his playing résumé. Van Scoyoc had changed all that.

This was a new assignment for Van Scoyoc. It wasn't one-on-one swing instruction or a job mostly in the front office. He would be in the clubhouse every day and would be responsible for a roster full of players and their hitting instruction. He couldn't just teach mechanics, but had to do all the other work expected of a hitting coach—like finding a way to get a team of hitters motivated and prepared for the rigors of a 162-game season.

"I never doubted for a second that I could do it," Van Scoyoc said. "If I did, I would have never taken the job."

He had a few things going for him that made the transition easier. First off, his track record. Robert Van Scoyoc might not have been a household name to the public at large, but in the baseball industry it was no secret that he had worked with J. D. Martinez, Chris Taylor, and so many others. Justin Turner, maybe the best hitter on the Dodgers, had turned into a star after working with Doug Latta, another outsider who honed his craft working alongside Craig Wallenbrock. Heck, Wallenbrock himself worked for the Dodgers. Who could argue with that track record?

"It's hard to ignore the results," Taylor said. "You see his résumé and the guys he's worked with that have had success at the big league level. I'm one of many."

The other thing Van Scoyoc had working in his favor was his support group. Though Van Scoyoc was the hitting coach, he was also a cog in what Andrew Friedman described as a "hitting department." Wallenbrock was the anchor at the center of it. To the Dodgers, Wallenbrock and the coaches who grew from his tree weren't outsiders. Not anymore. From the moment they hired Wallenbrock and Van Scoyoc as consultants, they were acknowledging that these were people worth investing in, people capable of improving an entire organization.

Alongside Van Scoyoc at the major league level was Brant Brown, a former outfielder who started working with Wallenbrock shortly after the start of his career in the mid-1990s. At the beginning, they would hit in an outdoor cage at Chatsworth High School, then review video on an old VHS machine inside a tool shed where the team kept the chalk to draw the baselines. He has known Van Scoyoc for almost 20 years, since Van Scoyoc was a high school baseball player with little talent but an enormous hunger to learn. In 2019, the Dodgers reunited the trio of

Wallenbrock, Van Scoyoc, and Brown and also brought on Chris Antariksa, another of Wallenbrock's apprentices, in a consulting role. Antariksa did such a good job that the Dodgers hired him on a full-time basis for the 2020 season.

Van Scoyoc's hiring certainly raised eyebrows, especially among fans who couldn't understand how somebody with his background could possibly be qualified for the job. He faced a barrage of questions from media through spring training. Van Scoyoc never feared any of that. For years he had argued that there was a better way to teach hitting than what the industry had been doing. Now he had the chance to prove it.

Van Scoyoc did just that. The Dodgers led the NL in runs, OPS, and homers in 2019.

"I've always had to earn my way by getting results and proving myself," Van Scoyoc said. "There was never any built-in equity like ex-big leaguers have, so I've had to build equity via getting results, which is very difficult to do. So why would I ever shy away from it?"

Still, it wasn't easy at first. Will Rhymes, who in 2019 was the Dodgers' director for player development, remembers Wallenbrock and Van Scoyoc during their first spring with the organization. They'd stand around, not quite sure what they were supposed to be doing. They rarely spoke. They had no agency. Or if they did, they didn't know how to exercise it. But then they got in the cage, and Rhymes no longer doubted. "I wish I had known Craig Wallenbrock when I was playing," Rhymes said. "I would have had a better career."

Craig Wallenbrock would probably chalk up the trajectory of his own career to what he perceives as the inherent randomness of the universe. That's how his mind works. Life is a collection of unconnected events that, in his case, led to him becoming a master of hitting.

But that would be selling him short. In truth, Wallenbrock created his own luck. He not only helped his players improve but cared about them as people, which made them want to somehow return the favor. His ability to connect with his clients explains how Joe Borchard led to Cord Phelps led to Jason Castro led to J. D. Martinez. It explains why Borchard brought Greg Walker into the fold, leading to Wallenbrock's first opportunities to formally coach professionals with the White Sox. It explains how, even though the baseball world wasn't ready for him at that time, he wasn't deterred and waited until his time came. He was a pioneer who laid the groundwork for others to follow in his path.

"The only thing I regret," Wallenbrock said, "is my age, that all of this stuff has happened so late. I wish I would feel like I had another 20 years to live, now that it's finally taking place."

As he said this, Wallenbrock sounded wistful, and understandably so. Then, in true Wallenbrock fashion, his perspective pivoted outside of baseball. When he starts feeling sorry for himself, he said, he thinks of a perhaps apocryphal quote often attributed to Supreme Court Justice Oliver Wendell Holmes Jr.: when Holmes, then in his nineties, saw an attractive young woman walk by, he is said to have remarked, "Oh, to be 70 again."

"So I guess you have to put things in perspective," Wallenbrock said.

Craig Wallenbrock has a unique perspective, cultivated from studying the paintings of Wu Li, the worldview of surfers, and the teachings of samurais. He believes that randomness governs the universe, and so, he would say, it was randomness that made him the pioneer of a movement that has changed baseball forever. But it wasn't random. Wallenbrock worked for decades to bring his ideas about the swing into the mainstream. And he succeeded.

* * *

As people like Craig Wallenbrock have undergone their transitions from outsiders into the mainstream, professional baseball has fundamentally changed. The version of the game played in major league ballparks across the country last season had no precedent in the sport's long history. Previously, no team had ever hit more than 267 home runs in a season, a record set by the Yankees in 2018, who had surpassed the 1997 Mariners' mark of 264. Four teams surpassed that number in 2019: the Twins, Yankees, Astros, and Dodgers, with the A's, Cubs, and Brewers hitting 250 or more. All told, 15 of the 30 teams set or tied their franchise record for home runs.

Without a doubt, the baseball itself is an enormous reason why. Nobody in the industry argues that anymore. Even Rob Manfred, MLB's commissioner, acknowledged last season that the balls are behaving differently than they had in the past, though he vociferously denied that it came at the league's direction. Regardless of why it happened, the ball is impossible to ignore.

But the ball isn't the only thing that's changed. The players have changed, too—and not just J. D. Martinez and Justin Turner. The leaguewide ground ball rate in 2019 was 43.5%, the lowest since at least 1987, which is as far back as Stats LLC has such data. In 2015, one season after Martinez and Turner first emerged with the Tigers and Dodgers, respectively, the ground ball rate was 46.2%, the highest on record. That isn't an accident. Players around the league saw some of their counterparts change their entire careers—and make boatloads of money—by learning to hit the ball in the air. Of course others would follow. In 2019, the average launch angle on all batted balls was 12.2 degrees, the highest since the advent of Statcast in 2015. Independent coaches like Craig Wallenbrock and Doug Latta are a big reason why.

Pitchers have started to adjust, in the unending cat-and-mouse game that makes baseball so compelling. Throughout the 1990s and 2000s, pitchers relied heavily on sinkerballs and sliders, keeping everything down in the zone. Uppercut swings were, at least in part, a response to that approach. Naturally, pitchers have now moved back toward featuring high fastballs and pairing them with curveballs, with some progressive organizations all but eliminating the sinker altogether. It has thwarted some hitters. For hitters like Martinez and Turner, the most advanced students of Wallenbrock and Latta, it hasn't mattered. These coaches scoff at the idea that what they teach can only work against low pitches, insisting that when executed correctly, their swings allow batters to cover the entire strike zone.

Not everybody in baseball is fond of the changes. Take Kevin Youkilis, a three-time All-Star in his career as the first baseman for the Red Sox. He frequently takes to Twitter to criticize these trends, arguing that modern coaching has resulted in the devaluing of experience. "The growing number of online self-proclaimed 'hitting gurus' that continually self-promote and take all the credit for hitters that succeed while never being accountable for their hitters that have gone backwards in their development is truly frustrating," he wrote in September 2019.

It makes sense that retired players like Youkilis would feel that way. The game, to many longtime fans, seems practically unrecognizable, and baseball faces a reckoning. There's no doubt baseball is smarter now than it has ever been. The question is whether "smarter" means "better," or, specifically, "more entertaining." Baseball is, after all, an entertainment product first and foremost. It could be dissected and studied in every conceivable way, but if fans don't like what they're seeing on the field, it hardly matters.

As home runs have soared, so have strikeouts. A whopping 35% of plate appearances ended in either a home run, a strikeout, or a walk in 2019, the highest rate ever. The average length of an MLB game ballooned to 3 hours, 10 minutes, an all-time record. With so few balls actually hit into the field of play—and games getting longer—it sometimes feels like nothing happens at all, except for the sudden burst of action when a player blasts a ball out of the park. MLB average attendance dropped for the fourth straight season in 2019, to 28,339, down from 30,517 in 2015.

This isn't to say home runs are the sole culprit for that. Manfred has said that the league's internal data says that a large portion of fans like the home run boom, while others prefer the older style of play, which featured more finesse, technique, and strategy. But the reality is that baseball isn't going back. Not anytime soon, anyway. In the modern game, home runs aren't just common—they're essential for survival.

Pitchers throw harder than ever. Their breaking pitches move in ways that seem to disobey the laws of physics. Data and technologies have made major league pitchers nearly unhittable. Seriously, just look at how the ball moves the next time you watch a game. What human being could hit that stuff? Meanwhile, teams deploy their bullpens more aggressively than ever before, meaning hitters almost never face a tired starter. Instead, they face an army of pitchers who all throw close to 100 miles per hour. A batter's one counterpunch is to hit the ball over the fence. The days of stringing together three or four hits in an inning to score off pitchers this good are over. That's why in 2019, about 45% of all runs scored in the major leagues were the result of a home run, the most ever.

Given all of this, how will baseball chart a way forward? This much is certain: The modern game is about power. Lots of it.

Home run numbers might not continue to climb forever, but for the foreseeable future, the revolution is here to stay.

Craig Wallenbrock isn't an outsider anymore. His teachings have been fully embraced by the establishment, and the Dodgers continue to make him an integral part of their hitting strategy. Thoughts about the swing that were once too radical to even share publicly are now commonplace.

For proof of that, look to Josh Donaldson. More than a half-decade after he changed his swing, Donaldson remains one of the premier faces of the swing-change revolution.

In August 2016, Donaldson visited MLB Network, where he was interviewed by Mark DeRosa, a former major league player. Over the course of eight minutes and 39 seconds, Donaldson presented the tenets of his swing to the world, offering anybody willing to listen a free clinic on high-level hitting. He took DeRosa through his swing frame by frame, providing insight into exactly what he is trying to do at every moment during the process. This was the money quote: "If you're 10 years old and your coach says, 'Get on top of the ball' . . . tell him no," Donaldson said, pointing emphatically to the camera as he spoke. "Because in the big leagues, these things that they call ground balls are outs. They don't pay you for ground balls. They pay you for doubles. They pay you for homers."

This was it—the fly-ball revolution in 75 words or less, and it was on national television for everybody to see. It was as if Donaldson had given every hitter in the world the answers to the test before they took it. And for anybody who missed it, Donaldson doubled down a few months later. On March 1, 2017, at 5:05 p.m. EST, Donaldson posted on Twitter a 23-second clip of himself hitting in a batting cage. The video was captioned, "Just say NO . . . to ground balls."

Donaldson has kept on hitting, blasting 37 home runs in 2016 and 33 in 2017. After the 2018 season, following an injury-plagued campaign, Donaldson signed a one-year, $23 million contract with the Braves, and he hit 37 homers in 2019.

Through it all, one person Donaldson hasn't talked about at all is Bobby Tewksbary. In his famous MLB Network interview, DeRosa asked Donaldson for the source of his ideas about the swing. Donaldson mentioned his former agent, Hunter Bledsoe, who also worked with him, then added that he "had a couple other people who got me into that."

Between Chris Colabello's suspension and his broken relationship with Donaldson, it had been a difficult time for Tewksbary. His internet presence diminished. He withdrew from the pro game and all but stopped pursuing major league clients. Instead, he returned to his roots, to where he started his journey from failed independent ballplayer to hitting coach for the greats: he went back to working mostly with kids and amateurs.

"I had to try to find joy in the game again," Tewksbary said. "I became just very disheartened about the game of baseball."

Even out of the public eye, however, Tewksbary continued to work in the hitting community. In 2017, he spoke at Pitch-A-Palooza, an annual clinic that brings together many of the nation's most progressive and innovative people in the realm of baseball coaching. Although he wasn't working in person with big leaguers very much anymore, he continued to help them indirectly, as plenty of pro players found his material online and used it to help themselves. Otherwise, Bobby Tewksbary went dark.

Then, in October 2018, he resurfaced. He posted on his website a video titled "State of the Union (Since 2016)." It opens with Tewksbary sitting on a black armchair in front of a blue wall saying, "What the heck have I been up to since 2016?"

For the next 23 minutes, Tewksbary tries to answer that question. He candidly admits that, after throwing in the Home Run Derby and achieving a level of fame, he discovered that things had "escalated and grown beyond what I was ready for." He speaks openly in the video about his disillusionment with the game he has loved for his entire life.

"I didn't really like baseball for a stretch," he says. "I hated the professional game because of what had happened to Chris."

At no point in the video does Tewksbary discuss his severed ties with Donaldson. To the contrary, he says right at the outset, "I'll forever be thankful to Josh," and, "There's no way to ever thank him enough or repay him." Later on, he acknowledges that he had "some fallout with different players that isn't important," but he never singles out Donaldson. He ends with a hopeful message: "I've come out of that dark cloud of hating baseball."

Tewksbary is comfortable remaining on the outskirts of the pro game. He has become fascinated with technology and the mental side of baseball, and he hopes to grow his facility into the ultimate training lab for hitters.

In the off-season before 2019, he interviewed with multiple professional organizations for potential jobs. His ideas about the swing continue to inspire top hitters across the industry. In June 2018, for instance, Tewksbary posted a video on his Instagram account of a swing by Mariners outfielder Mitch Haniger. Haniger saw it and left a comment: "I would be out of baseball by now if I never read your e-book on mechanics," he wrote.

Haniger is one of many players who have found success thanks to Tewksbary's ideas—even if Tewksbary himself is more circumspect.

"They're not my ideas. They've never been my ideas. They're nobody's ideas," he said. "They never needed to be validated, because the history of the game has said they're right."

In other words, Tewksbary doesn't view himself as a "guru" or some sort of groundbreaking innovator. None of the Swing Kings do. Bobby Tewksbary is just a guy who had brought a lot of heart onto the baseball field but wasn't good enough to make it there, and he wanted more than anything else in the world to know why.

He figured it out. They all did.

EPILOGUE:
SWINGING FOR GLORY

The sun shone bright over Yankee Stadium on May 31, 2019, bathing the Bronx's cathedral of baseball in the warmth of late spring. It was the morning of the media game. I was 31 years old, representing New York against the rival reporters from Boston. The time had finally come for me to take everything I had learned over the past 18 months and try to put it into practice in an actual, real-life game.

Our team manager, Ken Davidoff of the *New York Post,* made the lineup based on both seniority and past success in the media game. I had neither. We had 16 players in the batting order. I was batting 16th. I couldn't argue with my placement. My previous output had consisted mostly of weak grounders to second base. Still, I couldn't help but think about J. D. Martinez showing up for his last spring training with the Astros in 2014 after rebuilding his swing with Craig Wallenbrock. He knew he was different, but nobody would give him the chance to prove it.

My first at-bat came against Boston starter Rob Bradford, who writes about the Red Sox for WEEI.com. As I waited anxiously in the on-deck circle, the advice from more than a year of lessons swirled through my head. I remembered Ted Williams's upswing and Craig Wallenbrock's "lag position" and Richard Schenck's constant pleas to *snap it!* It became overwhelming, trying to keep all those ideas in my head at once while also preparing to swing a wooden stick at a baseball hurtling toward me. Right before I walked up to the plate, one of my teammates, Tyler Kepner of the *New York Times,* reminded me to try to keep my mind clear—and think about getting the ball in the air.

Looking to launch at the New York–Boston media game.

Leaving the batter's box, looking up.

As I settled into the box, my hands low and close to my body as Doug Latta and Bobby Tewksbary had shown me, I decided that I wouldn't let the home-plate umpire's inconsistent interpretation of the strike zone cost me. I would swing at the first good pitch I saw—and try to launch it. It didn't take long. Bradford's first pitch was a fastball just below my belt, on the outer half of the plate. I knew I could hit it. I swung. The ball jumped off my bat and flew into the air, soaring toward the Yankee Stadium outfield. I looked up, wondering if I had done it, only to see Boston's center fielder waiting comfortably for the ball to land. He had hardly moved a step. I was 0-for-1, but at least I hadn't hit a ground ball.

Still, I was running out of time. With so many hitters in the lineup, I knew I'd receive just one more chance to fulfill my mission. What if I failed? Would everything I had done over the past year and a half have been in vain? Would I be letting down my gurus, the people who had worked with me to show me a better way to swing? By the time my turn in the lineup came back around, I couldn't worry about all of that. Boston had changed its pitcher, replacing Bradford with Joon Lee of ESPN, and I had to prepare for him.

I felt a strange amount of pressure as I walked up to the plate this time. I wanted so badly to re-create the magic I had conjured at Dean Field in Scarsdale all those years ago. I didn't even know why. None of this *mattered*. I hadn't played competitive baseball since I was 18, and I never would again. I had a wife, a supportive family, and a good job. I didn't need any validation. Yet in that moment, nothing in the world felt more important than this at-bat. Maybe I just wanted to prove to myself that I could do it, that all the years of my life I had devoted to baseball, all the swings I had taken as a child with my dad on the mound, weren't for nothing.

As Lee entered his windup to deliver his first pitch to me, I went into my load, preparing to attack the first pitch I saw once again. At the last moment, I stopped as the ball, coming toward the plate low and inside, forced me to move my feet to skip out of the way. I took the same approach to the second pitch. Again I stopped. I thought of the "humming" drill Chris Colabello had mastered, a cue that reminded him to "swing until he wasn't." The ball nipped the outside corner. Strike one.

With the count at 1-and-1, I knew my time was now. I couldn't afford to let another good one pass by and give Lee the advantage. I dug into the box. Lee delivered. It was a good one. I swung up.

Crack!

The sound reverberated across the nearly empty stadium, echoing off the seats that later that night would be filled with 45,556 screaming fans. I heard my teammates in the dugout buzz with excitement, as the ball jumped off my bat and flew toward right-center field. I started to run toward first base and looked up for the ball. I knew I had hit it well. The noise alone told me that. For a moment, the vision of me rounding first base and cruising into second with a double crossed my mind.

Then I looked up. The center fielder, after my fly ball in my first at-bat, had taken a couple of steps back this time. My hit had chased him back even farther, sending him out toward right-center as he tracked the ball—which settled into his glove for a fly-out. In the box score, it would look just like any other out. I had gotten only two or three steps out of the batter's box when he caught it.

As I returned to the dugout, I was met with a line of high-fives, butt slaps, and fist bumps, reassuring me that I had simply fallen victim to a bit of bad luck. I had hit the ball hard. I couldn't have done anything else. That's baseball.

Still, I had failed. I had taken two at-bats, and neither of them resulted in the monster blast of my dreams. I felt dejected as I took my position at first base. I couldn't help but wonder if I had

really hit the ball all that hard. Maybe I was delusional. That's when the umpire stationed behind me at first base tapped me on the shoulder.

"Hey," he said, "that was probably the hardest-hit ball all day."

I smiled. I may not have re-created that day from my youth, but now it actually seemed like a possibility. I had at least learned to hit the ball in the air. This was progress.

That night I called Latta. The next game was only a year away.

ACKNOWLEDGMENTS

Swing Kings began its life as an article about the rise of independent hitting gurus that appeared in the *Wall Street Journal* during spring training in 2017. When the piece ran, I couldn't have even fathomed that those 1,100 words could serve as the basis for an entire book. But Lauren Sharp, my amazing agent, saw something greater. So for that, I have to thank her and the entire team at Aevitas Creative Management. Lauren guided me, a terrified first-time author, through this entire process from the beginning. She was the first person to believe this was possible, and I truly couldn't have done this without her help.

That same sentiment applies to Nick Amphlett, my incredible editor at William Morrow, who taught me how to write a book while I was actively trying to write one. In addition to answering my unending barrage of inane questions without ever mocking me (including the time when I asked how to write an acknowledgments section), Nick took my draft of *Swing Kings* and molded it into something to be proud of. He and the entire HarperCollins team deserve all my gratitude: Erin Reback, Eliza Rosenberry and Amelia Wood for their publicity and marketing genius; Rich Aquan and Bonni Leon-Berman for their artistic vision; Evangelos Vasilakis for making sure that everything came together; and Liate Stehlik for supporting this project from the start.

I need to thank all the people who generously gave me their time and expertise over the past three years. They allowed a complete stranger into their lives, sat for countless hours of interviews and trusted me with their stories. A special mention goes to Craig Wallenbrock, Robert Van Scoyoc, Doug Latta, Bobby Tewksbary, Chris Colabello, Richard Schenck, J. D. Martinez, and

Justin Turner, all of whom were beyond integral to the creation of *Swing Kings*.

Morgan Lawrence was an absolute lifesaver for transcribing all of my interviews quickly and professionally. The value of her work is immeasurable, and I can't thank her enough. The same goes for Will McCollister, who fact-checked the entire manuscript and repeatedly saved me from myself.

A huge thanks goes out to all my colleagues at the *Wall Street Journal* for allowing me to pursue this project while I continued to fulfill my duties as the newspaper's national baseball writer. It'd be impossible to name them all, but I'd be remiss if I didn't at least call out a few: Bruce Orwall and Jim Chairusmi, the remarkable editors responsible for what is the nation's best sports section; Rachel Bachman, Andrew Beaton, Ben Cohen, Brian Costa, Jason Gay, Laine Higgins, Louise Radnofsky, Josh Robinson, and all of the other insanely talented journalists who have been a part of *WSJ* Sports over the years; Sam Walker and Geoff Foster, the original Dynamic Duo, who hired me to my dream job and showed me how to be a reporter; and Bill Eichenberger, my longtime mentor, who has always believed in me even when I didn't know why.

Swing Kings wouldn't have happened without the support of my family: my parents, Carol and Jeff; my younger siblings, Justin and Elyssa; my grandfather, Allan; and all of the other Diamonds, Feinbergs, Geizhals, Marcuses, Herskovitses, and Racensteins who have always been there for me. They all took this journey with me. My wife, Talie, stands alone for her kindness, patience, and love. She never doubted that I was capable of this even when I did—and now she shares in this accomplishment.

Lastly, thank you to Jack Diamond, my dearly departed grandfather, for instilling in me a lifelong passion for this magical game we call baseball. He endured unspeakable atrocities to emerge as the patriarch of our family, and he remains a guiding light to us all.

PHOTO CREDITS

13) Nova Southeastern University Athletics; 17) Adam Davis/ Icon Sportswire; 25) Matt Brown; 57) Doug Latta; 69) *The Art of Batting and Base Running*; 71) Library of Congress; 73) Library of Congress; 82) Courtesy of author and Mike Bryant; 86) Courtesy of author and Mike Bryant; 126) Craig Wallen-brock; 147) Craig Wallenbrock; 187) Richard Schenck; 188) Richard Schenck; 204) top: Icon Sportswire; 204) bottom: Icon Sportswire; 210) Craig Wallenbrock; 235) Bobby Tewksbary; 264) Doug Latta; 278) Brian Rothmuller/Icon Sportswire; 304) top: Nick Amphlett; 304) bottom: Rebecca Seiner.

INDEX

Note: Page references in *italics* refer to photos.